"*Finding Freedom and Grace in a Broken World* is a comprehensive, exhaustive exploration, a deep dive into the world of knowing and trusting the God of Scripture. It examines divine grace from every imaginable perspective through 234 brief, easily digestible essays."

—MICHAEL CARD
Author of *Inexpressible: Hesed and the Mystery of God's Lovingkindness*

"Are you seeking answers to life's deeper questions? Perhaps you are tired of superficial answers that scratch the surface of life's concerns, but do not satisfy your profound issues. If so, I suggest you read *Finding Freedom and Grace in a Broken World*. This book will touch your mind, heart, and emotions. I'm certain you'll contemplate its teachings long after you have read the chapters. It's a proverbial gold mine for the soul."

—GARY L. MCINTOSH
Distinguished affiliate professor of Christian ministry and leadership,
Talbot School of Theology, Biola University

"*Finding Freedom and Grace in a Broken World* invites the reader to examine implicit values shaped in the soul by cultural assumptions of Western Christianity. The book stretches us to move beyond a performance-based Christianity to a deeply trust-based relationship with God himself. This multifaceted book with various entries covers well the gamut of the Christian life, written from the heart of a seasoned coach and a caring soul mentor."

—CHRISTY HILL
Professor of spiritual formation and women's ministry, Grace College and Seminary

"Thomas Stallter has created something new—a biblically grounded refresher in the essential truths of God and the way the believer experiences them, packaged in an easily accessible format for the lay person. He has chosen topics that are central to Christian life today and has provided solid, but short, reflections with full scriptural support. Contemporary Christians beleaguered by cultural messaging can return to the heart of the gospel with each reading."

—KATHLEEN MULHERN
Teaching fellow, Denver Seminary

"Got a few minutes to stop and think? About what? About our walk with God, our view of ourselves, and our view of life. In his unusual book, Thomas Stallter provides one-to-two-page reflections to 'encourage us to reboot our faith, modify our values, and reassign the influences of self and culture.' Wide-ranging topics include fear and anxiety, enjoyment, justice, worship, and unexpected providence. These short and thoughtful prods to new thinking can open up new vistas. Try it out."

—KLAUS ISSLER
Professor emeritus of educational studies and theology,
Talbot School of Theology, Biola University

"Thomas Stallter delivers on his promise to guide us into clear thinking that provides grace and godliness for our journey. The Christian culture may seek the clever or the comforting, but Stallter invites us into a deep and freeing interface of our core beliefs with difficult cultural norms. Prepare to think. Prepare to grow."

—JOHN ADDISON TEEVAN
Co-dean, School of Arts and Humanities, Grace College and Theological Seminary

"This book is a Godsend, in the way of the book of Proverbs, offering nuggets of wisdom for mind and heart. With the 'closing of the American mind' and the 'scandal of the evangelical mind,' it's clear that our society has deep needs. And Thomas Stallter delivers. The meditations and supporting Scripture references are gourmet: insightful, thought-provoking, inspiring, reassuring. Eat slow and savor the flavors."

—D. BRENT SANDY
Author of *Hear Ye the Word of the Lord: What We Miss If We Only Read the Bible*

Finding Freedom and Grace in a Broken World

Finding Freedom and Grace in a Broken World

A Journey in the Purposes and Providence of God

BY THOMAS M. STALLTER

WIPF & STOCK · Eugene, Oregon

FINDING FREEDOM AND GRACE IN A BROKEN WORLD
A Journey in the Purposes and Providence of God

Copyright © 2024 Thomas M. Stallter. All rights reserved. Except for brief quotations in critical publications or reviews, no part of this book may be reproduced in any manner without prior written permission from the publisher. Write: Permissions, Wipf and Stock Publishers, 199 W. 8th Ave., Suite 3, Eugene, OR 97401.

Wipf & Stock
An Imprint of Wipf and Stock Publishers
199 W. 8th Ave., Suite 3
Eugene, OR 97401

www.wipfandstock.com

PAPERBACK ISBN: 979-8-3852-0857-9
HARDCOVER ISBN: 979-8-3852-0858-6
EBOOK ISBN: 979-8-3852-0859-3

VERSION NUMBER 020724

All Scriptures are from Holy Bible, New International Version®, NIV® Copyright ©1973, 1978, 1984 by Biblica, Inc.® Used by permission. All rights reserved worldwide.

To Sharon, my good wife, and Nathan, Erin, and Megan,
treasured children meant by God for us.

And to Christopher, our son-in-law and Christie, our daughter-in-law,
gems brought our way by the Father of lights.

And to Annabella, Madeleine, and George,
God's good gifts to us who make me a happy grandfather.

"We are often unable to tell people what they need to know, because they want to know something else."

"Man finds it hard to get what he wants, because he does not want the best; God finds it hard to give because He would give the best, and man will not take it."

—George MacDonald

Contents

Introduction | 1
1. Choosing Grace | 11
2. Morality | 13
3. Our Names | 14
4. Feelings | 15
5. Survival Is outside Ourselves | 16
6. Freedom of Choice | 18
7. Joy Intended | 19
8. Trusting God's Way | 21
9. Obedience | 22
10. Material Blessings | 23
11. The Declaration and Mystery of Grace | 24
12. Worry | 26
13. Forgiveness, His and Ours | 27
14. Suffering | 29
15. The Peace of God Interrupted | 31
16. Emptiness | 32
17. Uncertainties Call for Trust | 33
18. God's Answers to Prayer | 35
19. Gratefulness | 36
20. Learning to Rest in His Grace | 37
21. Letting God Be God in Our Prayers | 38

22. Prayer as Part of God's Design | 40

23. Justice | 42

24. Feelings of Security | 43

25. Assurance | 45

26. Mystery in God's Purposes | 46

27. God's Freedom | 47

28. Purpose of Creation | 48

29. Providence at Work | 50

30. Enjoyment | 51

31. God's Purposes and Our Prayers | 52

32. God and the Mundane | 53

33. Personality and God's Providence | 55

34. The Journey to Knowing God | 57

35. God's Perfection | 58

36. Wisdom | 59

37. God's Wrath | 60

38. Information Only | 61

39. The Grace of Forgiveness | 63

40. Out of Darkness | 64

41. Striving Ended | 66

42. Human Justice | 67

43. Good King or Bad? | 68

44. Will Christians Be Punished for Their Sin? | 69

45. Adam's Sin and the Doorway of God's Grace | 71

46. Adam's Sin and Ours | 73

47. Cheated and Wronged | 74

48. Debts We Owe | 75

49. Guilty as Charged | 76

50. Becoming Perfect | 77

51. Purity | 78

52. Hopeless Feelings | 80

53. Salvation, Before and After | 82

54. Spiritual Faltering | 84

55. Calling Evil What Is Good | 85

56. Ultimate Decision | 87

57. Risking Our Relationship with God | 88

58. Limitations | 89

59. Distracted | 90

60. Secret Ways to Know God? | 91

61. Pride and Terror | 92

62. The Justice of God Waits | 94

63. Miracles | 95

64. Uncertainty | 96

65. Peace in a World of Suffering | 97

66. Spiritual Disciplines Gone Wrong | 98

67. Humility | 100

68. Control | 101

69. Legalism versus Grace | 102

70. Worship | 104

71. Unexpected Providence | 105

72. Our Calling to Trust the Providence of God | 107

73. Selfishness and Pride | 109

74. Stopping to Think | 110

75. Wounded | 111

76. Culture's Way | 112

77. Self-Awareness in Christ | 114

78. Ungratefulness | 116

79. Social Recognition | 117

80. The Anxiety of Doubt | 118

81. Doing the Right Thing | 120

82. Truth | 121

83. Nations under God | 122

84. God's Words | 124

85. Divine Communication | 126

86. Knowledge | 127

87. Conversion Takes Humility | 128

88. Freedom from Fear | 129

89. Materialism and Asceticism | 131

90. Spiritual Life Lived in the World | 132

91. Passion and Loyalty | 133

92. In Love with Self | 134

93. Hardship or Riches | 135

94. Reality | 136

95. Barriers to Our Search for God's Will | 138

96. Popular Christians | 139

97. Sacred Calling | 140

98. Biblical Christians | 142

99. Knowing God's Will | 143

100. Missional People | 145

101. The Nature of the Church | 146

102. Spiritual Gifts | 148

103. Special Guidance | 150

104. Hope | 151

105. The God We Know | 152

106. Kindness | 153

107. Syncretism | 155

108. Allegiance | 157

109. Loving God | 158

110. Empathy | 159

111. Choosing the Best | 160

112. Hidden Treasure in a World of Woe | 162

113. Loyalty to One Lord | 164

114. Resting in God | 165

115. The Old World | 166

116. Obedience Is a Choice | 167

117. Gifts of God | 168

118. Experience | 169

119. Culture and Conversion | 170

120. Love Your Enemies | 172

121. God in the World | 174

122. Defending the Faith | 175

123. The Process of Conversion | 176

124. False Teaching | 178

125. Salvation | 179

126. Complexity in Knowing God | 181

127. Judging Others | 182

128. The Worship and Love of God | 183

129. Legalism versus Relationship | 184

130. Conscience | 185

131. Judgment of Believers | 186

132. Superficial Christianity | 188

133. Perfection | 190

134. Good Works | 191

135. Painful Events | 192

136. Patience and Gratefulness | 194

137. His Way | 196

138. The Great Change | 198

139. "Good" Christians | 200

140. Trust and Love | 201

141. From God? | 203

142. Decisions | 204

143. Self-Worth | 205

144. Good Fortune | 207

145. God's Care in Adversity | 208

146. Judging Others | 209

147. Men and Women in Marriage | 211

148. Forgiveness and Dirty Feet | 212

149. Trusting God | 214

150. Life and Death | 215

151. Our Attention | 216

152. Another Day, Another Choice | 217

153. Rare and Fleeting Moments | 219

154. Always Busy Doing Something | 221

155. Individualism and Success | 222

156. Necessary Avoidance | 223

157. Simple Faith | 224

158. God Calls People to Himself | 225

159. Worn Out Words | 226

160. Right Thinking | 227

161. Religion | 228

162. Medicine for the Soul | 230

163. Knowing God's Will Is Not Complicated | 231

164. Choosing Good | 233

165. Pretending to Be Wise | 235

166. Desires and Needs | 236

167. Church Membership | 237

168. Hanging On | 238

169. A Sign from God | 239

170. Endangered Species | 240

171. Conscience Overloaded | 242

172. The Turbulence of Culture | 244

173. Tragedy and Pain | 245

174. Parents in an Individualist Culture | 247

175. The Mind | 249

176. Meditation | 250

177. Regrets Changed to Contentment | 251
178. Emotional Pain | 252
179. To Love Again | 253
180. Letting God Speak | 254
181. Wrong-Way | 255
182. Good Works in a Bad World | 256
183. Unity around God's Word | 257
184. The Great Deception | 259
185. Traditions Forgotten | 260
186. God's Ways | 262
187. Human Love Is Inadequate | 263
188. Seeking Approval | 264
189. Approval Achieved, but Not by Us | 265
190. Heaven | 266
191. Ingredients | 267
192. Pleasure | 269
193. The Basics | 270
194. Christian "Leaders" | 272
195. Change | 274
196. Kingdoms of Darkness and Light | 276
197. Transported | 278
198. Categories of People | 279
199. Motives for Beliefs | 280
200. The Works of Legalism | 281
201. The Sacred Gift | 283
202. Accepting Freedom | 284
203. God's Intentions in God's Way | 285
204. Knowing and Doing | 287
205. What, No Options? | 288
206. The Source of Thinking | 290
207. Wisdom over Culture | 291

208. Freedom and Its Limits | 293
209. Thinking about What We Know | 294
210. The Great Decline | 295
211. In Love with Christianity | 297
212. Popular Christianity | 298
213. Spiritual Adultery | 299
214. The Choice of Loyalty to God | 300
215. Eyes of Faith | 301
216. God Does Not Run Out of Time | 303
217. Knowing and Not Knowing God | 304
218. The Interference of Culture | 305
219. Cultural Wineskins | 306
220. God Speaks? | 308
221. All Sin Matters | 309
222. Time with a Fool | 311
223. The Conscience of a Nation | 312
224. The Golden Rule | 314
225. Survival | 315
226. Fear and Anxiety | 316
227. The Christian Life Is Not Natural | 318
228. God Loves the World | 319
229. The Knowledge That Leads to Godliness | 321
230. Dealing with Doubt | 323
231. Help for the Weary | 325
232. Mystical Experiences from God | 326
233. Knowing Yourself Is Important for Knowing God | 328
234. Anger, the Enemy | 330

Scriptrue Index | 331

Introduction

THE ABILITY TO REASON is an extraordinary human capacity. God gave it to his creatures in his sovereign providence, but it is not always a gift used to honor its Giver. We make that choice. Sometimes, "knowing God" is reduced to a cold, rational, informational domain that limits God to the extreme of naked intelligence. Other times, knowing him is cheapened at the extremes of sentimental simplicity or mystical secrets. But there is a correct use of our minds that results in understanding and faith, producing gratefulness, humility, loyalty, worship, and wonder. This way of thinking nurtures love for the Creator-God of the universe.

In these readings, I hope to open up the centrality of trust and freedom as we seek to live for the purposes of God. We must often recalibrate our thinking to reflect these realities of God in our lives. To this end, I have noted what I see as biblical thinking regarding various themes that inevitably come our way as we progress on our journey in the Christian life. My prayer is that it will be helpful to those who want to "have the mind of Christ" in their daily walk, those seeking to know God as he is, not as others try to make him. It is for people who want to move from Christian routines and rituals, from information about God to flourishing faith and trust, enveloping a living relationship with him in our broken world. I also hope some themes here will help people who wish they knew God but have not heard, in a relevant way, how to open that door.

I realize people read books these days more for entertainment and information than for exercising thought and even less for weighing the truth about themselves and God. If an author touches on the potential injurious influence of certain aspects of our culture on us in the pursuit of that truth, hidden sensibilities come to the surface. The defensiveness of our Western ways is not long in showing itself. But we must be open to these considerations. I am not sharpening my dagger to skewer the love of the reader for their church or their loyalty to their culture. God's purpose for the church and many of our Western culture's freedoms are also dear to me, and they serve our life in Christ well. I am not asking you to be critical of Western culture on the whole but to become sensitive to its less helpful, even detrimental, influences on our faith and its expression and on how we do church—to lean on wisdom where loyalty to the old ways our culture has given us might blind us to God's ways.

We must be, as most of you who have picked up this book are, thinking Christians who desire God's will on earth as it is in heaven and let him speak for himself on the matter. My concerns about this are detailed in my earlier book, *The Gap between God and Christianity: The Turbulence of Western Culture* (Wipf & Stock, 2022). Here, I want to turn our minds to trust and freedom in our walk with God. I want us to know God's grace, providence, and purposes in a way that changes our lives and experiences in this broken world from this day on.

We have been brought up within our culture, along with those around us, to see things a particular way—to interpret our experience and respond to events, people, and even to God in both cultural and personal ways. This has given us a frame of reference that undergirds all else we know and trust and love in life, as well as all we question, distrust, and hate. But that foundation is not without its cracks. It is a worldview we accepted without examination and have been blind to all our lives. But what if we took it out and looked at it? What if we tested it to see the realities of its relationship to our faith? Has human culture influenced us in the wrong direction? Is our faith controlled by our culture? Or have we put its function to govern our thinking and values under the influence of our faith? It is time for an inspection and appraisal of this foundation and framework. Things are not always what they seem; we need to see them as they are, not as our culture shapes them.

As the West continues to become post-Christian in its worldview, we need a revival of the mind. Christianity based on emotions fails us when the feeling is gone. Christianity based on tradition or family loyalties leaves enormous gaps in our thinking, does not answer the hard questions, and becomes tiresome over time. In these pages, I am aiming at the Christian who knows they need to move ahead in their faith, the person who has grown tired of only popular ideas about God in his or her life, those who want to think carefully and understand where they are and how to move ahead on their journey to maturity in Christ. There are none of us without the need to grow in our loyalty to Christ, our trust in God's providence, and our progress toward wisdom. Then, some need to consider the alternatives of knowing or not knowing the God of the universe. I want to get these, too, to stop and think.

Like a fair-weather friend, our culture often helps us but offers no real answers in the storms of life and can lead us down the wrong path with a smile if the right way looks difficult. With its appetite for novelty, search for pleasure, and denial of absolutes, our culture leads us away from thinking about God, indeed, away from thinking at all. We will have to put our foot down and make some decisions. Where is our culture leading us? Where is our life going, and where do we want it to end? Who can we trust at the wheel?

Because I am seeking an audience willing to think about God, I will occasionally mention theology. Yes, strange as it may seem in our postmodern and woke atmosphere, there are truths to consider—countercultural absolutes of immense importance—that will mark our way and set the boundaries for our thinking about God. But, we must always move beyond facts and information to the meaning God intends for us in them. Far from becoming a prison of dos and don'ts, the truth marks the way to forgiveness, peace, well-being, and freedom in Christ. There is rest for the weary and hope for the lost. What we seek is found in a relationship with God that he desires, but we must choose.

So, careful thinking is where our journey must begin. We often hear that it is by faith that it all begins for the Christian. Yes, but not faith in a vacuum. Not blind faith. No, it must be faith that knows something—its object. It begins with humility that recognizes our guilt before God and accepts his grace for us through the work of Christ. You'll notice I didn't use the word *believe* in this sentence. Our English word is mainly reserved for referring to things we think might be true. We don't use the term to talk about things like the earth's gravity or the North Star, for example. Beliefs may be weaker or stronger, but we are dealing with facts here. These are the realities God seeks to make known to us if we have eyes to see and ears to hear.

This is salvation, God's purpose for his creation. He means to rescue non-Christians and give rest to Christians who are tired and weary. He is the Creator-God who intends to have a relationship with humankind, though a gulf of enormous proportions separates them. He, and only he, provides the way for this to come about in Christ. Are there feelings involved? Yes, but they begin with grief when we understand our lost condition and arrive at an overwhelming sense of gratefulness for his grace—gratefulness that he did not turn his back on us. His being and actions then call for our trust in his words. Here, we must engage the mind. We must think deeply about the ramifications of knowing the Creator-God. All the godless explanations of the beginnings of humankind are a thin film of human defense against God, desperate efforts to wrench our destiny from his hand, and intentional attempts to erase him. But, though all the engines of atheism are leveled against him, he remains. Our Creator-God is not moved. There's not a scratch on the armor of the sovereign King of the universe.

Our usual ways of thinking superficially are problematic, to say the least, and they become habitual. We become lost in the everyday realities of life and our survival in society. We may be unaware we are in a rut and do not realize where our discontent or anxiety comes from or why God's word does not seem relevant, effective, or practical in our lives. God's ways are very different from ours. Our ways are shaped by our self-concerns and the patterns Western culture gives us for our survival, and, in this situation, God's word may not seem practical. Thinking habits are not easily broken, and our society reinforces our typical superficial approach to life at every turn. We must become aware of these thinking patterns we have been given and renew our minds. Yes, setting our minds on things above, we must look to God's way and turn from our self-absorbed thinking to knowing his will. To do so, though we can see a lot in his word, we must be content without knowing everything about his providential activities.

God's purposes in our lives and ministries may not fit our definitions. We may prefer black-and-white reasoning in our informational, compartmental, logical world, but he wants our trust. Two of the three central concepts in the Bible are grace and trust. Neither is logical to the Western mind, but both are essential for contentment in him. The third central concept is truth. Nothing about grace and trust makes sense without the truth about God and his purposes. By truth, I mean facts—not what we believe but what is and what nothing can change.

In a world where it seems new is always better, and change appears the way forward, I want to take us back to some old thinking of an era when wisdom was valued. The influence of the Psalms and Proverbs of the Bible can be felt today if we are still and listen. I will refer to them often. If we think we are past the old words in our modern world, we are distracted by our own cleverness and may lose our way. We can learn a great deal from those who have gone before, who are now part of a great cloud of witnesses. God has used these ancient writings in the lives of many; he can also use them in ours.

These thoughts may not be devotional for many in our widespread use of that term. I intend that they help us correct our thinking and turn our eyes toward God. They may or may not provide emotional support, but I hope they add to our faith and courage for what we must be and do for God. At the same time, I am concerned about anyone using them to overcorrect their views, causing the pendulum to swing to the opposite end of a continuum of right and wrong when the biblical perspective is not always so categorical. Though many essential truths are right and their opposites wrong, most of life lived for God within these certainties must be one of moderation, humility, and wisdom. Our freedom in Christ must not be cast aside, but it must, without fail, be expressed within the boundaries of love and gratefulness.

My hope is that this collection of thoughts about God and ourselves will encourage us to reboot our faith, realign our loyalty, modify our values, and reassign the influences of self and culture to their proper places. Persistent trust, unswerving loyalty to God, and relevant assessments of self and our culture's impact on us will renew our perspective of God's grace and providence and calm our lives. It is not a once-for-all fix. We must check our alignment with his way fairly often as we go along. And none of us will do this perfectly.

The church is made up of fallible people. One can expect certain weaknesses as people seek to grow in Christ and strengthen their faith. The great problem, weighty and often severe, is when they are not pursuing the goal of this alignment with God or the church does not encourage them to seek it. The salt will have lost its flavor, the light, its ability to show the way. God helping us, we can and must do better.

In putting my thoughts together, I have used some terms that need an explanation to give you my full intention. Let me list a few here. The word *syncretism* is critical in some of my comments. It is the main problem we face as Christians seeking to deal with our inconsistencies as we grow in Christ. Syncretism is when one belief or value system is mixed with another to become a new system. When cultural values and beliefs contrary to the Bible are combined with Christianity, the result is syncretism. It causes the distinctions of the truth to become blurred by cultural understandings and personal preferences. This may happen initially when the message of the gospel is not delivered carefully and with an understanding of the worldview of the audience. Or it may be a creeping syncretism, slowly infiltrating the church as the culture lures us toward its values and puts social pressure on us to conform to its expectations. Satan can use it to blackmail us with the risk of our personal happiness if we do not follow its lead.

Another word that is important in my thoughts is *mysticism*. I use this word in a particular way. I use it to describe modern subjective spirituality. Like the religions, organized Christianity can have its own "spiritual" approaches to God that combine wishful thinking and a human emotional approach with biblical thinking. It is a kind of magic—the enchantment of secret, spiritual discoveries through rituals and signs. It makes objective truth subjective, meaning what the adherents want or need in their interest. It is used to attain recognition, inclusion in a group, personal meaning, and feelings of self-worth. Mysticism has to do with personal experience and its emotional interpretation. It is risky, unpredictable, and subjective—not God's idea of walking in the Spirit.

We must also talk about *legalism*. I will do so with what some may feel is disturbing regularity. Legalism comes from expanded information about God and his will from outside his word. It is based on the teacher's personal preference for objectivity out of fear of ambiguity. It is then forced into objective cognitive categories with rigid boundaries. It is predictable and impartial, making people feel safe but guilty with its black-and-white interpretations and impossible lists of things to do and avoid doing. It adds regulations to God's intentions, ignores his grace, and leaves us on our own, seeking God's approval. It promotes addiction to information without the grace of God alongside. Its logic and order resolve feelings of insecurity with ambiguity, uncertainty, and change. The extremes of this requirement for conformity to the list of rules created by the legalist can become cultic. The relationship with God becomes one of a slave to his master even though he tells us that both grace and truth came to us in Jesus (John 1:14, 17). Why so much talk about legalism? Because it is death disguised as spirituality, skirting wisdom and destroying both the grace of God and our freedom in Christ. I would send the reader directly to topics 69, 129, and 200.

By *trusting God*, I mean to accept his truth and promises as they are, as he gives them, without always knowing how he will work in our lives. This means allowing him to be God and speak for himself. It means accepting his unconditional forgiveness of all our sins when we come to him in faith, however weak our faith may be. It means not forcing our human and cultural expectations on his ways or his providence in our lives. It means unquestioning loyalty to his power and authority while realizing "his ways are not our ways." It is a placing of ourselves, ordinary as we are, in his hands, realizing he has a purpose for us and can and will use us, despite our history and weaknesses, because of our forgiveness and position in Christ. It means that in our most mundane routines of life, the mountains are still full of horses and chariots of fire (2 Kgs 6:15–17).

In the editing process, I was asked what I mean when discussing *honoring God*. We live in a culture that accentuates guilt and innocence instead of honor and shame. This removes us somewhat from the cultural contexts of the Bible that emphasize this honor or shame dichotomy. Honor concerns the infinite worth and importance we attribute to God—who he is, what he does, his being, power, grace, providence, and judgment in his relationship to his creation. It makes his position as creator and sustainer of the universe of ultimate significance in all our earthly affairs. We must honor him first in our lives and love those he puts in our circle of influence. In loving them, we are loving him. When we honor God, we show his glory (the "weightiness" and significance of his being and works) in praise and worship and in how we live our lives for him. We acknowledge him in all we do, live a life that trusts him, and make him known to those around us.

The *providence of God* is a central theme in these readings and needs comment. I have used the terminology over 140 times. You may become numb to it, but I assure you it is a predominant theme of the Bible and fundamental to our faith. By it, I mean God's discerning activity and proactive wisdom in our lives. He works in our lives in perfect foresight, providing and governing all he knows we need for his purposes, even using our experiences before we know him. He provides and controls what we cannot manage for his ends. His providence gives us gratefulness for his grace, peace in his control of events, and rest in his trustworthiness as he accomplishes his plan for us and for the world. By it, I do not mean a sovereignty that smothers all human initiative but works in and through it, as we allow him, for his purposes. Our faith, good works, and prayers are tools in his hands as he works in us.

One more term needs some explanation. I often use the words *popular Christian* to describe people who call themselves Christians but are so superficial in their understanding it is not evident they actually know God. This is a broad category of people who like Christianity. They are shallow in their faith, and their lives may be filled with "Christian" trinkets, rituals, and superstitions. They have a somewhat tit-for-tat understanding of God's ways: "I do this for you, so you must do that for me." I use the term in contrast to those I call "biblical Christians," people whose trust and loyalty to God allow him to speak for himself without imposing rules or our personal or cultural expectations on him. They know they are imperfect and do not expect God to exempt them from his boundaries for believers, but they experience freedom in Christ unknown to popular Christians.

A popular Christian's beliefs are carelessly combined with their cultural and personal values. This is the syncretism mentioned above. They are in love with their church or with a form of "Christianity" instead of with God. They lack a personal and motivating relationship with God, perhaps through ignorance or because they have not yet experienced his grace. The goal of faith should be to move from this condition to that of a biblical Christian seeking to honor God through faithfulness to his word. One of my goals in this book is to help popular Christians in this process. I don't deny it will take some thoughtful reading and an open and humble heart.

My thoughts here will not be conventional to everyone. Readers will identify with some entries more than others. We are all so different, and I am only human. But I ask you to give them time. Each topic has taken a piece of my life to develop and may fit a part of yours, but you may not see it immediately. In addition, your own thinking may take you to new places in your applications that I cannot imagine. So, I am leaving the application of these thoughts to you.

I realize some of these comments can be taken the wrong way and turned into ideas I have not intended. If you think a comment is going off the rails of traditional conservative Christianity, you may be right. Traditional for us has become somewhat mired in our cultural preferences. Our ethnocentrism screams loyalty to the old ways of saying things, the culturally comfortable standard way of arranging our Christian lives. But if you think I am leaving behind a conservative stand on salvation by grace, the truth and inerrancy of the Scriptures as originally given to us, or the need to make disciples, relax. Put that paragraph aside and come back to it another day. My way of articulating these thoughts is an effort to get the reader's attention. We are often numbed to certain aspects of the truth by the old ways of saying it, our culture's preferences, or personal blindness. Let it cool off, and then come back to it.

Furthermore, these thoughts are not bedtime reading. The statements in a paragraph are dense as I have sought to distill the considerations necessary to the topic and compress them into a small space. This makes the flow of the content more direct and less relaxed. I don't think this will be entertaining; my purpose is to cause us to think. Some concepts may seem repeated several times, but each time, I add to or develop that idea, showing some additional angle or perspective from which to view that truth or connecting it to some new concept or experience in our lives. Again, you may profit by giving certain thoughts here some time, coming back to them weeks, even months or years, later. We grow in our perspective as we go along in the Christian life. In the spring of our lives, we see things one way, and in the autumn, we are surprised at how we have changed. These thoughts are reflections during the autumn of my life as I look back at years of God's providence and grace along the way.

Each topic is followed by Scripture verses that stand behind the comments, so you may go to the Bible directly for help. There, you can go further and deeper on your own journey and see those verses in the larger context of the original, God-inspired author. I have used the 1986 New International Version to select these verses. You may find another version or a modern paraphrase helpful. The number of verses mentioned at the end of each theme is not exhaustive, and the ones listed may not always be those you expect. Some directly relate to the paragraph's themes, while others are indirect or add more context. Others are somewhat tangential and touch on a lateral meaning. These may suit the more inquisitive reader. But in each case, go to the source. Like the Bereans, examine the Scriptures yourself to see what is true.

Some passages from the Bible come up over and over as basic themes over broad areas of life and apply to differing scenarios. This will benefit those who read these thoughts topically rather than in sequence. Some verses come from a context in the Bible that seems quite different from the subject of the paragraph, but they show us something of God that is true for that topic as well. Some concepts have more verses than others, depending on the nature of the subject matter, and some passages are longer than you might expect, to provide more context for better understanding. Again, give them time and thought.

I hope you will see new applications of old and familiar verses that have lost their impact in our day. You may see the connection later as you go along and then look back. You may spend a week considering the verses given for one paragraph. Please note the verses are listed in their biblical order, not in the order of the concepts they accompany in the paragraph. In no way are these paragraphs and the verses cited a complete commentary on the subject. They are not intended as such. Neither is every topic of the Bible represented. There is much more in God's word than mentioned here. My purpose is to make an impression on us in our day of need, to help us reflect on what kind of people God purposes for us to be, to help us turn our personal thoughts to God and his ways, to see ourselves in the light of his word, and finally, to further reflect his image in a desperate world. These comments are only a beginning. They may take shape in your life in ways only you and God can understand.

I did not intend a one-sitting reading of these comments. At least I did not design them to be read that way. I expected the reader to take them in small doses. That is how I interact with the material I read, just a few pages at a time, noting my thoughts in the margins. Give yourself time to digest each topic. For those of us ordinary people, too much of a book in this format at one time blurs the vision as ideas run together, and we forget individual points we might do well to remember. My great inspiration is God's word itself, and I hope my efforts here will lead you to pore over his word more often, more deeply. Allow yourself to explore your mind and heart in the shadow of the greatness of our God.

So, stop and think. In our culture, it seems that only poets have time for that sort of thing. But you will benefit from it. Stop your motion for a few moments and read a paragraph or two. Go to the Bible verses that relate to the concept. Add a few that come to your mind. Make a note or two of your own as you read. Read the paragraph over again the next day. Add to your observations. These notes will remind you of your thoughts in your busy life. I hope these moments of consideration for you will not just vanish but will one day become thoughtful moments for others. Keeping a journal helps many people think through life's events, feelings, thoughts, and directions. The margins of the books I read are full of my notes. Do whatever works for you.

My goal in these pages is not bigger churches but Christians of a sturdier faith. I pray for more freedom in Christ, more unity around the essentials of our faith, and steadfast loyalty to God and his purposes and providence in our lives and in this broken world. Not that I have achieved all this myself. I write for us individualists who need insight into our thoughts and ways, humility in our hearts, and a greater trust in him to better serve our Lord. In many cases, the paragraph is a sermon to myself, rethinking where I am and where I want to be and how to better express my gratefulness for his grace. I might add that the thoughts here are written by an introvert and may look different to an extrovert. But we are all in this together. I am intending for us to be in touch with our inner selves, which may be more difficult for some but is beneficial for all.

Do not accept the paragraphs in this book as complete or final for you. Though they are statements of what I believe God's word says to us, I cannot, as I have said, apply them specifically to you. Only you can do that. These are broad strokes. Make your own observations that touch you where you are in your life. Each of us has his or her own journey with God. But God's providence is at work in all of us and can be trusted completely. I sincerely hope some of these comments will be helpful to you on your journey.

I have one more suggestion. Though some of us read alone, reading these entries with a friend or spouse might be more meaningful for others. Also, studying the Scripture references for their connection with the paragraphs is a good way to stimulate thinking in a small group as you reflect together. I pray they will help you make God's word the starting place for a growing commitment to him, the starting blocks of a race run for him. The stakes are too high, and our lives are too short, to do otherwise.

1. Choosing Grace

> "Do not conform any longer to the pattern of this world, but be transformed by the renewing of your mind. Then you will be able to test and approve what God's will is—his good, pleasing, and perfect will."
>
> —Romans 12:2

We must choose how we think, and we must also let God be God. He is a God of grace, but we may not have allowed it to touch our lives in the deepest ways. The undeserved favor and forgiveness of grace are not found in religion, only in God himself. He provided for it while we were his enemies, dead in our sins. The mystery of this grace is that, though none deserve it, it is available to everyone, yet each person must choose to own it. Each must want it more than the alternatives of their own achievement, survival, or success. Our confidence must not be in our efforts to gain his approval but in the offer of his inconceivable grace to such as us, its unconditional love, its far-reaching forgiveness.

    This is an offer to all the lost to find the way—held out to those who can never earn or purchase it on their own. But they must see their need, which will be a humbling experience. They may, and most will, reject that offer and choose the broad road of the rule of self, the values of their culture and its rewards, or the unrestrained ways of the world. They "want something else." But they must decide, and so must we as Christians. It is not for us to love the world or the things in it, not to worship the self, but to put it in perspective. We who think we are okay as Christians will not truly know him except through the humble acceptance of his grace each day. It is the difference between being a Christian on the popular level or being a biblical Christian who honestly trusts God's grace.

After arguments among the disciples about who was the greatest, Jesus put a towel around himself and washed their feet. Peter's pride would not allow it, but Jesus said that if he did not, Peter could have no part in him. The alternative to God's grace in our lives is separation from him—what the Bible often refers to as death. Even many who know something of Christianity continue in pride to peer down the broad road while he waits for them to trust him. Grace is within reach, but we must, in humility, accept it—allow it to wash over us and make us clean, forgive us unconditionally, and give us the security and freedom we long for.

If we want to know God but still long for the rewards of our culture, our misery will be multiplied. But God will be persistent in seeking our attention. We cannot serve two masters. He will use that misery to draw us to himself. Again, it is our choice to open ourselves unreservedly to him. After seeing Jerusalem besieged and destroyed because the people would not look toward God, Jeremiah tells the remaining Jews to examine their ways and return to the Lord. As Christians, we may also need to humble ourselves among the ashes and return ownership of our lives to the Lord. (Ps 130:3-4; Prov 14:12 and 16:2; Lam 3:40; Matt 18:12-14; Mark 9:33-37; Luke 16:13-15, 19:1-10, 22:24-26; John 1:10-18, 3:14-21 with 36, 5:24, 13:1-17; Rom 3:20-24, 5:6-11; Eph 1:3-8, 2:1-10; 1 Tim 1:12-17; Titus 2:11; Heb 4:14-16, 10:26-27; Jas 4:10; 1 John 2:15-17)

2. Morality

IT IS NOT ABOUT boasting at the end of your life, "I have never done an immoral thing." No amount of traveling down that road will get you to your desired destination. It may seem like you are gaining God's approval, but legalism is not the road he has given us. In the end, the achievement of legalism becomes the goal itself. It is about what we have accomplished, the self-discipline of mastering our inclinations, not about him or what he has done for us. Legalism is the body without the soul.

Life with God is about living out one's faith in the humility and honesty that knows very well we have *not* been righteous people, but we have God's grace and forgiveness. Pride is the enemy. We must learn our way out of legalism and false guilt and walk gratefully in the freedom of his grace and the enjoyment of all things he has created for us. God is more interested in what we are than in what we do. Morality is not about our record of outward achievements. It is about being someone who knows their weaknesses but trusts God's strength, wisdom, providence, and grace. It is less about us and more about him. (1 Chr 29:17a and 18b; Ps 51:16–17; Prov 16:2, 21:3, 28:26; Isa 42:1–3, 66:2b; Hos 6:6; Mic 6:8; Matt 9:9–13; Luke 18:9–14; Rom 14:1–8, 13, 16–18, 22; 1 Cor 8:8–9; Gal 5:1, 13–16; Eph 2:1–10, 5:15–21; Col 2:16–23 with 3:1–4; Jas 1:22–25; 1 Pet 2:15–16)

3. Our Names

We may have fallen in love with our name. It can be music to our ears in the mouths of those we love. It can be an encouragement or a rush of relief when those who love us hear it. It can also be the satisfaction of our pride to hear it mentioned above that of others, to see it listed among those who have achieved success. For good or for ill, our name identifies us and brings to mind for others not only who we are but often what we are. In biblical cultures, names themselves had meaning. In our individualist culture, they are primarily labels that distinguish you or me from someone else, but they are still very significant.

God knows your name and my name. Imagine hearing it spoken by him. Our name is written in the Book of Life. Each of us belongs to him and is very special to him. We are so important to him that, when we enter heaven to be with him, he will give each of us who knew and followed him a new name that says something special about our relationship with him. We are the particular focus of his love now, and our new name, known only to him and us, will forever establish an intimacy we have yet to know with him.

In the meantime, we may give an over-importance to our name here. In our Western culture, it is left to us to achieve an identity in the eyes of those around us and the feelings of self-worth that come with it if we succeed. Many of us feel insecure if we are not known for some accomplishment. And it is never enough. In our culture, one must keep achieving more to maintain that identity. But as Christians, we are free of that demanding social value on popularity, winning the attention and affirmation of others. We have an identity in Christ; we are "hidden with Christ in God"; he gives us worth the world cannot duplicate. He knows all about us, things others do not know, and he still loves us and wants us near him. We are not perfect, but we are his, and he wants us to dwell with him forever. (Pss 16:5–11, 139:1–6; Prov 3:3–4; Isa 43:1–3; Luke 12:6–7; John 14:1–4 and 20–23; Phil 4:3 with Rev 20:15; Col 3:1–3; Heb 13:5–6; Rev 2:17)

4. Feelings

EMOTIONS ARE INCONSISTENT, UNPREDICTABLE, and temporary. You can seldom have the feelings you want when you want them. If you are led by them, they will betray you just when you need them. They are not to be ignored entirely and can be a great blessing, but they are unreliable, and we must learn some emotional self-awareness so we do not allow them control without supervision. Only the truth remains when all else fails us, and it will stand by us in the difficulties of life. We can depend on God's word and providence in our lives, though we may not feel anything like we would expect or want. He stands by us regardless and will be there when all else has faded. He is the foundation of this truth. To know him is to know the truth and freedom from discouraging and anxious feelings on the edges of our everyday lives.

We are no longer defined by our feelings but by what God says about us: in Christ, secure forever, loved unconditionally, part of his plan for the world, and headed for eternal joy with him. This understanding of truth allows us peace in difficult circumstances and unpromising situations. Ambiguity and uncertainty can be set aside when we trust his truth and welcome the freedom it gives us. We will know he has a purpose in the world and for our lives and will carry it out. All is in his hands if we entrust our lives to him. (Pss 9:7–10, 16:1–11, 37:1–6, 42:5; Prov 3:5–7, 20:24, 28:26; Isa 41:10, 13, 43:1–3a, 46:10, 50:10–11; Matt 8:23–27, 11:25–30; John 14:6 and 27 with 20:19–20, 16:33; Phil 4:6–7; Col 3:15; 1 Pet 5:6–7)

5. Survival Is outside Ourselves

Our own efforts do not get us out of our self-centeredness. We are selfish and petty while thinking we are generous and grand, or we pity ourselves for the harsh life that is ours while living in plenty. We may resent what we see as unfair or become bitter about the suffering that has come our way when others seem free of it. Some become angry with God about their circumstances and turn away from him, but there is no other help. Others turn to religion to fix their world, but rituals are not the answer. We can try to look strong and confident and do good things to look like better people, but the problem is deep in our hearts. We are resisting God and, eventually, we must realize that, if we fight him, we are going to lose.

We must come to know God as he is and ourselves as we really are. Then, if we are willing, through humble faith, to take his way, he will lift us out of our self-absorption and helplessness. Though we cannot forget our former selves or hurtful experiences, we will be released from the penalty of our guilty state by his grace and made new to see life from his perspective. Few become effective for God who have not suffered in some way, even to the point of despair. They might not have come to him any other way, but when they do, the hopeless find hope; they see how that suffering has shaped them for God's purposes. We will live on a higher plane, above the small things of this world. We will face difficulties with the perspective of his hand on every detail of a bigger picture—his purposes, his movement in the world to bring about his ends. Our anxiety over the temporal things will fade; his providence becomes our guide, his way, as much as possible, our way.

Of course, we must live our day-to-day lives with an effort to allow this trust in him to have its way in each difficulty that comes. "Each day has enough trouble of its own." Yes, life in a broken world has its suffering, trouble, and sorrows. But he is with us through it. Perfection is still ahead of us, but its recognition changes our perspective and draws us away from insecurity and worry to the assurance and calmness of his grace, power, and providence. (Pss 9:7–10, 33:16–22, 37:1–11, 23–24, 28, 91:1–2, 14–16; Prov 3:5–7, 5:21, 16:2, 21:30, 28:26; Matt 6:25–34, 11:28–30; John 3:35 with Matt 28:18; John 13:3, 16:33, 17:15–19; Eph 1:22–23; Phil 4:4–7; Jas 4:10; 1 Pet 1:3–9, 5:6–7 with 10–11)

6. Freedom of Choice

GOD DOES NOT *MAKE* us always desire good or always desire him. Desire comes from within us. This freedom to love and be loyal to him makes the relationship real. Grace is a gift from God, but we choose to have faith. Without choice, there is no love; there can be no loyalty; we cannot know good. We must be free to decide, even though we sometimes choose wrongly. In an unspoiled situation, Adam and Eve had God's perfect love and attention, but they wanted more. He allowed them to make that choice on their own after clearly giving them his will for them. They chose loyalty to self over loyalty to God. They took what they desired, though the results were devastating for all of creation.

But God did not abandon Adam and Eve for their terrible decision nor take their freedom away. Though the distressing consequences of their sin were sudden and permanent in this life, there was also grace for the way forward based on the promise of One coming who would strike the serpent's head. Jesus Christ would bring forgiveness and hope for all who believe in him, those who, turning from self, humbly choose to be his. This grace and truth came to us many centuries ago when he fulfilled that promise. Through what he would do in Jesus, God forgave them that day in the garden. That same forgiveness is offered freely to all, though all are undeserving. Nothing can change his offer or remove those of us who have chosen it from his hand. The world continues to know suffering and proud rebellion, but for us, on the narrow way, our gratefulness can know no limit. And one day, all suffering will be removed again. (Gen 3:1–19; Ps 130:3–4; Isa 65:17; John 1:14–18, 3:16–21, 10:28–30, 16:33; 1 Cor 2:9; 2 Cor 3:15—4:7; Eph 2:1–10; Jas 1:13–18; 1 Pet 5:10–11; Rev 21:1–4)

7. Joy Intended

We must come to know God's intentions for us and choose his way. We will not always feel like it, but feelings are not the primary concern nor always very helpful. Seeking to honor him is his will for us. Although we will not be perfect in carrying out our desires, he sees our hearts and their intentions and motives. As we seek to be faithful, we will discover and delight in the many beautiful and satisfying things he intended for us. We are free to enjoy all things created with gratefulness. He calls them good, and though their abuse is often evil, we should not call what he has made good bad. The imperfection is in us, not in what he has created for us. We often love the things he created for us in place of the God who created them. This can be a selfish love; when it is, it will misuse what he has given us. We must love the Creator first to enjoy his gifts as he intended. If we do, we will see he has not withheld anything good thing from us.

As in the last paragraph, I have often mentioned how we will not be perfect in our walk with God. Though that is true and may comfort us to realize it, it must send us to him for his grace and forgiveness. We must be growing in our relationship with God in ways that bring improvement so that we might walk "worthy of the Gospel." We all have sins that God's grace must wash from us daily. Paul talked about his own struggle, Jesus washed the disciples' feet when they struggled, and John talks about God's faithfulness to forgive us. But this does not mean we cannot be better people for him. The Bible calls us to a higher plane. We each have a human and selfish nature that we must deal with to honor God and desire what he desires. Indeed, we will not be perfect, but we must allow God more influence in our lives—if we are to flourish in our faith and trust. Knowing very well our weaknesses, we also know we *can* do better. It is a battle with the self and its desires—to set them aside for God's will in our lives and relationships more than we do now. God intended joy for us, but we may be keeping much of it at a distance by not trusting him more and self less.

Despite being human and the abuses of God's good creation, we can fully enjoy all God created if we do so with discernment for his intentions, a desire to honor him, and consideration for the needs of those around us. Love for God and for others must rule our hearts more and more. When we put off virtue and commitment for our human inclinations, we put off peace and happiness for another day. Our lives will be upset with frustrated attempts at superficial satisfaction while lasting fulfillment is within reach—his grace and forgiveness are always nearby. Joy is intended for us, but we will have to take its path even though we stumble at times.

When we strive to take his way, his purposes will be fulfilled in us. The fact that we struggle with the human desires of the old self and will do so until we leave this world does not mean that we do not desire to honor him and are not making progress in our loyalty to him. It means we are human and need his grace as much now as when we first believed. He knows this about us, and yet his purpose is to use us in his plan. Like a tree by a stream, he plans for us to bear fruit in the appointed seasons and endure the elements with green leaves. We get our strength from roots that are near the living water. We are his, and he intends to give us joy in himself amid the trials, difficulties, suffering, and sorrows of this broken world. (Ps 1:1–3; Isa 43:1; Matt 7:13–14; Mark 9:33–35; Luke 22:23–34; John 1:4, 8:12, 13:6–10, 14:6; Rom 7:14–25; 1 Cor 6:12, 10:23–24 with 31; Col 3:17; 1 Thess 5:21; 1 Tim 4:4; Titus 1:15–16; 1 John 2:15–17)

8. Trusting God's Way

Trust is what God wants from us more than anything else. Noah believed God and built the ark. God saved him and his family. Abraham was justified by his faith in the most trying way. By trusting God, Moses stood in his weakness but in God's strength before the pharaoh of Egypt. On and on goes chapter 11 in Hebrews, for without faith—knowing that he is and trusting what he says and does—it is impossible to please God, experience his grace, or know his peace. Though he gives us countless opportunities to look to him, rest in his grace and strength, trust his providence, and experience his care, he will not force his way. God desires us to walk by faith, and we must do so to be in his way. There can be no trust where there is no insecurity, ambiguity, or trouble—a reason to trust him and the choice to do so. In the throes of these negative emotions and adversities, we must choose not to be anxious. These are the opportunities God puts before us. We are in his hands when we trust him; that is precisely where he wants us, though he never abandons us when we waiver.

Unfortunately, trusting him is not irresistible. We must choose to go to him, humble ourselves, and seek to honor him though we may not recognize his help when it comes. As characters in his story, we must let him write the part we are to play. Though we make many choices in how we will do that, some of them not so good, his providence guides us in the way as we let him. He is not looking for perfection but for a heart that trusts him. It is a consistent theme in Scripture—God's unconditional grace for all who know and trust him. It cannot be overcome even by our sin or Satan's strategies. When we trust him, we belong to him, and nothing can change that. (Num 23:19; Pss 20:7, 28:6–9, 33:16–22, 37:3–5, 40:4, 139:1–18 with 23–24, 146:3–6, 147:10–11; Prov 3:5–7, 11:28, 21:31, 28:26; Isa 43:1–3a, 50:10; Mic 4:5; Hab 2:4; John 14:1, 16:33; Eph 1:17–23; Phil 1:9–11; Col 1:9–14; 2 Thess 1:11–12; Heb 11:1–39; Jas 4:10)

9. Obedience

BEING HONEST, JUST, CONSIDERATE, loyal to him, and forsaking the need for recognition are ways of becoming the person God wants us to be. It is not a list of things to do or avoid as much as attitudes of the heart that he seeks in us. From a good heart, people seek to do what honors God, even if they do not always succeed. In the sermon on the mount, Jesus showed us God's will concerning the outward law of the Old Testament. It, too, was a matter of the heart. Throughout the Old Testament, he looked into his people's hearts for loyalty and the desire to honor him, though their behavior might not be perfect. But God did not always find what he was searching for. Evil hearts led to evil behavior.

We may not find emotional desire the most effectual motive for obedience to God. It is more a matter of the will. We desire to be loyal and to do what God puts before us because we choose to. Feelings come and go. God knows our desires; still, we must not lean on emotions but on chosen loyalty to influence our life with God and others; we must seek to walk in a manner worthy of his love. If feelings come with it, it is a blessing. They *will* come after it in contentment and peace. Once again, obedience is a matter of trust. But he is worthy of it in every sense. (1 Sam 13:14; Pss 40:6-8, 51:17, 78:7-8 with 35-37; Prov 10:9, 21:3; Mic 6:8; Matt 5—7; Luke 6:43-45; John 14:15, 21-24, 15:9-14; Acts 5:1-11, 13:22-23; Eph 4:1-3, 4:17—5:2; Phil 2:12-16a; Col 1:9-12; 1 Thess 2:12; 1 Tim 1:5-7; 2 John 4-6)

10. Material Blessings

We know all things worth having come from God. All else is temporal and short-lived at best. God provides the everyday things we need for this life, not that we should set our hearts on them, but to help us fulfill his destiny for us—his will. If moth and rust corrupt things, envy will equally corrupt our hearts if those things are too important to us. If we crave the status that the possession of things will give us, the acids of greed and pride will eat at our souls. All things are given to those who believe for their help and encouragement, for their joy and pleasure, for sharing with others, and for their use in giving honor to his name. Our need is to be grateful and let love rule. (Prov 3:9, 11:25, 28, 22:9, 23:4–5, 28:26; Matt 6:19–21, 25–34, 7:7–11; Luke 12:15; Rom 8:31–32; 1 Cor 10:23–24, 31, 13:1–13; 2 Cor 9:6–11; Col 3:17; 1 Tim 6:6–10; Titus 1:15; Heb 13:5–6; Jas 1:16–17, 5:1–6; 2 Pet 1:3–4; 1 John 3:17–19)

11. The Declaration and Mystery of Grace

GRACE FROM GOD IS at once both fact for the mind and assurance for the heart, at the same time both declaration and mystery. What we greatly desire and desperately need is beyond our comprehension yet overwhelming in our experience. It was a mystery even to the angels, now revealed—his eternal purpose opening the way to himself through the grace rendered freely in the sacrifice of Christ who bore our sins. If you reject God's grace because it appears unreasonable, illogical, or too good to be true, you will be left with nothing in a wasteland of only human solutions that cannot satisfy. Days and months go by without assurance or help. Guilt nags, and insecurity is always at the edges of experience without God. When your life is required of you, you will have nothing on which to stand; you will not stand at all.

Grace is not logical, but it is complete, leaving nothing unforgiven, no stain when you come into his presence. For when we humble ourselves and accept his grace, we receive the righteousness of Christ and come in his name. God is faithful to respond to us, and his justice is perfectly served in forgiving us. Grace is unconditional for the one who knows God in this way.

But the new wine will not fit in the old wineskin of personal achievement. Pride must be shattered in the acceptance of grace. Those who know it deep down will be characterized by humility, for they know their old self and its ways. And they know that he knows, but that he still forgives and wants them to be his own in an intimate relationship. The old wineskin must be put aside for a new one. Prior things have passed away, and all things are new. We go from thinking we are something to realizing we are nothing to knowing a new identity in Christ that gives us everything we have ever needed. We will not be perfect, but we will see everything from this new perspective, and there will be no end to our gratefulness. (Pss 25:8–9, 130:3–4, 139:1–6, 145:13–14; Prov 21:3, 28:26; Mic 6:8; Matt 5:3, 9:16–17,

18:1–4; Rom 5:1–2, 11:33–36, 12:3; 1 Cor 10:22–31; 2 Cor 5:15–17; Gal 6:3–5; Eph 1:7–10, 2:1–10, 5:22–27; Col 1:27; 1 Tim 3:16; 1 Pet 2:24–25, 3:18; 2 Pet 1:3–4; 1 John 1:8–10)

12. Worry

GOD WANTS OUR SOULS to flourish. But we often allow worry to eat away at us—letting trust dwindle until our joy and freedom are consumed. We are responsible for what we do right now, but God has not yet given us tomorrow. If all the time and emotional energy spent worrying about things we have no control over were used for the important matters we must care for today, we would have more than enough to honor God with our lives. We could use that energy to meet the needs of our family and friends and accomplish valuable things that will affect the future.

We cannot control the future, but we have seen God's faithful providence in our lives over the years through thick and thin. He has kept all his promises, his grace has surrounded us, and he has carried us through many struggles to this day. Though we may have scars, we are his now and can trust him for tomorrow. We can then notice this moment, its blessings, and the important concerns God placed in it for our attention.

The struggle against worry will be ongoing for many of us, even as the disciples of Jesus struggled with it in the storm on the sea. So, we must remember that the events of our lives are not out of his control, though he may want us to learn from him as he takes us through difficulties. He often wants us to learn to trust him in small matters so we are ready to trust him in the more weighty events in life. Moreover, his providence in our lives may not be evident from our perspective; it may not look like we expect it to. But we must trust him. He is with us in our boat, and the storm is not too much for him to handle. Worry must be set aside, for it does not allow the soul to flourish. (Deut 31:6, 8; Pss 37:1–11, 42:5, 63:1–8, 91:1–16, 139:7–12; Prov 3:5–8; Matt 6:31–34, 8:23–27, 16:5–12, 28:18 with 20b; Rom 8:28–39; Phil 4:4–9; 2 Thess 2:16–17; Jas 1:2–4; 1 Pet 1:3–7, 5:6–7)

13. Forgiveness, His and Ours

God's forgiveness is not like ours, but ours can become more like his. His is complete, consistent, and without conditions or limits when we come to him through Christ. For us, it is a process that may take some time. For him, it is now and forever. We often put forgiveness on an emotional plane. We think we must feel forgiving if it is the real thing. But God does not base his forgiveness on feelings. Yes, he has compassion on his own, so much so that he sent his Son to die for us. But, based on this sacrifice, God's forgiveness is an act of his divine will. It is an act of his to move us from the deplorable and helpless state of our sinfulness to the righteous position he gives us in Christ.

When we forgive, we may never forget, but God removes our sins from us as far as the east is from the west. However, forgetting is not necessarily part of forgiveness. In fact, we are told to "remember therefore what you have received . . . ." Paul reminds the Ephesians how they were dead in their sin. For us, forgiveness is knowing full well the damage someone has done to us. It is not walking into further abuse but being cautious. We need to act with wisdom to avoid becoming their target again if possible. Our forgiveness is not returning the unkindness but waiting for the right moment to show kindness again when an opportunity arises. It is not to ignore, overlook, or condone the hurtful action but to acknowledge the wrongdoing fully and choose not to act in anger, exact revenge, or wait for an opportunity for payback. It is to respond in compassion as God did for us.

However, societies cannot exist without law and its enforcement. God put human governments in place to serve him and protect the community. Though some do this much better than others, and all are subject to human corruption, we, as Christians, are part of society and should support what we can of the legal system for detainment and correction of criminal and destructive behavior. Lawful detainment may be necessary when people harm us. It is not a sin or the opposite of forgiveness to do this. Our personal forgiveness cannot disregard the evil it causes in society. Antisocial people must be stopped from habitual behavior that harms others. In doing this, we are not exacting payback from harmful people. We do not seek to bring about our own vengeance or vindication. No, we leave these things to God and act out of love for others. We are using the government put in place by God to stop them from destroying other lives. We hope it will also give them time to consider God's way and allow him to work in their hearts. Of course, not everything in the human legal system is moral or just. Legality or normality does not make unbiblical actions right. So wisdom and discernment in our "free" society is necessary.

God's forgiveness is greater than ours, for his kindness is there while we are being unkind, selfish, vengeful, or dishonest. His love and grace are then lavished on the undeserving when they turn to him, and such are we. (Pss 32:1–5, 37:5–6, 103:6–18, 130:3–4; Prov 3:3–4; Matt 6:14, 7:6; Acts 5:29; Rom 11:33–36, 13:3–5; Eph 1:6–8, 2:1–5; Col 3:13–15; 1 Pet 3:14b with 18; 1 John 1:9, 3:1–3)

14. Suffering

WHEN THERE IS NOTHING left, there is still God. He is with us in a world of suffering that he never wanted to be that way. The knowledge of good and evil God sought to withhold is a terrible fate to desire, and it is ours without our consent, a choice of our ancestors. But do not think we would not have chosen the same as they. For, though God wanted a world without suffering, he intended for people to be free to choose so there could also be love, loyalty, honesty, and compassion—virtues that cannot exist in a vacuum. They involve personal choice of action where opposite values exist, where there are temptations like the forbidden tree in Eden.

But, though God gives us good things, shows us beauty along the way, brings stillness amid the confusion and disorder, and provides relief from suffering and grief, we also sometimes suffer in prolonged and intense ways and in the darkest tones. That is when our trust is proven. We must cling to the fact that he is there; he never wanted this for us and is preparing a place where it can never touch us again. But we must trust the Lord our God. Jesus suffered for us and uses our struggles and sufferings to get our attention, shape us, and train us—for our good, the growth of our faith in his providence, and our gratefulness for his grace. Jesus is the perfector of our faith in these ways.

So, God sometimes allows suffering to strengthen our faith, as with telling Abraham to sacrifice Isaac. Other times, it is to glorify himself (make himself and his way known), as with Joseph being sold as a slave, Daniel being taken captive to Babylon, or the blind man in John 9. Then there are times when he wants to show us that his grace is sufficient, that his power is made perfect in weakness, and that he is at work in us for his purposes, as he told Paul. He wants our trust in him to give us peace and our patience and endurance to be an example to the world. When he is shaping us in this way or correcting our shortcomings, he may need to get our attention in ways we do not like. But it is worth the discomfort to grow our trust in his good purposes for us, our loyalty to his ways, and our confidence in his careful providence.

We must also realize that we often bring much of our suffering on ourselves through our individualist ambitions and self-assertion; we are compelled by our love for ourselves. Much of this we can correct if we will humbly come to terms with God's way for us. It is not an easy path for the Western individualist, for whom survival has always been a matter of personal achievement. That is why Jesus says the seed must die if there is to be any fruit, that whoever wants to save his life must lose it. Our minds must be renewed. Our old wineskin will not serve the purposes of God in our new lives. We have a new wineskin, a new frame of reference for meaning and personal worth in the circumstances of life.

Much of the time, however, suffering is simply part of living in a fallen world. It shapes the context within which we must live for God by faith, and it will help us focus our hope on the world to come. We must not let suffering come between God and us but bring us closer to him. The correct perspective will give us wisdom, remembering that his way is not ours. His purposes must be fulfilled. But, if not here and now, he will still heal our broken hearts and bind up our wounds. The raging storms of this life will become still in time. All will be well again if we take his way through it. (Gen 3:8–13, 50:18–21; Job 2:9–10; Pss 23:4, 119:67–71 with 92–93, 138:6–8, 139:7–12, 147:3; Isa 65:17; Matt 9:16–17, 28:20b; Luke 9:23–25; John 9:1–41, 12:24–26, 17:15–19; Rom 5:3–5, 8:28–39, 12:1–2; 1 Cor 2:9; 2 Cor 5:6–9, 12:7–10; Phil 1:6, 2:12–13; Heb 10:32–38, 12:1–12; Jas 1:2–8; 1 Pet 1:6–12, 3:13–18, 5:6–11; 2 Pet 1:3–11; Rev 21:1–4)

15. The Peace of God Interrupted

WE ALLOW MANY THINGS to come between God and us. The smallest trouble, the slightest loss, a pleasure postponed, concern for our reputation, and worry about the future create emotional confusion. Our minds fog over, and we can't see past our circumstances. We become nervous and irritable. We are afraid we will not be happy unless things go our way. This is letting concerns for self come between God and us, family and us, other Christians and us, and between those who need our help in the world and us. One's self has become the frame of reference, the foundation for decisions and behavior.

These concerns are often shallow, inconsiderate, and insignificant. But we do not see them that way and allow them to preoccupy a good share of our waking moments. Our minor concerns allow essential things to pass us by in the rapidly vanishing days of our time on Earth. But from the perspective of God's grace in our salvation, his providence in our lives, and his work in the world, the lesser things fade in their importance to us. You see, we seek happiness for ourselves when it lies outside the self in knowing and trusting God and understanding and serving others. It is not that self has no importance; it is the need to put self in perspective, trusting God that we are the object of his love, grace, and providence in every circumstance. The peace of God can and will guard our hearts and minds in Christ Jesus. We must remember that unimportant matters are just that—unimportant. (Matt 6:25–34; Luke 6:46–49, 9:23–25; John 12:20–26, 14:27, 16:33; Rom 6:6–7, 12:1–2; 1 Cor 6:19–20, 13:4–7; 2 Cor 5:15; Eph 4:22–24; Phil 2:3–4, 4:6–7 and 8–9 with Col 3:1–4; Jas 3:13–18; 1 Pet 4:6–11)

16. Emptiness

THE FEELING OF EMPTINESS can grab hold of us and hang onto our souls if we take our eyes off God and his way. It may seem he does not care about us or our situation. Feelings can be wonderful; however, they are woefully unstable compared to his constant care outside our awareness. If we seek God's help, we will have to let him be God instead of trying to fill the emptiness by making him the answer we want for ourselves. Feelings of emptiness can be an avenue to God, an opportunity for us to know and trust him, to motivate us in his direction. His providence and grace come together in our salvation and an ongoing relationship with him. But we can keep them at a distance with our concerns for feelings of happiness. We must receive his grace on his terms, and that begins with trust. Trust in him can fill the emptiness with gratitude for his grace and love, rest in the protection of his good providence, strength when we are emotionally exhausted, and peace as we see the world in which we live from his perspective instead of ours. We must look up, setting our minds on things above to see things on earth as they really are. (Pss 42:5 with 84:1–12 and 100:1–5, 90:10–17, 91:1–4; Prov 3:5–7, 16:9; Isa 26:3–4, 42:1–3; Matt 11:28–30; John 14:27, 15:5–8, 16:33, 20:19–20; Rom 5:3–5, 12:1–2; 2 Cor 12:7–10; Phil 2:12–13; Col 3:1–3; Heb 4:9–11; Jas 1:2–8; 1 Pet 1:6–12)

17. Uncertainties Call for Trust

WHAT IS MORE NAGGING than doubt that God might act on our behalf? It is true we will suffer various things as a matter of course in this broken world. It is the natural result of sin, as God said it would be. But doubting his goodness is not worthy of us who have been saved by his grace through the sacrifice of his Son. How is it that he would not also care for our needs in his own time and way, that his purposes would not be carried out in us in this world? Selfishness and pride are the greatest of the sins, but doubt is in a category of its own and is often used by Satan, as he used it in Eden, to lead us further away from God. But, if we allow it, it can also trigger our self-awareness of an opportunity to trust him. Bred of our insecurities, doubt is a weakness in our relationship with the one who cares more than we can know and can do more than we can imagine.

Jesus prayed not that the Father would take us out of the world, where the troubles that cause doubt abound, but that he would protect us from the evil one, where doubt begins. Don't take the fruit. Don't doubt God's ways. It may look like something we really want lies in that direction, but doubt can bring suffering, luring us away from God and the good things he has for us. So, we must trust him even when we do not know all the details and life feels uncertain.

There is mystery in God and much he has not told us. Paradox and irony are in his ways, for they are not our ways. But we should be neither threatened by uncertainty nor afraid of ambiguity, for our lives are in God's wise and loving hand, and he is not absent in the experiences we encounter. Uncertainties call for trust; without them, there could be none. Trust is what God wants from you and me more than anything else. It will take humility and courage to say, "I don't know, but I know who does, and I trust him to carry out his purposes in my life." And if you are serious about walking with God, you will get plenty of practice saying it. (Gen 3:1–7; Pss 4:8, 20:7, 21:7, 28:7, 37:3–6, 111:4–7, 115:3, 125:1–2, 127:1–2; Prov 3:5–7,

28:26; Isa 26:3–4, 55:8–9; Matt 14:28–32; Luke 24:36–49; John 14:1, 16:33, 17:15, 20:24–28; Rom 8:31–35; Phil 1:6 with 2:12–13 and 1 Thess 5:23–24; Jas 1:2–8; 1 Pet 1:6–12, 2:24–25, 5:6–11)

18. God's Answers to Prayer

WE ASK GOD FOR help, but sometimes it seems he is looking the other way. Is he distracted or unmindful of us in our situation? We are told that he answers all prayers with a yes, no, or not now. Why does it seem there are so many "no" answers? The truth is, there are not that many times God says no, though we don't always recognize a positive answer. His ways are not our ways, and his providence has often shaped some of the answers to our prayers before we pray and continues to shape them afterward when our patience has run out, and we are looking the other way. But if he does say no, it is not like a distracted parent wanting to give their attention to something else. It is like a parent who knows the gift is already under the tree. Some of those gifts are for the near future, and some are further off when, done with needs, we will enjoy him and those we have known and loved for all time without end. It may be harder for those who have not had a loving father or mother in the home, but Jesus gives us the picture of one who truly loves us and responds to our needs every time we bring them to him. (Pss 37:1–11, 85:10–12; Prov 16:9; Matt 7:7–12; Luke 11:9–10; John 15:5–8; Rom 8:32; 1 Cor 2:9; Eph 3:12; Jas 1:16–18; 1 John 5:13–15)

19. Gratefulness

WE ARE OFTEN PAINFULLY aware of our needs, faults, pride, or selfish behavior. Hopefully, they will drive us to God for the forgiveness and help we need. The woman at the well, Nicodemus the Pharisee, the man born blind, or the woman taken in adultery were people in these situations—arguing, selfish, proud, or needy—when Jesus came into their lives. Then, they were humbled, thankful, and indebted, though they all came to him in various ways and showed their gratefulness differently. Another, the rich young man, refused to see his need to turn aside from his wealth and walked away. Not everyone will follow Jesus. Pride, materialism, or social success will often block the way. We can only come into God's family through the sacrifice of Christ with humility. Those who seek him in truth will be overcome with the knowledge of his grace and our unworthiness—his unconditional forgiveness. They will become known for their gratefulness.

We do not become perfect and will regret self-centered behavior after his grace has been poured out on us. But that regret shows us we are his and draws us back to his grace and his way. How good is our strong God and caring father whose forgiveness is without boundaries! He never turns away. When we stray from his way, he waits for us to return to him. If we are his, we can never wander too far off the path, searching for our own idea of happiness. His love and grace are always there for us, drawing us back to him. Humility and gratitude make us less likely to move away from him again, but he is still there for us if we do. (Ps 103:10–14; Jer 29:13; Lam 3:40; Matt 7:7–12, 19:16–24; Luke 15:3–7, 8–10, 11–24; John 3:1–21, 4:4–26, 8:3–11, 9:1–38, 10:27–30; Rom 7:18–25, 8:35–39, 11:33–36; Col 2:6–7; Jas 4:6 with 10; 1 John 1:8–9)

20. Learning to Rest in His Grace

WE KNOW EVERY BREATH is from him, and every blessing and gift is from above. But sometimes, when our emotions let us down, we act like it's not true; we become preoccupied with our circumstances and forget to thank him for his goodness. Our ungratefulness causes us to sink deeper. We must remember. We must wake up to the grace he has shown us—the greatest blessing of all. Through that grace, he gives us all we need. We can rest "under the shadow of the Almighty," for he is "our refuge and strength," removing all fear and the anxiety of our souls even in the most trying difficulties. Though we have done nothing worthy of it, his grace is there, and we are not required to have earned it. It is free, and he calls us to embrace it. We would never be worthy in ourselves, but we have that worthiness in Christ. No circumstance can change that. We can rest in his grace anywhere, anytime. In our most trying moments, we must consider this great gift from God. We must lean on it and not on our own achievements. But the choice is ours to remember.

Rest is found in turning from the search for recognition to his way, realizing our feeble inadequacy and his good providence, desiring to honor him, seeing ourselves from his perspective, and finding our joy in his grace. The world may never know our name, but he does. Our perspective may be limited, our logic fall short, our feelings unhelpful, but we are his, and he will never leave us outside his purposes or abandon us in our human circumstances. Knowing this is resting in his presence, power, and providence. (Pss 23:4, 46:1–3, 62:1–2, 5–8, 11–12, 91:1–16, 107:13–16; Isa 42:1–3, 43:1b; Matt 11:28–30; John 14:27, 20:19–20; Eph 5:14; Phil 4:4–9; 2 Thess 2:16–17 with 3:16; Heb 4:1–2 with 8–11; 1 Pet 5:6–7)

21. Letting God Be God in Our Prayers

We often hear, "Prayer changes things!" or "Prayer really works!" But these exclamations move us away from God instead of toward him. They are the Western excitement of finding solutions and fixing the broken things in our lives. Prayer does not change things; God changes things. Prayer does not work; God works. If the ritual becomes its own answer, our relationship with God is needy. We long for spiritual feelings and think they are the assurance that God is with us in our need or listening to our prayers. But it is not about emotional feelings. They are wonderful, of course, but they come and go while God does not. He remains. His grace and power to help us do not need them. That he loves us and has bathed us in his grace are facts that do not change with the weather. That is our God, and we must let him be and do what he will in our lives, for all he does is out of love for us whether we feel like it or not.

As we have often said, more often than yes, no, and not yet, God answers prayer in another, more common way, though we hear little of it. It is the answer to our request in ways we do not recognize, ways we do not expect, and timing we do not anticipate. Our expectations are for an answer we have already fixed in our minds, the way he should act on our behalf coming from personal preferences and cultural values. But his methods are often outside our logic, beyond our expectations, and include what we do not want in order to give us what we really need. What we anticipate seems normal to us for an omnipotent God. But we do not know ourselves very well or understand the influence of our culture's values on us. They are fragile indicators of the answers we need in his design for us. Neither do we understand his providence on our behalf—what events will bring about his purposes for us and how that affects our future. God wants the best for us, but we have made plans for him to achieve that from our limited human perspective.

21. LETTING GOD BE GOD IN OUR PRAYERS

We must let God be God. How could the Creator-God not know best what will meet our needs? It is not that our preferences are unimportant, but that we must see them as secondary to his way, and we do not know what lies ahead. We are invited to come to him with our heart's desires and pressing needs. He is always there, and he is always attentive. But we must trust him. He moves in ways that we may not understand now. It is his way of giving what is best, though that may not be what we seek at the moment. (Gen 45:4–8, 50:19–21; Ps 37:3–6; Prov 3:6–7, 16:9, 20:24; Isa 55:8–11; Jer 29:10–14; Matt 6:9–13; John 14:13–14, 15:7–8; Rom 8:31–32, 11:33–36; Phil 4:6–7; Heb 11:6; 1 John 5:13–15)

22. Prayer as Part of God's Design

SOME TODAY EMPHASIZE GOD'S sovereignty in a way that does not allow people to have a part in his work in the world, but he invites us to do just that. Though sovereignty should cancel out prayer in our all-or-nothing logic, that is not his design. We are invited, even called upon, to pray. We pray for change regarding those things that disrupt his ways, deface his message, cloud his image in the Bible, and hinder our part in serving him. We pray for basic necessities in our poverty or for his control over the powers of evil and the suffering they cause. Our prayers may be the groans of our own pain or sorrow, seeking relief, or for the welfare of those we love. In this way, he gives us a part in his work, though we may not see how it plays out in his plan.

All our humble prayers are heard by the sovereign God of the universe who delights to help us. He planned that we would commune with him, worship him, lay our petitions before him, and he would listen to every word. It is part of his design—something he wants and seeks from his own to meet their needs and give them a role in his work in the world. He does not need our help but wants a relationship with us and gives us every attention. He meets our needs, shows us how our needs make us better servants for him in his purposes, or shows us that in our weakness, he is powerfully at work to carry out his plan. We can trust him even if we do not recognize his help at the time.

Though his design from the beginning was for the best things to happen, the world is spoiled by sin, and some things will not come about while we are here but are reserved for us in heaven. Other blessings he brings about in his way and time or gives us the grace to endure our time in our frail bodies and this broken world. In the ups and downs of life, on the bright days, and on the dark paths, we have a God who cares. We must be grateful and pray for his will to be done on earth as it is in heaven. (Gen 1:31, 3:16–19; 2 Chr 7:14; Pss 19:1–6, 23:4, 130:5–6, 139:7–12, 145:18; Matt

6:9–13; John 1:1–18, 15:5–8, 17:15–19; Rom 11:33–36; Phil 4:4–7; Col 1:15–20; 1 Tim 4:4; 1 Pet 1:3–9, 5:7–11)

23. Justice

"If God is good and omnipotent, he would not allow suffering in the world." So say the proud and angry of heart. They blame God for the suffering in the world and put him on trial when humankind is guilty of desiring and choosing evil over good for our world. He created a perfect place and gave it freely to the man and woman in the garden, along with the costly gift of freedom to trust him or go their own way. He gave us perfection; we destroyed it, and we blame him. We should thank him for not turning his back on humankind after their distrust of his goodness. We would have done so. But he, at great sacrifice, offered help, a way back to himself, and forgiveness of our preoccupation with ourselves, our sin of not trusting his word. We cannot deny it; we were dead in our sins, unresponsive, and he brought life to us. His grace is active today and poured out on anyone who trusts him.

The world may seem out of control. It may not be kind to us. But we are not of the world and its ways. We in Christ are of a higher court, not subject to the world's judgments. Our case has been dismissed by his stepping in to take the sentence for our guilt. He endured the separation from God in our place so that those of us who believe may never be separated from him. In him, we are acquitted by the Judge of all humankind. God's justice has been carried out, the curtain between us removed, our appointment to an eternal destiny with him declared. (Pss 37:3–6, 89:14, 99:1–5; Prov 19:3, 21:3; Mic 6:8; Matt 27:45–54; John 14:1–4 and 23, 17:13–19; Rom 3:21–24, 5:1–2; Jas 1:13–18; 1 Pet 1:3–12, 3:18, 5:10–11; 1 John 1:5–10, 2:17, 4:1–6)

24. Feelings of Security

INSECURITY IS A MAJOR hurdle for Christians in individualist cultures. The Western cultures of North America and Western Europe teach us that our emotional, social, and even physical survival is entirely up to us. These expectations for us are nearly overwhelming. Parents socialized in this world of individualism often fail to help their children navigate these powerful cultural expectations and establish feelings of security in their identity and self-worth. Most people spend a lifetime coping and using everything possible to reach the goal—often to their ruin and that of those around them.

In this battle, individualist people are never quite sure they are achieving enough for the survival and benefits they need. Someone else is always performing better, achieving more, and upping the bar. We try to gather and hoard material things to feel secure, but they are fragile and temporal, no matter how much we accumulate. We then offset disillusionment with more achievement. So, doubt breeds insecurity, leading to more achievement, resulting in more doubt, continuing the cycle. It is hard for individualists to risk stepping away from this effort for survival to trust God's way. David tells us that "some trust in chariots and some in horses." In the West, we trust in our achievements. David goes on to say, "But we trust in the name of the Lord our God." Only a willingness to risk all our culture has promised us for survival will bring lasting security under God's wing.

Trusting God's word, grace, purposes, providence, and love will overcome our insecurities. All has been achieved for us in Christ; we cannot add to his work. And in Christ, God has given and will give us all we need. Our feelings are not often the best indicators of true security. It is more a matter of determined trust. Jesus was in the boat with the disciples on the day of the storm. They were secure, though they did not feel like it. We can trust him completely each day and in each circumstance. He is always in our situation with us. (Pss 16:8, 20:7, 23:4, 63:1–8, 91:1–4, 139:7–12; Hab 3:16–19; Matt

6:19–21, 25–34; 8:23–27, 19:16–26; Luke 12:13–21, 22–34; John 10:27–30; Rom 8:31–39; Phil 4:13; Col 3:1–4; 2 Pet 1:3–8)

25. Assurance

SEEKING TO KNOW GOD'S will through feelings of self-confidence is a faulty pursuit. It is not a feeling that can tell us the true story—or not all of it. Assurance is found not in emotions but in the truth we find in God's word, in his promises, purposes, and providence. It comes down to a matter of pure trust, which, in turn, results in the assurance we seek. We can also look back and see God's providence in our lives as a source of assurance and confidence. He carries out his intentions as he works in our lives. They may not have been your purposes, but they reflect his faithfulness and love and turn out far better than yours. His purposes may be unclear to us and often undetected until much later. They may come out of what we consider the worst times of our lives, times when we nearly gave up. We may still endure the residue or pain of certain events in our lives. Some have been called upon to trust him for more than others in our broken world. But his grace is sufficient. We may be saved as those snatched from the fire when all else is gone, or he may bring flowers out of the ashes, but we must trust him.

God's intentions do not always look like they could be his. But our trust in his providence and care will bring beauty where once there was devastation. He has been transforming us who know him for a long time. We do not yet know everything he has done and may not until we are with him in heaven. But we can be assured of his work to good ends in our lives. We are his purpose for creation. (Pss 8:3–9, 37:23–24, 89:8, 91:1 with 9 and 14–16, 95:6–7, 100:3, 139:1–6 with 13–16; Prov 16:9, 24:15–16; Isa 40:28–31, 41:10, 48:17; Rom 8:28–39; Phil 1:6 with 2:12–13, 3:12—4:1; 1 Thess 5:23–24; 2 Thess 1:11–12; Jude 17–23)

26. Mystery in God's Purposes

WESTERN PEOPLE DISLIKE UNCERTAINTY in nearly any domain, but it is especially troublesome when it touches on their personal happiness. This causes unbelievers to view the Bible with skepticism. They don't want to risk what "happiness" they have achieved. Christians in the West may try to minimize what is ambiguous to them in the Bible. Some even change the meanings of obvious words or add details not in the text to clarify passages that seem unclear. Uncertainty is an illness in our minds and rational, comprehensive, black-and-white categories, our medicine. We seek to give everything meaning in a logical, consistent system that we can master—one that fits our preferences—our theology. The Jewish leaders had this problem with Jesus. His actions did not fit their Oral Torah or their interpretation of the prophecies for the messiah.

Before we package God up in our preferred logical system to "understand him," we must consider his ways. We forget that he has not told us everything, that there is mystery in his being, and that much of his truth comes to us in paradox or shines a light on the irony of our human preferences. His intentions and purposes are his, and we know them as he desires us to, not more, not less. We must not add what he has not revealed. He is not obligated to us in this matter. It is often not ambiguity we need to resolve but mystery he intended. It is part of the wonder of worshiping him who is so far above us in every respect. It requires our full trust in him and a humble, dependent attitude. We need some theological modesty in our day. (Job 5:9; Ps 139:6; Isa 40:28, 46:9–10; John 4:23–24, 8:1—10:42; Rom 11:33–36; Col 2:2–3; Heb 12:28–29; Jas 4:10)

27. God's Freedom

GOD GIVES US THE freedom to choose his ways and experience his blessings or to choose our own ways and live with the results. But we find it hard to grant *him* freedom. Our culture trains us to seek to control everything around us to our advantage for emotional, mental, social, and physical survival. We are told to be proactive and self-assertive; ambition and achievement are admired. But we must intentionally choose to let God be God in our lives, in everything, if we are to know peace and security, identity and self-worth—the survival of our souls. We must not lock him into our expectations or designs for him.

We want him to be part of our plan, but he wants us to be part of his. We must choose. We are very limited in our understanding of life and its events. We know even less of the effects of our background on our thinking, the influence of our culture on us, or what tomorrow holds. It sounds like a terrible risk, but he knows the end from the beginning and knows us better than we know ourselves. We must give our needs and desires to him and then allow him the freedom to providentially bring about his plan in all things regardless of the circumstances. The God who gives us freedom must be free to work in us and bring about his good purposes. (Gen 2:15–17; Deut 32:4; Pss 43:3–5, 46:10, 139:1–18; Isa 46:9–10; Matt 7:12; Gal 5:1, 13–15; Phil 1:6 and 2:12–13 with 1 Thess 5:24; 1 Tim 4:4; Heb 4:12–13; 1 Pet 2:16)

28. Purpose of Creation

ALL THINGS GOD HAS created display his greatness and are there for humankind to enjoy. People were not just added as missing pieces; they were his purpose from the beginning, his crowning act in the first week of the world surprising even the angels. Creation reveals God's desire for us. We did not just happen in the course of human history; we each were his purpose from the beginning. And we remain at the center of his interest, love, and loyalty, as was the first couple created and as no other part of creation. This intimate connection of the created with the creator gives meaning and purpose to the gift of life. We were not designed to flourish or even survive without an ongoing relationship with him. Any substitute will take us down the wrong road without meaning or purpose, leading to spiritual death—an everlasting separation from the creator.

Many things created in that first week were for our delight, and God called them all good. We must not allow false guilt from legalism to distort his purpose for us to enjoy his creation, nor permit the abuses of his gifts to discourage our delight in them. This freedom in Christ comes from our trust in God's grace and his love-filled purposes in creation. Its only requirements are our gratitude for his gifts and a discerning love for those around us.

God's purpose was a perfect existence, which included giving humans free will to choose between good and evil. Adam and Eve chose pain and suffering instead of trusting him in Eden. They found they had come to know the good of all God created and the evil of its abuse. Yes, we are created good in the image of God, and what is evil is our abuse of that gift of goodness. As we come to know him better and the truth that we are created in his image, we will become more acutely aware of the sin of our abuses and how evil—opposite of God—they are. But he still cares deeply. He has given his Son to open the way for us to be right with him again. His undeserved lovingkindness is everlasting.

28. PURPOSE OF CREATION

When we trust him, we can enjoy his creation anew despite the pain and suffering we have caused. His blessings abound even in a broken world, where most have turned their backs on him as the people of Israel often did. Satan rebelled against God first, and, like him, those who reject him today to make themselves gods take this world to its destruction. But God's intentions are not ruined. He is not finished, though his created beings bring about disintegration by the free will he gave them. By his hand, the earth will be made new, and his people raised up. We will inhabit a new creation and, once again, enjoy his purpose of perfection as he intended it. (Gen 1:26–28, 2:15–25, 3:1–7; 1 Sam 2:8c; Pss 8:3–9, 89:5–18; Prov 16:25; Isa 14:12–15, 45:12; Jer 2:5–13; John 14:6, 15:4–5; Rom 8:18–25, 31–32, 12:9–19, 14:1–22; 1 Cor 10:23–31, 15:51–54; 2 Cor 5:17; Eph 1:9–10; 1 Tim 4:1–4; Jas 1:22–25; 1 Pet 1:12, 5:10–11; 2 Pet 3:11–13; Rev 21:1–5)

29. Providence at Work

THOUGH THE PERFECT EXISTENCE still awaits those who trust God, his providence cares for us now in our imperfect world. He is at work in our lives before we ever know it, and nothing we do, no choice or mistake, can obstruct his desire to shape us for his good purposes. If we stop trying to make him part of *our* plan and step into *his*, he will work in our lives to use us in his design. We can smother his Spirit's work in us when we look away, put something else in his place in our lives, something outside his intentions for us. But he waits for us to return, forgives us when we do, and, in his perfect wisdom, can use even the most difficult things of our past to glorify his work in and through us today. This battle with the old self will go on our entire lives, but he is at work, and we are growing stronger as we see ourselves better and see his grace and patience with us along the way. We move toward maturity in Christ, some of us more slowly than others. But we are his, and nothing can change that.

He remains in the background of the events and activities of our world, allows all humankind to make their own decisions, yet is always in control of history, involved in the lives of his people, and directs the destiny of all things. Nothing is impossible for God. Though some try to deny his existence and authority, nothing can stop his actions in the universe. His plan to "bring all things in heaven and on earth together under . . . Christ" will be accomplished. This same providence that controls the universe is at work in our lives. We belong to him, and he keeps it that way. (Gen 50:18–21; Exod 1:15—2:10 with 3:9–10; Esth 1—10; Pss 115:3, 135:6; Prov 16:9; Isa 14:26–27, 43:1, 45:5–6, 9–12, 46:10 with 48:17; Lam 3:40; Dan 1:1–7 with 2:48–49, 4:34c–35; Matt 6:33; Luke 1:37; John 9:1–41; Rom 7:14–25 with 8:28; Eph 1:9–10; Phil 2:12–13; Col 1:15–17)

30. Enjoyment

OUR EARTHLY ENJOYMENTS MAY be small and limited compared to those ready for us in heaven, but Jesus took an interest in them during his time on earth. The excellent wine he produced at the wedding at Cana was an example among many. He had dinner at the homes of tax collectors, interrupted the moaning at funerals, gave hungry crowds an endless lunch, and brought healing, life, and joy back to many. Though he was primarily interested in their souls and the faith that would save them, he also gave his time and effort to many joyful moments with people.

God created the universe and our five senses with intention. Our ears for music and the voices of our loved ones, our eyes for beauty and coordination, our sense of feeling for the gentle breeze and soft touch, our sense of smell for the scent of flowers, and our ability to taste for the sweetness of honey and the enjoyment of seasoned cuisine. Mind and heart, given to us by God, come together in their use of our senses to create works of art and beautiful music, produce goods of quality, delight in relationships, and manage life and work. All are given to us to honor him by their use for the enjoyment of his creation with thanksgiving and love for those around us. These gifts of God give us moments of rest and pleasure amid frequent pain along the way, the results of Adam's choice, and sometimes our own wandering from God's path. Jesus cares about these moments of enjoyment. We are invited to unselfishly experience the goodness of God's creation, giving thanks to the creator. "To the pure, all things are pure," and in time, "they will see God." These words are not given to perfect people; there are none. But those who desire him will see God's hand in all he has created, enjoy it to the fullest, and, one day, live in his presence forever. (Gen 1:31; 1 Sam 2:8c; Matt 5:8 with Titus 1:15; Matt 6:33–34; John 2:1–11, 10:10b; 1 Cor 10:31; Gal 5:13; 1 Tim 4:4–5; 1 Pet 2:16)

31. God's Purposes and Our Prayers

GOD'S ANSWERS TO PRAYER never interfere with his design for creation while bringing change to our lives and circumstances and to others. As strange as it may seem, he accomplishes his purposes while responding to our needs. It is part of the mystery and paradox of God's ways. His attention to our prayers expresses his love and grace for us in that creation, spoiled though it is by human sin. His responses to the needs we bring to him will go beyond our expectations of what he should or will do. They may not always look like they could be from him; they may seem like things going wrong, like it appeared to Abraham, Joseph, Esther, or Daniel, so we must be aware and confident in his sovereign providence.

Jesus' mother knew he could help with the lack of wine at a wedding. She had no idea of the extent of that help and only shadowy thoughts of its purpose in his mind. Sometimes, God does not respond with the miracle we desire, meeting a great need on our terms, but that does not mean he did not respond. Our expectations are pretty shallow for the God of the universe. We know very little of his design for us or our situation; sometimes, his answers are not apparent until much later. We must ask him for help but trust him for his way of giving it. We must let God be God. No power can stop his hand or thwart his purpose when he moves to answer our prayers, and answer them he will. (Gen 22:1–2, 37:28; Esth 2:8–9; Pss 37:23–24, 138:6–8; Prov 16:9; Isa 40:28–31, 41:10, 43:11–13, 44:6–8, 46:10, 55:8–11; Dan 3:16–18; Hab 1:5–6 with 12, 3:16–19; John 2:1–11; Eph 3:12; Phil 1:6, 2:12–13; Heb 11:6; Jas 1:6–8)

32. God and the Mundane

DOES EVERY EVENT IN our lives, every decision we make, have some divine purpose? No. But what does and what does not? If I use a little more salt and my wife a little more pepper (and garlic) on our potatoes, tie certain of my shoes with a double knot, or forget to take the trash out on the given day, these actions seldom alter divine providence in the direction of our lives. This morning, I had two cups of coffee instead of one while writing these thoughts, and I will go on about my day the same as usual. And I might just put off cleaning the garage one more day and regret that decision tomorrow. Many everyday decisions do not matter, but our attitude in mundane routines and chores does. As long as our hearts are set on honoring God and loving others, we can go about our everyday lives with confidence. We may not always succeed; we make mistakes, but our purpose to honor him is our desire and motivation, and his grace our strength. God is interested in our hearts, not our harmless habits. It is the pure in heart he seeks; they will see him.

Our awareness of him in day-to-day life and desire to fulfill his purposes in all we do is what matters. We must also remember that God can and occasionally does step in and use events in our everyday routine to affect our lives or the lives of those around us. He is moving in the background while we go about what are to us the mundane activities of life. Our kindness, confidence, and calmness are signs of walking in the Spirit as we go along in the things God sets before us, even when we mess them up. Our attitudes are signs of living everyday life with a different perspective than those without God and can encourage others. He is looking at our hearts, not whether our trash made it to the curb on time or whether the company arrives before we can clean the house. Anyway, the unexpected visit will be more meaningful and encouraging if our visitors receive kindness than the impression that we have everything under control. (Prov 27:23–27; Acts 2:46–47; 1 Cor 10:31; Gal 5:16 and 25 with Eph 5:15–20; Col 3:17, 4:5–6;

1 Thess 4:11; 2 Thess 3:6–13; 1 Tim 2:1–4; Titus 2:1–8, 3:14; Heb 6:12; 1 Pet 2:12 and 15)

33. Personality and God's Providence

GOD WILL ACCOMPLISH HIS overall purposes for us if our hearts are set on him. He made us unique in the wisdom of his design; we must seek to honor him in the expression of that individuality. Our emotions, reasoning, personalities, and decision-making are part of being created in his image. We are gifted in various ways. Some of us have emotional intelligence, sensing the needs of others with empathy, but are not as good at seeing the logic of an event or argument. Others have logical intelligence, with the ability to arrange information into sequential systems, arriving at clear conclusions, but are unaware of how others feel about a situation. A few people have cultural intelligence and are able to set their own cultural values aside to grasp the who, what, and why of human behavior in another cultural system. There are many more kinds of abilities and combinations of them; in each case, there are strengths and weaknesses and introverted and extroverted expressions. But we all need to honor God in the use of the abilities he has given us. Each person sees themselves, others in their lives, and the world around them differently. Each thinks and acts with a unique personal expression influenced by the intensity of their trust, doubt, or rejection of God.

God constantly reminds us and encourages us to make good decisions within the boundaries his word gives to us—loving him and those around us—regardless of the strengths and weaknesses of our personalities. This is using wisdom while remembering we are different from one another—the activity of faith does not look the same in each person's life. This is why we are often called to unity and harmony in the body of Christ. He can use the talents he has given us in the events and affairs of our lives for his plan for us or others as we seek to honor him, but we must be faithful to honor others in the body, however different from us they may be. Individual people think differently from one another and do different things to serve those around them. And God determines the results of their service, though we may not recognize his hand in the outcomes until much later.

We are not robots with a computer chip programmed for every movement and decision. We are free to decide and act using the gifts he has given us within the boundaries of his word. On the other hand, we may not be aware of what God is using us for; some incidents in our lives may be for someone else's benefit. Our role is to be faithful, trust God in all things and every circumstance, and go forward with what he puts before us with confidence in him and sensitivity for others. In his own way, he will care for what we cannot. (Pss 37:23–24, 138:8; Prov 16:9, 24:16; Hab 3:17–19; Mark 12:28–34; Luke 10:25–37; John 17:20–23; Rom 8:28, 12:1–2, 9–16, 15:5–6; Gal 5:1–6; Phil 1:6 with 1 Thess 5:24; Col 1:9–14, 3:12–17; 1 Thess 1:2–3, 2:11–12; 2 Thess 1:11)

34. The Journey to Knowing God

SEEKING GOD NOT FOR what he can give us of this world's benefits but for who he is remains the first step to knowing him and, therefore, toward wisdom. But a word of caution: there is a cost. It will mean facing yourself. When you begin to see God as he is, you will start to see yourself as you are. If you are willing to take a good look, it can be disturbing, for some of us, as staggering as it was for Isaiah in the throne room of God. But as hard as this is on us, it, too, is a step toward wisdom. The next is, in our humility, to thank him for his extraordinary grace toward us in our situation. Finally, we begin to see God in his concern for the world around us. He is not to blame for the evil humankind brings into the world. He could have turned his back on his creation or destroyed it all with a sweep of his hand. That would have been justice, but here we are, we who know him: bathed in his grace, comforted by his love, secure in his providence, saved by justice from outside our world.

Human logic does not serve us well, systematic categories fall short, and our expectations fail when we consider his grace beyond anything we deserve. We will stumble sometimes, but we must pray that we will walk worthy of this grace, though we can never deserve it. There will always be mystery in him and his ways in the world, but this is the beginning of knowing God. There is much more to know, and for what he does not tell us, he asks us to trust him. (Pss 16:5–11, 91:14–16, 111:10; Prov 1:7, 3:5–7, 9:10, 14:27, 28:26; Isa 6:1–7; Jer 9:23–24, 29:13; John 1:4–5, 10–13, 8:12 with 10:28–30; 14:6 with 21–24, 17:3; Rom 3:21–26, 5:1–2, 11:33; 1 John 1:9, 5:12)

35. God's Perfection

GOD'S PERFECTION IS POORLY measured by our human standards. Our culture and its values and categories are inadequate. His justice is shaped such that our human measuring sticks fall short. We cannot put him under our cultural microscope or on trial in human courts. He is over and above our limited understanding. There is mystery in his greatness and perfection beyond our informational domains and systems, beyond our logic. We must bow to the divine way of not revealing all but know that he is worthy of our complete trust. He wants it more than our attempts at endless explanations from our finite perspective. Furthermore, he wants more than repeated rituals in our behavior. He is not seeking legalistic obedience. Worship his majesty, accept his mystery, trust his goodness, have confidence in his greatness, be loyal to his purposes, and be grateful for his grace beyond our deserts and in our weakest moments.

Knowing him is the key that unlocks the door to the survival and flourishing of humankind. Many in our day are trying to throw that key as far away from themselves as possible. They want to control their own lives and create their own values. As Eve wanted to know good and evil for herself, and Adam joined her, those of our day want to know life without God's interference. But throughout history, they have always failed. Only he can give meaning and purpose to life and fill it with the well-being he intended for us. Yes, his ways are perfect. (Gen 3:6; Deut 31:6 and 8 with 32:4; Pss 18:30, 27:13–14, 29:1–11, 96:6–9, 139:6; Isa 40:28–31, 44:6–8, 55:8–9; Mark 12:28–34 with John 3:23–24 and 17:3; Rom 11:33–36; Eph 2:1–5; Col 2:13–15; Jas 1:17; 1 John 5:11)

36. Wisdom

TO SEEK TO BE a person of wisdom is a tall order in terms of the time, experience, and self-knowledge it requires. It may well mean the sacrifice, along the way, of things we think are dear to us. But it will increase the value of things that do matter, things he created for our blessing and enjoyment, which outlast all we now know. Letting go of our own ways and our culture's expectations will be hard. It will take endurance and humble trust in God's grace and providence. Our weaknesses make the road difficult. But knowing God intimately, realizing his presence in our experience, and having his perspective of the world, life, and human culture is worth any price. It is a jewel for which we can never pay too much.

If we trust God instead of our own understanding and acknowledge him in all our ways, he will make the path ahead of us known and possible. This trust in him is the heart of wisdom. It does not make obedience to him automatic. It teaches us, instead, how much we need his grace. We must still seek to choose the best and right things. But we will know what they are and what we ought to do, even if we fall short. It is not a plateau we reach in our lives but a growing awareness of his providence and, as we said, trusting him in all things. Learning that his power, grace, and providence are all we need. (Pss 25:1–21, 90:10–12; Prov 3:5–6, 8:10–21, 15:33, 16:9, 25, 28:26; Eccl 9:17–18; Hos 14:9; Luke 9:23–25; John 14:23–24; Rom 8:31–32 with 2 Pet 1:3–4; 1 Cor 1:18–31; Eph 5:8–17; Jas 3:13–18, 4:10)

37. God's Wrath

GOD'S WRATH HAS OFTEN been used to scare Christians into conforming to a legalistic, human standard sprinkled with Christian vocabulary and Bible verses. But true Christians will never experience his wrath. We may be poor Christians, but if there is trust in him, though we may need his discipline, we will never see his wrath. His vengeance is reserved for rebellious unbelievers, false teachers, and enemies of the faith and faithful. The category of false teachers may cause us some confusion because they may claim to be one of us. But those who use Christianity for their own gain, take advantage of simple believers, lead them astray, or control them for their own selfish ends will answer for their deception of God's people at the judgment. Their insincerity does not go unnoticed. To harm one of God's own, to deceive his children, or take advantage of their needs is to be in the eye of the storm of God himself. What could be worse? But this vengeance is God's alone. We must do what is in our hands to protect the church from these, but vindication or retaliation is not ours. We must leave it in his hands. And we must never forget that no one is beyond God's grace. Whatever he forgives through true repentance will be washed away eternally. There is always hope. (Pss 37:6–9, 103:10–14, 130:3–6; Matt 7:13–29; 13:36–43, 18:1–6, 25:31–46; John 3:16–21 with 36; Rom 1:18–22, 4:6–8, 5:6–11; Phil 3:17–21; 1 Thess 5:8–11; 2 Thess 1:5–10; 2 Tim 4:1–5; Titus 1:10–16; 2 Pet 3:1–12)

38. Information Only

THE PERSON WHO DOES the little they know of God's will for them is well ahead of those who know volumes of information and can parcel it out, and even those who get paid to do so but for whom it does not touch their lives. Being knowledgeable alone or a professional in ministry is not to be envied. These, unless their knowledge changes their lives for God, are deceived. They mistake their knowledge for salvation, their profession for being in God's will. They, as well as we, must approach God with humble trust, knowing that all we are and have is from him and for him. We must seek to become what the information God has given us tells us to be, knowing we will not do so perfectly. As James says, we must not look in the mirror and then walk away, forgetting what we saw there. What we now know must change our hearts and then our actions. So, learning is not the end of the matter; it is the beginning.

In short, we must go beyond information to experience God. Knowing the recipe and putting it together to make a chocolate cake may be commendable, baking it tantalizing to our sense of smell, but the experience is in the eating. In that experience, something happens to our knowledge of chocolate cake and how to make it. We taste it and now know something more than all the information about it can tell us. In the same way, David tells us to "taste and see that the Lord is good." We will have to trust the recipe and the baker of the chocolate cake enough to eat a bite, but if we do, we will know if it is good. Like any human illustration of the Divine, this example may not be the best metaphor. It might turn out that the baker left something out or mismeasured an ingredient. But our God is perfect, and to trust him enough to taste and see brings the deepest blessings of a relationship with the God of the universe. Yes, you and me, belonging to the ultimate, absolute King over all, as his children and his people at work in the world for him. Information only about God is not enough; we must experience the reality of God himself. (Pss 34:1–22, 37:3–6, 51:6, 16–17, 111:10;

Prov 1:7, 9:10, 21:2; Hos 6:6; Mic 6:8; Matt 6:1–8, 7:15–23; John 12:24–26; Phil 3:13–14; 1 Tim 1:3–7; Jas 1:17, 22–25, 4:10; 1 Pet 2:1–3)

39. The Grace of Forgiveness

MANY HAVE TROUBLE ACCEPTING forgiveness in Christ or, knowing his forgiveness, have trouble forgiving themselves. They are weighed down with guilt for past sins and fear God's punishment. But in Christ, we are forgiven, not on the basis of being good enough each day but on his perfect righteousness. We are given his perfect standing before God. With our trust in him, all sin is forgiven, never to be mentioned again, washed away in the flood of his grace. We will not answer for forgiven sin at the judgment seat of Christ as some preach. To think that is to degrade God's grace and forget his promise to forgive the sin of all who seek it in Christ.

We need to recognize that we fall short of his will in our daily lives and confess to him the weakness of our faith. It is sin to reject his will for us in selfishness and pride when we forget his grace and take our own way. But we can accept his grace anew, which had not wavered though our faith did. Not accepting his forgiveness makes his word a deception and all his grace and sacrifice for us in Christ of no account. Not forgiving ourselves is then an offense against that same grace. We must confess and renew our trust in him and then get off our knees in joy, bathed in his grace, fresh and clean, to serve him again. (Deut 31:6-8 with 32:4; Pss 27:1, 32:1-5, 51:16-17, 91:1-2, 103:12, 130:3-8; Isa 1:18, 42:1-3, 43:25; Matt 18:21-35; Rom 3:21-26, 5:6-11; Eph 2:1-10; Col 2:13-15; 1 John 1:5-10)

40. Out of Darkness

God holds out his grace to the stone-cold will of men and women who refuse him. But we must not be mistaken. Though he is still there and waits, he will grant their wish to be left alone one day, to have their own way. We do not know the hearts of these and must always trust God for them, praying for them and encouraging them toward repentance and transformation. We, too, would be lost with them if we had not accepted his grace.

God's providence in our lives is overwhelming. He sought us out and waited for us as a father, his lost child. As younger people, some weakness or trouble, severe event, early negative experience, or abusive situation may have pushed us away from God. But, though he never wanted this for us, his intention is that it should push us toward him. He is there. Later in life, at our worst moments, he is there. In the tragic accident, the profound loss of a loved one, and the awful news of disease, God wants us to turn to him. These events are like landmines on our path through life—Satan's landmines. He hopes to trip us up, turn us away from God, and make us bitter, angry, anxious, or revengeful. Sometimes, he wins in people's lives. But God would have it otherwise.

When we are numb from the sudden explosion of disaster, run out of strength, and have no tears left, he is there, waiting. He intends that, in our difficulties, sorrows, and anxieties, we lean on his help and grace to move from the darkness to light. He waits for many who say they are his, but tragic events have dimmed their hope and weakened their trust in him. Darkness is crowding in again, but he is there. His providence is at work to use even those dark days to carry out his purposes in those who are his. He waits for others who have never looked his way to find the path, to discover the light in their darkness. He is there with grace and hope—life where there is only death. (Pss 53:1, 107:14; Prov 16:9; Isa 9:2 with 6–7, 42:1–3, 50:10–11; Lam 3:22–26; John 1:1–5, 3:16–21, 36, 8:12, 11:17–43, 16:33; Acts 26:15–18;

Rom 1:18–22; 2 Cor 4:6; Eph 2:1–10; Phil 1:6 with 2:13; 1 Thess 5:1–11, 24; 1 Pet 2:4–12, 5:6–11; 2 Pet 3:9; 1 John 1:5–10 with 2:9–11)

41. Striving Ended

IN OUR GROWTH IN Christ, we don't want to sin, but we must take the emphasis off striving against sin and put it on living in his grace. Those who know his grace will be painfully aware of falling short of his will. We cannot ignore it. We don't need to strive but to go to him for forgiveness and be strengthened, encouraged by that forgiveness, and renewed in our loyalty to his way for us. Knowing his grace, we will want nothing more than to live more fully for him each day. Life in Christ is to be lived in the joy of his grace, not in the guilt of past sin. All is forgiven for all time, once under his grace. Christ's death is adequate for us, past, present, and future. So, go to him. He longs to forgive and restore. He waits to fill our lives with himself. If we lose our way, forget his will for us, or become insensitive to his guidance, he will act to bring us back; he will wait for our return. Though getting our attention may be painful, his purpose is restoration, and the motive nothing but love. Because of this grace, striving can give way to peace; anxiety can give way to trust and hope. (Pss 37:23–24, 103:10–14, 130:1–8; Prov 24:16; Lam 3:40; Matt 11:28; Luke 15:11–24; John 3:16–21, 14:27; Rom 3:22–24, 6:8–14; Phil 4:6–7; Heb 4:14–16, 9:11–15 with 26b; 1 Pet 3:18, 5:6–7; 1 John 1:8–10)

42. Human Justice

THERE ARE MANY TIMES when human justice is not applied to a situation as we would hope. It falls short of our expectations of fairness. Then there is the corrupt judge and the miscarriage of justice, the political leaning that weaponizes the system in its favor, which can frustrate the strongest heart or hurt us deeply if it is our case. We may forgive, but the unjust simply move on to their next target. It is all too common in this life.

Human justice falls short and does not go unnoticed by God, especially when the injustice concerns his own people. But God's justice is perfect. We can rest in this promise and wait for his hand to move in vindication and final reckoning. Wait on the Lord. Patient faith instead of self-assertion is the better path—the path he intends for us. God can use the suffering of injustice to strengthen or shape us for his purposes. While we wait on God, we hope the unjust will turn to him and repent of their ways. How much better if they come to know God and give their lives to him, the just Judge of all. (Deut 32:4, 35; Pss 27:13–14, 37:1–11, 130:5–6; Prov 20:22, 21:2; Eccl 7:8–9; Isa 10:1–4, 42:1–3; Lam 3:22–26; Zeph 3:7–8; Jas 1:2–8, 5:7–11; 1 Pet 1:3–7, 3:14–17, 5:10–11; 2 Pet 3:8–10)

43. Good King or Bad?

THE KING'S HEART IS in the Lord's hand; the ruler is his servant. They rise and fall at his command. But these servants do not usually recognize God's hand on them in this way. To them is given a position to do good or ill to the people. If they abuse the power granted to them, it is of eternal consequence. If the king's arm becomes weak and no longer wields the sword in right judgment of the people's affairs, he will answer for it. Weak and pathetic are those rulers who cannot or will not govern for the welfare of the people, whose justice no longer punishes the wrongdoer or honors those who do good, and whose moral compass points to the opposite of God's intentions. These use the people for political or military advantage or to enhance their power and wealth. Twisted justice will ruin the kingdom, though they think it is for their profit. What could be worse than rejecting God's hand on your course in life? But good king or bad, our responsibility is to obey all we can of their authority and pray for them to understand the burden of ruling God has given them. We must pray they would come to know God himself. In the meantime, we are to live responsibly under their rule as much as possible, using wisdom and discretion to honor God first. (Ps 89:8 with 14; Prov 21:1, 24:21–22; Eccl 5:8–10; Dan 3:8–18; Hab 1:1–6; Matt 22:15–22; John 19:11; Rom 13:1–7; 1 Thess 4:11; 1 Tim 2:1–4; Titus 3:1; 1 Pet 2:13–17)

44. Will Christians Be Punished for Their Sin?

WE HAVE ALL HEARD people say that even Christians will answer for every misspoken word, every detail of their lives that is not in accord with God's standard at a future judgment. Though these people confess their sins and say they are forgiven, they also say Christ will publicly expose those sins on that day. But this is entirely outside his grace for the truehearted believer. There is indeed no escape from his watchful eye, but he is not looking for every misstep or stumbling. He wants our obedience for our sake but is looking at our hearts for loyalty, not perfection. Of course, we do let him down. We sin against his desire for us. But his forgiveness is always ready when we come to him. He orchestrated the greatest tragedy in the history of the world to provide for us the greatest act of grace possible: his Son for the forgiveness of our sins against him. He longs for our every expression of trust in him, knowing that it brings us security and contentment in the worst circumstances and storms of life. Trusting him, we will not fear the terror that may come in the darkness of the night or enemies that may attack us in by day. He wants us very much to be free of fear, including the condemnation some say we will suffer even after we have experienced his grace in Christ.

His holiness is satisfied in Christ; once his grace is bestowed, his forgiveness is forever. Those who do not realize this do not yet know him as he is. Relationship and legalism are opposites, and legalism undermines grace. His discipline may be necessary to bring the best things into our lives, but it is his guidance, not punishment. Unconfessed selfishness, pride, legalism, and the abuse of his word and people by those in the church who claim to be in Christ will be exposed at the judgment seat of Christ. Some who claim to be Christians will be separated out with the goats on his left. These were not his. But for his sheep, never will forgiven sin again be mentioned. (Pss 51:6, 16–17, 91:5, 14–16, 103:10–14, 130:1–8, 139:1–12; Isa 1:18; Matt 7:21–23,

25:31–46; John 3:16–18; Acts 20:28–31; Rom 3:21–26, 5:6–11; Titus 1:16; 1 John 1:9; Rev 21:1–4)

45. Adam's Sin and the Doorway of God's Grace

ADAM WAS MADE PERFECT and placed in an ideal environment. But he chose not to trust God's word and fell from perfection into a world of sin and suffering. The second Adam, Jesus, though the uncreated, eternal Son of God, was also a perfect human. He came into a world spoiled by Adam's choice, a place of suffering and evil. But amid this, he remained perfect and did so on our behalf. It was the unlatching of a door back to God by his grace. We can be redeemed in this world; with all our imperfections and stumblings, he will carry on his work in us. If we trust him, he will give us peace and shape us into his man or woman along the way, and we will enter perfection at the end of the journey, as will every aspect of the creation.

It is one of the great paradoxes of God's way that he would create perfection but give humans the freedom and ability to destroy that perfection in a single moment by their choice—a decision not to trust God. They had known the good of all creation and, in that moment, came to know the evil of its abuse and the suffering that evil would bring. And to fill out that paradox, his plan to fix the tragedy was that his Son would have to die. He would come to his own, and they would torture and kill him. But Jesus would die for us willingly. Such was his desire for us to be part of his kingdom.

Through such a "disaster," God made a relationship with himself possible for sinners. It is a willing and lasting relationship of love, loyalty, grace, peace, and trust, as imperfect as we may be. There had to be free will to reject that encounter and relationship with him if there was to be free will to accept it. A door had opened, but it was a back door, one often overlooked or rejected as the only way. His perfection through grace came to us from heaven through the paradox of an animal stall and a used feeding trough, the visit of dirty shepherds, the later visit of Zoroastrian priests, and the ending of his earthly time in a criminal's execution. The perfect Son of God came to his creation, but only those who had eyes of faith to see knew it was him. He overwhelmed the imperfection of their souls and released from guilt all who believed from that day on. (Isa 53:1–6; Matt 1:21, 7:13–14, 21; John 1:1–18 with 8:12 and 10:9–10; Rom 15:13; Phil 4:7; Heb 13:20–21; 1 Pet 3:18; 2 Pet 1:1–2; 2 John 3)

46. Adam's Sin and Ours

WE SEE A PATTERN of themes in the creation: Adam and Eve received life and experienced perfection, but instead of trusting God, they chose mortality, leading to suffering for all humankind. Jesus, though God, was born and lived a life of perfection in our situation. He experienced the death Eve and Adam chose, but resurrection brought him back with redemption for humankind before God and eternal life for all who believe in him. We are born into a broken world set in motion by our ancestors. We follow their pattern and inherit the curse they brought upon humankind.

But though we were among the walking dead, we chose life in Jesus and now have his perfection before God while in this world of sin and suffering. Before we are too hard on Adam and Eve, we must remember that we have often chosen not to trust God's words and still do after experiencing his redemption. We would have done what they did. We must always be humbly grateful for God's forgiveness and ongoing grace in our lives. (Gen 1:26–31, 3:1–24, especially 15; Rom 3:21–25, 5:6–19; 1 Cor 15:3, 20–28; Eph 2:1–10; Col 1:15–20; 1 Pet 3:18, 5:10–11)

47. Cheated and Wronged

IN THIS LIFE, THERE are many times when someone will take advantage of us, hurt us without cause, or injure us with deception and injustice. Sometimes, this comes from even those who claim to be "Christians." Trusting God for these offenses is difficult, especially for individualists trained by their culture to look out for themselves, assert their rights, and defend their reputations. These are the weapons our culture has given us for our survival. But God will not have it so. We must break those cultural chains and experience freedom in Christ from bondage to our human feelings and expectations. These bring anger and the desire to get even. But God tells us our vindication is not always in the present.

Forgiveness on our part can seldom, if ever, forget, but it can set us free of our own prison of hurt by giving it to God and waiting on his day to reveal the truth. We must be patient, for he is at work in us. Hard experiences are bricks in the building he is making of us, and he intends to finish it. (Pss 17:2, 27:13–14, 33:20–22, 34:17–19, 37:1–9, 23–24, 27–28, 34a, 130:1–6; Prov 16:32, 17:1, 20:22, 24:29; Eccl 7:8–9; Isa 40:28–31; Lam 3:26; Matt 18:12–35; Luke 17:3–4; Rom 12:17–21; 1 Cor 6:19–20; Eph 4:32; Phil 2:12–13 with 1:6; Col 3:12–14; Jas 1:19–20)

48. Debts We Owe

OUR DEBT TO GOD is cared for in Christ by his grace—our model for showing grace to others. He will care for us. Our debt to others, however, is our concern. We must trust God for wrongs done to us, but being aware of it, we must deal with our offenses to others. We need no special guidance from God as to what to do. Whether it is unpaid gratitude, an apology owed, or forgiveness due, the more quickly we act in grace, the better. The sooner done, the sooner we are free from the distraction it may bring, for we are fulfilling the law of love—the greatest commandment—and our conscience must be clear to do our best.

    Showing grace to others is possible because of God's grace in our lives. But judging others can be a bad habit for Christians when they forget the grace shown them. Though discernment is necessary for avoiding false teachers, it is easily turned into criticism of others on their journey. We often try to make ourselves look better than them. We do not see our own failures but notice the least of theirs. Yes, other Christians can do wrong, but forgiving them is of primary importance. Jesus talked of the worst possible outcomes for the unmerciful servant. God's grace is a serious business. He has forgiven us much and continues to do so. Though there may be contentment when we have used the opportunities he gives for good and not ill, there cannot be pride. He has shown us compassion, and we must be compassionate toward others. We must be loyal to his purposes and cannot take credit for his work of grace in us. (Pss 95:6–7, 100:3; Matt 7:1–2, 18:21–35, 22:34–40; Luke 6:37–38, 18:9–14; John 13:34–35, 15:12; Rom 13:8–10; 1 Cor 6:7; Phil 2:12–13 with 1:6; 1 John 2:9–11, 3:16–20, 4:7–12, 19–21)

49. Guilty as Charged

THOUGH MANY TODAY WANT to use the suffering in the world to say there cannot be a God, it is we who are to blame for the pain and misery that evil breeds. Our sins have results. Our guilt and shame are not just systemic from the fall; they are personal and need fixing. The Son of God is perfect and, as such, is the only one who can remedy our situation. By a justice beyond our human reasoning, Jesus' death is substituted for what we deserve, and God offers his perfection and merits to us so that we can stand before him in righteousness. We are desperate, and he is there. We have no resources for our hopeless predicament; he has all we need in himself.

We cannot fix ourselves in this matter. We must humble ourselves and turn to the One who can. And he will. He will give us his purity, and we will begin a journey with him at our side, making the way before us in his wise and purposeful providence. The poor in spirit will be part of his kingdom; the pure in heart see God. There will still be suffering, injustice, and persecution in the world, and he does not remove us from that context. In it, we can extend the grace we have received and show compassion for others; we are needed as light and salt. It is a situation where we can be peace-makers—leaving justice in his hands and showing we are the sons and daughters of the God of grace. For justice and grace are both his. (Pss 24:1–6, 32:4–5, 37:23–24, 91:14–16, 130:3–6, 145:18–19; Prov 16:9, 19; Isa 42:1–3; Matt 5:3–10; John 5:13–16 with 16:33 and 17:15–19; Rom 3:21–26, 5:1–8; Eph 2:4–5; Phil 2:12–13 with 1:6; Jas 4:10; 1 Pet 3:18, 5:6; 1 John 1:9)

50. Becoming Perfect

HE IS AT WORK in us to accomplish his will. It started when Jesus closed the gap between God and us by taking our condemnation on himself. It moves through our trusting him for his grace shown us in the act of his sacrifice, on to his work in us to shape us into his desire for us. Not that we reach perfection in this life, but living as we can for him, we are destined for it in the next. At present, we share in Christ's perfection before God. Our clothes may be dirty and stained, but before God, we wear the brilliant robes of Christ himself. Do not expect perfection in your life now. It is a terrible letdown nearly every day. But we must not get discouraged. We must bathe ourselves in his grace anew and pick ourselves up for the next task he has for us.

Because of God's grace, we are not without hope. He is at work in us for his purposes and will accomplish them if we desire him. We will get better at revealing his grace in our lives as we work out our salvation each day. Meditating on his word, remembering his providence, and reminding ourselves to trust him, we grow in the wisdom and knowledge of our relationship with him. We grow in our trust of his hand in our lives. (Pss 25:4–5, 91:1, 138:8; Prov 2:1–11, 16:9 with 20:24; John 13:6–10, especially 10a; Rom 7:14–25 with Phil 3:12–16; 1 Cor 2:9–10; Eph 2:10, Phil 1:6 with 2:12–13; Col 2:1–3; 1 Thess 5:23–24; 1 John 1:9)

51. Purity

SOME CHRISTIANS TALK A lot about purity but tend to limit that purity to sexual behavior. However, purity is a much broader topic and goes considerably deeper into our lives. An over-emphasis on moral purity limited to sexual activity abuses God's intentions and masks a shallow view of our relationship with God. It also places this one category of moral behavior at the center of God's will for us. It leans toward the legalism of not doing something and disregards the heart's condition—its inclination toward self and away from God in many aspects of life. Our heart's desires are God's primary concern for us.

Sexual sin is an indication, a symptom of a wrong heart, and the tip of the iceberg of a general disregard for God and his ideals for us. It forgets the virtues of love and loyalty, within which boundaries God designed intimate relations as their fulfillment in marriage. Love and commitment combined with intimacy deepen and strengthen his design for that relationship. Failure to fulfill these purposes of God in marriage is as serious as seeking satisfaction outside it. Either is a failure of love for God for the spouse he provides and his gifts to us. But failure in this area is only one of many that break the law of love. Selfishness in this and many other areas of our lives is at the core of our need for his grace. It is a concern more important than doing or not doing something. It is a motive of the heart that can show up in many behaviors; unbounded love of self is spiritual adultery. Selfishness and pride lie at the root of all sin.

Purity is love for God, loyalty to his purposes, trust in his good providence, love for others, and personal humility. It is being unpolluted in our motives and desires. We are not perfect, and purity needs upkeep and protection in our lives. If you own a home, it will require certain maintenance, upkeep, and protection from the elements—a new coat of paint from time to time after exposure to the sun, wind, and rain. Living in the world will leave its residue on our lives as well. As Jesus washed his disciples' feet, we who are his need his grace daily to keep our hearts clean. It can remove any stain, repair the damage, and restore purity. Though some scars may remain, they remind us of where we were and of his grace bringing us through the storm. This purity is central to knowing God at all. (1 Chr 29:17a and 18b; Pss 15:1–5, 33:11; Prov 16:2; Eccl 7:20; Jer 29:13; Hos 4:12b; Matt 5:8; John 13:1–17; Rom 6:5–14; Eph 2:1–5; Phil 2:3–4; 1 Thess 4:11; Titus 1:15; Heb 4:15–16; Jas 3:13–18; 1 John 1:9)

52. Hopeless Feelings

EMOTIONAL DEPRESSION DOES NOT mean that God has stopped being God but that a cloud of flat emotions has taken over and hidden the truth from us. They have come between God and us—caused us to stop recognizing who he is and what he is doing. It is not something we want, but Satan is blinding our minds with feelings of emptiness and hopelessness, much like he blinds the minds of unbelievers to keep them from seeing the light of the gospel. But feelings do not change facts. They accompany many events and experiences in our lives but do not make things true or false. Sometimes, they are wonderful, and our hearts are glad; sometimes, they let us down, and we are disappointed; sometimes, they go flat, and we feel nothing. But the fact remains that God is at work in the world and in our lives. His love, grace, and providence are as real as ever, and he longs for you to trust him. He wants to bring you under the safety and security of his wing, the warmth and assurance of his shadow.

There is much pain, suffering, loss, and injustice in the world. Humankind has loved darkness rather than light, but God will do away with all sin and suffering in the coming days. In the meantime, he is with us through it and seeks our trust that he might fill all the emptiness with his love and care, assure us of our place in his heart, lavish us with his grace, and bring about his purposes. He reminds us of our destiny in him when he will make all things perfect again. Then we will know joy beyond our imagination. For now, we must trust him, even if we don't feel like it. We have one foot in this broken world, but our other foot is in the spiritual universe, for we belong to his spiritual kingdom, though we are on mission in this physical one.

There are valleys along the way; some seem dark and lonely to us, but he walks through them with us and takes our pain on himself if we give it to him. When we are distant from him in our feelings, he is waiting for us to look in his direction. He wants us to see his purposes as central in the world and not be confused by those who seek their own agenda. He wants our hearts, desires our trust, and forgives our failures as we come to him. Christ is the light in the darkness, the cause for joy in the empty heart. Loyalty to him in the darkest moment fills us with meaning, purpose, and hope.

When the Aramean military surrounded Dothan, where Elisha was staying, his servant was afraid, but his fear did not mean God was absent. Though not seen by the Aramean soldiers that day, God was very powerfully present—surrounding them all with horses and chariots of fire in the mountains. We must remember that God is powerfully present with us, for we are his. From our valley, the mountains are still full of horses and chariots of fire for our eyes of faith. (2 Kgs 6:15–17; Pss 23:4, 34:4–10, 40:1–4, 42:1–5, 91:1–4, 14–16, 119:105, 130; Prov 16:2, 20:27, 21:2; Isa 44:18; Matt 4:12–17, 5:1–10, 28:18 with 20b; John 1:1–14, 8:12 with 16:33, 14:23 and 27; 2 Cor 4:6; 1 Pet 5:6–11; Rev 21:1–4)

53. Salvation, Before and After

SALVATION IS A PROCESS rather than an event. It may begin long before we choose to trust Christ, culminate in that decision, and be followed by years of growing in our faith and learning to trust him. Many passages in the Bible tell us that we are accountable to God for what we believe about Jesus. Salvation is available to all, but we must be convinced in our hearts of Christ, each one of us. We must believe he can save us just as those who were sick and dying among the people of Israel trudged across the vast desert camp of their people to look at the serpent on the pole to be healed. We must come to him as the centurion who knew he could heal his suffering servant without ever entering his home.

God's moral will for all of us is that we know him and live forever in his love and grace, but each person may accept or toss aside that destiny. God does not do it for you. Each will choose to trust God and accept Christ and forgiveness, or they will not. However, many things lead up to that moment. God's work in our lives begins long before our choice. For some, it is a longer path than for others. Events and experiences, things we would never suspect as his hand in our lives, are at work to bring the choice before us and shape us ahead of time for his purposes should we choose him. When we consider him the only one who can save us, we must trust him and know and believe what he has said and done for us. But though we are in Christ the moment that choice becomes genuine, and our guilt is washed away, it is only a beginning. It starts a series of discoveries about him and about ourselves, a series of surrenders as, inch by inch, we become the person he desires us to be in our hearts. Our behavior reflects this change in us more and more until we, one day, go to be with him.

Though the benefits of our salvation are available to us the day we trust him, we seem to appropriate them in stages—realizing them more and more along the way. It is the process of becoming, not just knowing or even believing. It is moving deeper into God, beyond the self, beyond the concerns of this world, living as a child of God in his house, leaving syncretism with the world behind. It is growing in the central matter of our new life: *trusting* him. But it starts with choosing God and his way through Christ. It is open to all, and whoever believes has life—forgiveness, freedom, and security in him. Not choosing God, and solely that refusal, causes people to be forever separated from the life he gives. (Ps 139:13–17; Jer 1:4–5; Matt 8:5–13, 19:16–26; Luke 15:1–24; John 1:4, 10–13, 29, 3:16–18, 36, 4:14, 8:12, 10:10, 14:6; 2 Cor 5:15–17; Col 1:6 with 2:12–15; 1 Tim 2:5–6; Jas 1:22–25; 1 John 2:15–17)

54. Spiritual Faltering

WE MUST NOT BECOME too discouraged with ourselves in our walk with God. We battle our culture's demands, the stringent expectations of legalistic believers around us, our human inclinations and pride, and our past experiences. But we must realize we have stepped into the circle of God's grace where those influences are no longer in control. We have chosen a new master. For many of us, it was a growing awareness of our dissatisfaction with ourselves that one day, in some way, became an awareness of God—a sudden and unexpected interruption of life as we have known it, a sudden appearance of grace where there seemed no possibility, and it changed everything. Yes, born again. Then and there, we began a journey of growing in Christ.

Unfortunately, many people in Christian circles spend more time dealing with guilt than appreciating God's grace. We will not be perfect. We will not even meet our own expectations in our early steps, but we should be in love with his grace and eager to move in his direction, however faltering our steps. Legalism, guilt, and anxiety must be left behind, and forgiveness and freedom in Christ must take over. Forgetting what is behind us, we move ahead in the grace God has freely given us, costly though it was to him. Though we have our weak moments, doubts should never rule our lives again. We have trusted the God of the universe and Christ's sacrifice for us. He never said we would be perfect on this journey. Our concern about pleasing God shows we are his children, safe and secure in him. We must trust him, not ourselves. (Ps 16:5–11; Isa 42:1–3, 43:1; Matt 11:28–30, 14:22–32; John 3:17, 8:12 with 14:27; John 13:8–10; 2 Cor 5:17; Phil 3:12–16; Col 3:1–3; 1 Tim 1:12–17; Heb 4:9–11, 14–16; Jas 1:5–8; 1 John 1:8–9)

55. Calling Evil What Is Good

WE READ THAT ALL God created he called good, but we are not always in agreement with him. Our physical bodies are an example. How many of us are discouraged by our looks? We can see, hear, taste, smell, and feel, yet we complain. We always want something else, something more, something different. Most of this is from the expectations and influence of our individualist culture. We are taught the lie that we must compete for the acceptance and respect of others on their terms to have an identity among them and feelings of self-worth. When we do this, we only see our bodies as good if people around us say they are. We could take care of them better, but they are miracles created by God, and he called them good. Only good gifts come from him; trust in the fact comes from us.

The same is true in our thoughts about his purposes for physical intimacy in marriage. Together, God intended that man and woman be one body and that they be fruitful, increase in number, and fill the earth. But God's intentions for marriage as a life of intimate oneness were twisted when our distrust of him in the garden had its way with us. Now, it is the abuse of physical relationships that God tells us we must avoid. Selfish desperation, deteriorating cultural values destroying the virtues God intended, misplaced loyalties and affections bring sorrow and destroy God's design. He calls it humankind's love of darkness instead of light. The attraction is both a human appetite and an old trick of Satan.

But, an over-emphasis on sexual awareness as dirty often puts the good God created in the category of human error and sin. Because of so much abuse of sex outside God's design for marriage, parents are afraid for their children. This leads to years of over-emphasis and legalistic teaching and yields the collateral damage of a humanly conditioned Christian conscience. This, in turn, keeps many from realizing God's special place for the physical bond in marriage. The intimacy God intended remains misunderstood and tainted. Then, we are surprised by unhappy marriages, unfaithfulness, high divorce rates, and even gender confusion. We must use better, healthier ways of training our children in the way they should go.

For some, the only way to avoid abusing something is to paint it entirely as evil. So it is that we, to use an over-tired example, say that if drunkenness is against God's will for us, then wine is evil itself and must be avoided entirely. Those who say such things think this will keep people from the potential of wrong behavior. But we are reacting to sin by destroying the intended good. Like wine with dinner, many try to remove the element that is a blessing for those who accept it from God with gratefulness. We must stop avoiding the responsibility of disciplining ourselves for appropriate behavior within God's boundaries of gratefulness and love. Interestingly, we would not toss out eating because of the risk of gluttony. We do not do away with money because some fall into greed. Anything good can be abused. We must call good what God calls good, and sin only what God calls sin. Adding to the Scriptures is a serious failure to accept God's way. (Gen 1:27-28 with 31; Prov 4:20-27, 22:6, 30:5-6; Mal 2:14-15; Acts 11:9; Rom 14:5-8, 16-18; 1 Cor 6:12—7:5, 10:23—11:1; 2 Cor 4:4-7; Eph 5:22-31; 1 Tim 4:4; Titus 1:15; Heb 13:4; Jas 1:16-18; 1 Pet 3:1-7)

56. Ultimate Decision

CREATING MEN AND WOMEN who can know and trust him if they choose, receive his grace, love those around them, and appreciate the wonder of his works was at the center of God's purpose in creation. For those with eyes to see and ears to hear, the realities of God and his creation are all around us, awaiting our acknowledgment and appreciation even in a world broken by sin. Humans were the crown of God's skillful activity of bringing it all to be. Only they are free to turn to God's grace so that he might awaken their souls to a relationship with him and gratitude for all he has given us. It is not love that does not choose its object freely. Trust and loyalty cannot be forced from a person but must come willingly, from deep within. Where there is no freedom to choose, there is no responsibility, no justice, no compassion. To choose warmth, one must know what it is to be cold. One chooses light to avoid darkness. Love is choosing to be loyal, and hate chooses betrayal.

Creation and life on earth are pointless unless men and women are free to choose God over self, his ways over cultural expectations, and his gifts over temporary things of the world. "For what will it profit a man if he gains the whole world and forfeits his soul?" Yet many choose the alternative to God's grace—the ways of culture and personal preferences over freedom in Christ. Their empty souls sleep. They have closed their eyes and ears to God, his creation that shouts, and his voice that describes his greatness and grace. Pride, self-centeredness, and greed block their way. For some, aggressive assertiveness seeks control without God. Many of them are openly God-haters. For others, passive agnosticism and a life of ease blind their minds. When God speaks, they are deaf and dumb; like a fence post, they do not respond. These receive the consequences of their decisions now and for eternity. (Isa 29:16, 50:10-11; Matt 7:13-14, 21-23, 16:24-28, 19:16-30; Luke 6:46-49, 9:23-25, 12:16-21; John 1:10-12, 3:16-21, 14:6; Rom 1:18-25 with Jer 2:13; 2 Cor 4:4; Eph 5:14; Phil 3:17-21)

57. Risking Our Relationship with God

THERE ARE ALWAYS THE risks of self-interest, the influence of culture, and legalistic, mystical, or syncretistic views of the Bible that are limitations to knowing God and being part of his work in the world. If these alternatives are allowed to dictate their expectations for us as believers, we will never experience God as he intends. Self-assertion, fear of rejection, and the demand for achievement will set the boundaries of our trust, and we will never know freedom in Christ. If we let our faith drift into legalistic or mystical human definitions of God, we will never know him as he is. Each person must be on their guard and allow God to speak for himself in his word. Some try to live as if he was outside of us, could not see our hearts, and was limited to what people say about him. But he seeks to be known and deal with us individually and personally. If we allow him in, we can experience the freedom to let go of old anxieties and trust him for difficulties. We will realize his desire to lavish his grace on us, undeserving though we are. We will be free to serve others in the ways he provides us.

We each have been prepared to serve God and reveal him to others in a unique way; our part in his purposes is a special privilege of his grace. We must not risk missing his will by seeking satisfaction, approval, or assurance where it cannot be found. Instead, we must "set our minds on things above," and from there, all we need will come to us. Instead of earthly rewards, we will be comforted and shown mercy; ours will be the kingdom of heaven, and we will see God as his sons and daughters, having been filled with the righteousness of Christ. (Ps 139:1–18, 23–24; Jer 29:13; Matt 5:3–10, 6:33 with 7:7–12; John 1:12, 14–18; Rom 5:6–8; 2 Cor 1:21–22, 13:5, 15:9–10; Eph 1:3–8, 2:4–7; Phil 1:9–11, 2:12–13; Col 3:1–4; Heb 3:12–15, 13:20–21; Jas 1:16–18; 2 Pet 1:3; 1 John 2:15–17)

58. Limitations

WE CAN BE SEVERELY limited in our Christian lives by our cultural frame of reference, perspective of our personal experience, human inclinations, and the agendas of false teachers and legalistic influences. If we are to be what he wants us to be, we must step outside these limitations so apt to ensnare us and know the freedom of his grace. The human expectations and false guilt they rouse are roadblocks to the peace and contentment found in him and happiness with those he gives us. We must let God be God, not our old ways of serving ourselves, not the expectations of others, not even our own expectations of him, or we will limit his work in our lives. In giving ourselves to him fully, the limitations are lifted, the shackles fall off; we have freedom in Christ, security in God's grace, and peace in his providence. (Ps 37:23–24 and 28; Prov 16:9, 24:16; Matt 7:13–23; John 1:12–13, 8:31–32, 36; Acts 20:28–31; 2 Cor 3:17, 5:15–17; Phil 3:12–16; Col 2:16–23; 1 Tim 1:3–7; 2 Tim 3:1–5; Jas 1:22–25)

59. Distracted

WE OFTEN BECOME DISTRACTED in our pursuit of God by our interests and plans that give us feelings of personal achievement, worth, or belonging to a group. Some lose interest when there seems to be no attraction—when we do not feel spiritual in our thoughts about God. When distracted or without the spiritual feelings we count on, we often try to substitute for them. We sometimes substitute church or Christianity for God himself because it is easier to feel good about ourselves in that arena than in our personal relationship with God. We are so accustomed to feelings leading our spiritual lives that boredom is a risk when they are absent.

We try various methods to create more excitement in worship, more enthusiasm in prayer, and more fulfillment in ministry. But we are depending on feelings instead of on truth and the person of God. If we allow God to be God entirely, and if we trust him wholeheartedly—core concepts of the fear of the Lord—there would be less superficial activity, less noise, a steadier approach, a calmer view of life and what he has given us to do. We would have less concern for ourselves and more for his plan for creation, more resting in his providence, and less confidence in our plans. We must trust his grace in a relationship with him rather than our feelings, reputation, or achievements. It is the beginning of emotional health, the basis of our confidence in life, and the onset of wisdom in the life of the believer. (Pss 20:7–8 with 21:7 and 33:16–22, 23:1–6, 25:1–3, 90:12, 111:10, 116:1–2 with 118:6–9; Prov 1:7, 3:5–8, 4:5–13 with 23, 9:10, 15:33, 16:9, 28:26; Isa 32:17, 33:6; Luke 9:23–25; Phil 3:7–9; Jas 3:17–18)

60. Secret Ways to Know God?

IF WE CREATE SECRETS around God, we will miss the essence of his being. Outside the unique name he reserves for us when we get to heaven, he is not keeping secrets from us. There is no secret way to know God that we must discover in a particular way only a few understand. All we need is before us, though we must pay attention to his word and his way and trust him to see it. That does not mean, however, that there is no mystery in God. There are his ironic ways with humankind and the many paradoxes of his purposes, and there is much he has not told us. If we needed to know more, he would be free with us about it. We must be content with what he gives us and trust his way—his providence in our lives and the world around us. We must allow him to be God beyond our limited definitions and see him with eyes of faith, full of awe at his greatness, power, love, and grace. That he gives us a standing of worth and significance in his presence in Christ may sound impossible, but it is no secret. He does not keep secrets. As he brings all things to their appointed destiny, we may not know all the details, but we know no one can thwart his movement in history or stop his arm of justice. All will be right again in his way and in his time. (1 Sam 2:4–9; Ps 37:5–6; Isa 43:10–13, 46:10, 48:17, 50:10–11, 55:8–11; Mic 6:8; Matt 11:25–30; Rom 11:33–36; 1 Cor 1:26–31 with 2:14–16; 1 Tim 3:16; Rev 2:17)

61. Pride and Terror

MEN AND WOMEN DO not naturally seek God. Their culture has its own solutions for enduring life's problems and suffering or a religious system that takes God's place. People who seem to succeed in their culture become heroes and champion its ways as examples of its capacity to make survival and "success" possible. Many cultural heroes have no purpose but to serve their appetites for pleasure, leisure, wealth, or control. Many find their success in getting others to do what they want, buy their product, follow their advice. They shake their fists at God, become enamored with their achievements, and reject giving up control of their lives. They put all their energy into alternate theories of how we got here and where we are going. But all their cultural achievements have no meaning for their ultimate survival when their soul is required of them.

Others avoid God out of fear of finding him. They must not let it be true. They take heart in others like themselves who run from him, especially if they are cultural heroes. They react irrationally to those who say they know him, for these remind them of their insecurities and of his potential demands on their lives as they have heard them preached by legalistic Christians. They throw insults at him and label him a superstition that has ruled their lives for too long, thwarting their selfish designs and causing guilt from their pleasures; they are blinded by the influence of their own god. The uncertainty and terror that God might indeed exist eat away at their souls. They are desperate to terminate this Jesus.

All these turn their worship toward humankind and assert their "rights" that they will have under any conditions as long as God is kept out of it. Uneasiness troubles the day, and desperation haunts the night. But they crave the control of their souls and harden themselves against it. They are the willing victims of a counterfeit worldview. It is Satan's deception, the same he used on Adam and Eve at the dawn of the universe. When they die, and it is too late, their eyes will be opened, and they will see that behind their plan for survival lies eternal separation from the goodness and grace of God.

It is a grim story but does not have to end that way. When the rich man saw Lazarus in paradise, nothing could be done. But today, there is still time, and God's far-reaching grace awaits them. They will have to come to the end of themselves, humble their hearts, and turn to him through Christ to finally know true peace and security. But his grace will overwhelm them if they allow him his way. They will then know the One they dreaded, find all they have needed in him, and wonder at the deception that has been done away. In the meantime, God waits. (Pss 14:2, 40:4, 127:1–2; Prov 15:25, 28:26; Matt 7:13–14, 23:37; Luke 12:15–21, 15:11–24, 16:19–31; 1 Tim 4:1–4; Heb 12:28–29; Jas 4:4–10, 5:7–8; 2 Pet 3:1–9; 1 John 2:15–17)

62. The Justice of God Waits

MEN AND WOMEN CAN know righteousness in Christ. God freely gives it to all who choose his forgiveness. These can become leaders of justice in our societies, but their fight is against the god of this world and his deception of men and women who follow all kinds of injustice if it fills their selfish appetites. Satan's poison is sweet, and many do not believe in its lethality. What was once called pagan and heathen in the darker corners of our world is today called development and progress. The old deeds of infanticide, corruption, obscenity, and mutilation are once again shameless practices of our day as we enter the final stages of freedom from morality and the loss of meaning for life. Those under the spell of the god of this world no longer have eyes that can see or ears that can hear. Their hearts have become calloused. They have closed God out of their lives. His grace is still available to give them the miracle of life, but they refuse it for death.

Virtuous men and women leaders cannot prevail long unless God intervenes on their behalf. God has given humankind the precious gift of freedom for their choices in life, and most love darkness rather than light. He waits. Evil will have its way until it fulfills its limit, or these destroy themselves in their burning cities and crumbling nations. His people must wait on God; his delay will not endure forever. Rebellion and injustice do not escape his eye. He waits that some of them might turn to him, experience his grace, and know his goodness. But he will not wait forever. (Ps 97:1–2; Prov 5:21–23, 14:2, 16:1–6, 32, 17:3–4, 21:1–3, 25:4–5, 29:4; Eccl 5:8–9; Isa 56:11–12, 59:12–15; Lam 3:31–33; Mic 6:8; Hab 1:4, 2:9–11; Matt 13:11–17; John 3:19–21; 2 Cor 4:4; Jas 1:14–15; 2 Pet 3:9)

63. Miracles

OUR BODIES ARE FULL of the miracles of God's creative power in our senses, reasoning, will, emotions, and physical capabilities. We see beauty in nature and those we love, hear music and the sounds of the created world, taste the sweetness of honey, smell the scent of flowers, touch softness, and feel touched. Through these gifts, we, too, can become creative.

In his wisdom, God designed the family where the abilities and aptitudes of a man and a woman come together, enriching both. Together, he gave them the ability to reproduce lives with these same endowments and nurture these children in the God-honoring use of these aptitudes and abilities. The person, the combination of all these wonders and their use toward goodness and love, is the greatest miracle of all. A person loving God and those around them is beyond scientific explanation, a rare beauty, and a treasure to hold in high regard.

Nature and the animal kingdom also magnify God; all their wonders come together to tell us of the creator and inspire our admiration, humility, and wonder. God's power called it all into existence, all of it good, all of it outside the abilities of men to create. These miracles of the human being and the world around us are given to us—unworthy vessels made worthy in Christ. And what shall we do with the miraculous gifts of God in creation? They can be terribly abused, but we who are his must use them to honor him. We have but an hour on the stage of life, but in this short time, while we have these gifts, we must use them to call attention to him, be creative with them in revealing his grace, to love those he gives us, and lift up his name among our neighbors and among the nations. In this way, we glorify God with the life he has given us. (Gen 1:27–28, 31, 2:20b–24; Pss 8:1–9, 19:1–14, 57:7–11, 90:4 with 10 and 12, 139:1–18, 23–24; Prov 22:6; Matt 22:34–40, 28:18–20; 2 Cor 4:6–7; Eph 5:31–33; Jas 4:13–17)

64. Uncertainty

UNCERTAINTY IS THE NECESSARY environment for trust. Just as cold shows the necessity of heat and darkness, the blessing of light, so uncertainty and ambiguity, with their typical companion of doubt, are parts of life that can help us understand trust in God and the certainty it provides. Without these worldly concerns, we would never look further and never consider his grace and providence more deeply. On the other hand, nothing is more prominent in Satan's arsenal. From the beginning, his lies have influenced the hearts of humankind, and he continues to sow the seeds of doubt in men and women without stopping. But we overcome the world and our enemy himself when we trust God in the face of the cruelest doubt. Uncertainty will never be a friend, but it will become a familiar reminder of where certainty lies. Our feelings are no gauge of the unchanging truths of his presence with us, his purposes in our lives, and his desire for our well-being.

Without need, there can be no trust. Without a challenge, there can be no loyalty. Real love is best displayed when another lets us down or seems unloving. Worry about tomorrow, the temptation to return to culture's old solutions, and impatience and anger when needs are not satisfied immediately result from moments of weakness in our faith. But we must trust God at the worst of times to know him in the best. (Deut 31:6 and 8; Job 13:15; Pss 20:7, 23:4, 33:16–19, 40:1–4, 55:22, 115:11, 146:3–6; Prov 3:5–7, 16:9; Jer 17:5–8; Dan 3:16–18; John 14:18, 27, 15:18–21 with 16:33; Rom 12:21; Phil 1:6, 4:4–9; Jas 4:7; 1 Pet 5:6–7; 1 John 4:4, 5:1–5; Rev 3:4–6)

65. Peace in a World of Suffering

THERE ARE TIMES IN this life when we sense something outside it. For a brief moment, we have a notion of a better place, a peace that cannot be upset. It is a moment or two outside ourselves when all is well, and no worry or anxious thought is present. Even if it is only a wave of emotion, we long for this better place of peace, and that longing shapes our life in this one. But we walk on, having tasted it, in a world of suffering and injustice. This is what humankind, deceived by self and Satan, has made of God's creation. Sinful and destructive human behavior is everywhere, and despite what trendy criticism is in the air against God, his intent is not to change the world for now but to change people within that broken world when they come to him. He will give us peace and freedom now, here, in this world, though we may also know suffering and be on the receiving end of injustice and hatred. Peace in suffering? Yes. Knowing him, experiencing his grace, and trusting him, our hope is satisfied in him now, and we realize the world will not always be this way. Every anxiety that punctuates our lives and calls for renewed trust in God will be laid to rest permanently. (Gen 3:1–19; Pss 37:3–7, 119:71; Matt 11:28–30; John 14:27, 15:18–21, 16:33 with 17:15, 20:19–20; Rom 8:22–25, 15:13; 1 Cor 15:50–58; Col 1:3–6; Heb 4:9–11, 11:1, 6, 13; Jas 1:2–8, 22–25; 1 Pet 1:3–9, 5:10–11; 2 Pet 4:2–19; 1 John 3:11–13; 4:1–6)

66. Spiritual Disciplines Gone Wrong

SPIRITUAL DISCIPLINES OF PRAYER, Scripture reading and memorization, self-control, and even worship can go wrong. For some people, they become the problem instead of the help they need for their souls. When we drift into feelings of achievement, enjoy secret satisfaction in others knowing of our efforts, or see ourselves as more spiritual than those around us, the self has taken over where God should be central. While thinking we are spiritual, we actually display ignorance and arrogance. Our value on personal achievement is an old tool of our culture for personal survival. Before we met Christ, we used it to compete for social position and affirmation, to gain feelings of worth and personal identity. It was the basis of feelings of security, however temporary, and its chains are not easy to break.

If spiritual disciplines let our old need for achievement take over, pride has found its way onto the stage. When loosed from its cage, the appetite of self for social survival and success is never satisfied. Even what should produce the most unassuming spirit in us can become the enemy, powerful and deceptive. Our pride, greed, and selfish ambition may be unknown to others but not God. He wants us to deal with it. He does not intend to do it for us but waits for our hearts to recognize it, repent, and return to him in humility.

Spiritual disciplines are essential in helping us to grow in Christ. The less formal and systematic they are, the better their benefits blend into an expression in our daily lives. If there are interruptions to your "quiet times," you may need to try other times or locations, but if they make you angry, you are missing the point of growing in Christ. We must be on our guard even in our best moments. We must let go of the anxiety for self-survival and trust in God rather than our achievements. Spiritual exercises should be in secret, and our love and service for our neighbor and our brothers and sisters in Christ be the outward manifestation of a heart given to God. If they do not produce good works, they are empty rituals, something for which Jesus had no use. (Prov 28:26, 30:7–9; Matt 22:34–40, 23:25–28, 25:31–46; Luke 10:25–37, 18:9–14; John 13:34–35 with 15:12; Gal 6:14; Jas 1:19–27; 1 Pet 5:5–8; 2 Pet 1:3–11)

67. Humility

HUMILITY, ESPECIALLY IN OUR individualist society, is rare, even among Christians. Our culture has powerfully programmed us to "watch out for ourselves" to take care of "number one." This socialization is not easy to overcome. Humility involves a contrary view of ourselves. It is a virtue that results from realizing the depth and breadth of God's grace in our lives and our desperate need for it. We must recognize that we cannot trust ourselves in our best moments not to dip into self-centered thinking or pride in our personal achievements. We must acknowledge his complete and perfect forgiveness and unconditional love. It includes the realization of his providence in all things in our lives. There is a consideration of our personal needs that is normal and expected in the Christian life. But humility goes beyond this to giving up our efforts to achieve social rewards for the self and realizing that our true well-being comes from him. If we experience the affirmation of others, it will not be because we have sought it but because God has chosen to use it in our lives for his purposes, perhaps for guidance, encouragement, and help, and perhaps to give us practice in humility.

In the Old Testament, humility is a natural result of what is called the fear of the Lord. The same God who created the universe, whose word brings light and life out of darkness and death, who named the stars and shaped the hills, looks for and delights in the humble, for they have recognized him. They have found the treasure in the field, the pearl of great price—theirs is the kingdom of heaven; they will inherit the earth. Humility is the expected result of accepting the truth about ourselves and knowing God and his way. It's no use trying to drum it up on our own, apart from an awareness of the great paradox of his lavish grace for undeserving sinners. (Pss 25:9, 69:32, 147:2–6, 10–11; Prov. 11:2, 15:33, 18:12–13, 28:26, 29:23; Eccl. 5:1–3; Isa 66:2b; Mic 6:8; Matt. 5:3–10, 13:44–46, 18:1–4, 23:11–12; Luke 14:11; 2 Cor 4:6–7; Eph 4:2; Phil 2:3; Col 3:12; Titus 3:2; Jas 1:17, 3:13, 4:10; 1 Pet 5:5–6)

68. Control

IN INDIVIDUALIST SOCIETIES SUCH as North America and Western Europe, we are trained to control the environment to advance ourselves. Our culture gives us no other way than to achieve our survival through competition, self-assertion, and manipulation. But what could be less like Jesus' words about love, unity, and trusting God? This survival technique is at its worst when some control others in the church for their advantage. It is a powerful cultural urge, and nowhere is it more ugly than among God's people. Yet there it is. For them, the world is entirely about themselves, while they try to display the opposite attitude by church membership. It is one more reason the world disdains the church, and some Christians leave it looking for an authentic Christianity. Other people leave Christianity altogether. Self-interest must give way to God at the center of our lives before he can be the center of the church. Our social survival, identity, and reputation must be in his hands. Self-assertion and social competition deny the truth of the gospel and destroy our message of God's grace to the world. It is not by our words alone that the world will understand who Jesus is. We are part of our message. Stepping back from a need to control our surroundings opens the door for the love and grace of God to become evident in our lives. (John 3:22–30, 13:34–35, 17:21 and 23; Rom 12:9–10; 1 Cor 10:23–24 with 31–33; 2 Cor 5:15; Gal 2:20, 5:13–15, 25–26; Phil 1:21, 2:1–4; 1 Pet 3:18 with 4:2, 5:5; 1 John 3:16–20)

69. Legalism versus Grace

LEGALISM GIVES CONTROL OF our lives to someone or something other than God. It is adding our preferences for black-and-white statements and rules to the Bible as he gave it to us and making the new mixture "God's will" for us. This mixture hardens like concrete around its adherents, keeping love, grace, and freedom in Christ on the outside. Legalism in the church pushes thinking people away, especially the younger ones in our world today. It is not God's way. He makes us his sons and daughters and tells us we are free in Christ, bound by loyalty and trust for him and by love and ministry for each other. Whether out of insecurities or the need to control people, legalism is death when God intends to give life.

There is a paradox concerning black-and-white judgments of sin in the Bible. While sin against God and his people is clear and judgment sometimes fast and final, the overriding theme is that he looks at the intentions and motives of the person, not the outward appearance, that true worship is inward. Obedience is, first of all, a matter of the heart. Ritual or location are not the concerns. We see that one's standing with God is proportional to one's faith, not church attendance, displays of spiritual discipline, years in ministry, missionary service overseas, or a complex understanding of theology. He looks for pure, simple, unquestioning faith. But this way of God creates uncertainty for those who trust black-and-white categories instead of trusting God. It makes many Western Christians anxious and insecure. Their logic does not stand up against the truth that comes with—and is never to be separated from—grace. For them, there is no grace—only right and wrong, and everyone else is wrong.

Truth must not stand alone, for the law came through Moses, but truth and grace came through Jesus. For example, Jesus forgives the woman caught in adultery (grace) but not the rich young man (truth). We might be tempted to do the opposite. He forgave those the religious leaders would not; he allowed Nicodemus to find his way to the truth. This combination

69. LEGALISM VERSUS GRACE

of grace and truth is seen in his conversations with a Samaritan woman at a well, tax collectors in the city streets, and lepers on the edges of town. He touched the untouchables.

Grace is God's way within the boundaries of faith, love, and trust. It is a matter of the heart. It is not predictable how God will work in one person's life or in that of another, for though the truth remains the same, his grace is at work in people, and humans have different needs and must make personal choices. (1 Sam 13:14 with 16:7 and 13 and Acts 13:22; Pss 51:5–6, 16–17, 145:17–19; Prov 17:3, 21:3, 30:5–6; Hos 6:6; Mic 6:8; Matt 5:3–10, 19:16–26, 22:34–40; Mark 7:6–7; John 1:14–18, 4:19–26, 8:1–11; 1 Cor 1:26–31)

70. Worship

THE WORSHIP OF GOD is an honest and humble attitude of the heart that comes out in various expressions. It is not everything we do, but something specific with a purpose, displaying God's goodness, grace, and greatness and our gratefulness for all of it. And it is more. It recognizes his otherness, acknowledges his mystery, and submits to his providence. He is not like us, though we often bring him down to our level, making our worship shallow and our expression of faith thin. He is above and beyond us. We dare not forget our finiteness controlled as we are by our human nature, culture, and, often, poor theology.

We stand before the Creator-God of the universe, who alone is worthy, and in his grace, he welcomes us through the merits of Christ. This marries humility to the fear of God. It gives worship its perspective and puts our dependence on him in the foreground of our expressions. It removes all preoccupation with the self and our achievements, resulting in a natural and non-negotiable humility in his presence. This is worship in spirit and in truth. (Deut 10:12; 1 Sam 2:3b; Ps 100:1–5, Prov 14:12 with 16:2, 21:2, 22:4; Isa 6:1–8, 66:2b; Mic 6:8; Matt 18:1–4; John 4:23–24; Jas 4:3 with 7 and 10)

71. Unexpected Providence

GOD'S WAYS IN THE world and our lives are very different than we might imagine, prefer, or expect. We often attach human definitions to his being and set limits for his behavior in our theologies. The Pharisees in Jesus' day did that too. We find it hard to let him be God when he does not fit the limitations and guidelines we set for him. His providence is one of those problematic areas for our theology, often inscrutable and paradoxical from our vantage point. But in his word, we find he is moving in the universe to bring about his purposes. We are told he is working for the good of his own people in all things. We will not necessarily like or understand all that he uses for our good, but he intends to bring his work in us to completion according to his purposes. We are part of his plan for the world. We will have to trust him for many things along the way as he shapes us and uses us to shape others. For there is much he has not told us. There is mystery when we want everything to be objective and fit into a predictable pattern—a neat system with all the loose ends tied up. But we can, if we are willing, trust him for that mystery, and in the end, we will know all, and all will be for his glory.

He cares for us when we least think about it, as well as in our deepest needs. He shapes our circumstances without our awareness to fulfill his purposes for us. We cannot escape it, nor would we, in a sane moment, want to. It is, however, still up to us to join his plan, desire his intentions for us, and allow his purposes to be worked out in our lives.

We must often look back over our lives to see how God has brought us through many difficulties, provided for many needs, encouraged us through friends, used us in ways unknown to us at the time, and brought us to this moment in our lives. Our journey has taken many turns. Where we have resisted him and taken our own way, where we have made a mess of things, he can turn even those disasters into what serves his purposes. Many times, when he was directing our path, it did not look like we might have expected.

It did not seem supernatural at the time. Our role in his plan may look different than we could ever have imagined because he is in the background implementing it . . . and his ways are not our ways.

As the Jews were always to remember God's deliverance of them from Egypt, we must remember that he has also delivered us from darkness and never left our side. Though sometimes waiting for our attention, he never gives up being there for us. The Jews were to remember God's act of deliverance, mentioned hundreds of times in the Old Testament. We, too, must remember his hand in our lives, moving us from darkness to light. Contentment is in trusting this great providence. It is grounded in his love, inseparable from his grace, and powerful enough to move mountains. (Exod 13:3; Lev 11:45, 22:33, 25:38, 26:13; Num 15:41; Deut 4:20, 6:12, 20:1; Josh 24:5–7; Pss 28:6–9, 37:3–7a, 23–24, 28, 80:8, 138:8, 143:5–6 with 119:71; Prov 3:5–7, 16:9, 28:26; Jer 29:10–14; Acts 26:15–18; Rom 5:8, 8:28; Eph 2:1–5; Phil 1:6 with 2:12–13 and 1 Thess 5:24; Col 1:13–14, 2:13)

72. Our Calling to Trust the Providence of God

WE OFTEN HAVE A longing for a better place. We have experiences of God's hand on us, his wise providence, and we are reminded of that place where all is well and joy will never end. But his purposes have us here, and Jesus prayed that God would not remove us from the world but protect us from the evil one. There is purpose in God's providence in our lives in our present context. We can feel peace about his purposes in our lives, but those feelings may escape us when things get hard and complicated. However, his providence remains in control even when there are no feelings or we have bad feelings. We must have confidence in his all-knowing care and trust his Spirit for strength when there is no vision, no special moment, no particular sensation. His care for us is the same in the happy times as it is in the routines of life, the responsibilities he has given us, and the difficulties along the way. Our calling is to be faithful to our great God, for he is faithful to us. What looks like just another day to us is really quite remarkable, for he gave it to us as another day to be loyal to him—another day to fulfill our calling.

This providence of God is related to God's will. God's moral will consists of his desires for us, what he wants for us, and what he knows is best for us if we follow his way. But there is another side to God's will—his decreed will, his plan for the universe that will be accomplished whether humankind loves or ignores him. Between these two sides of God's will, leaning on both and intending to bless and use us in his plan, is his providence at work in the world and our lives. Here, there is mystery and hope, power and security, law and love, sovereign control and confident freedom. That hope, security, love, and freedom begin to be ours when we reflect on God's way with us in the past, though it may not look like we would expect. It continues to become our possession when we allow his hand in our lives today, though we don't know all his intended outcomes. The central concept for us is *trust*, for God arranges and regulates all things so that they serve his purposes in us and in the world. The psalmist talks about it as dwelling "in the shelter of the Most High" and resting "in the shadow of the Almighty." He says he is his refuge and fortress, "my God in whom I trust." Under the shadow of his wings, we are secure and loved, have both freedom and hope. We can trust his providence as it embraces us. It is his all-encompassing love and the power of his work in us and in everything that surrounds our lives.

When commanded to love the Lord our God, the word "love" emphasizes loyalty, commitment, and action. The God of all power, wisdom, and trustworthiness has covered us with his grace and called us to serve him. The loyalty he wants from us in this calling is based on trust throughout the Bible, from cover to cover. God is not commanding us to feel something. There will be gaps of time when it does not seem like he is still there, but we are not to act based on what appears to be or not be. He has promised he is *always* there. He will always act as necessary on our behalf for his purposes in our lives and will do so in power, grace, and love regardless of our feelings. Our calling is to trust that promise. (Deut 31:8; Josh 23:14; 1 Kgs 8:56-61; Pss 36:7-10, 37:23-24 and 28, 61:2-4, 91:1-2 with 9 and 14-16, 139:7-12; Prov 3:5-7, 16:9; Hag 1:13; Matt 28:18a with 20b; John 14:15-18; Acts 18:9-11; Rom 8:28-39; Phil 2:13; 1 Thess 5:23-24; Heb 13:5b-6)

73. Selfishness and Pride

SELFISHNESS AND PRIDE ARE our enemies. Other sins are petty in comparison and are rooted in these. If we can get to this core and cut the root, we can kill these weeds and prevent their seeds from spreading. We must have God's help, and we will be less than perfect, but we must nevertheless act. Our self-deception will not serve us. Covering it over with a show of spirituality, using devotional rituals to offset it or legalistic declarations to defend it will only let the root go deeper. And killing a seed here and there will not resolve the problem. The root is the problem. Even church attendance can be for self, or worse, the deceptive love for another. Only a humble recognition of it before God can cut that stubborn root, restore the soul, and prepare the soil for a crop that bears a generous harvest of good fruit.

Of course, any crop must be weeded regularly, and if we are sensitive to God, we will find ourselves on our knees doing that more than we expect. Resistance to selfishness and pride is an ongoing battle. We must declare war on the enemy. We must be alert as our adversary uses tactics beyond our sensitivities to deceive us. In this life, we will not be free of the skirmishes with self, but each time we take a hill here and a bridge there, we move toward our objective—maturity in Christ. (2 Chr 7:14; Ps 112:4–7; Prov 11:25, 22:9, 23:6–8, 28:26; Jer 17:5–10; Matt 13:18–23; Luke 12:13–21; John 15:4–8; Phil 2:1–4; 1 Tim 6:17–19; Jas 3:13–18, 4:7, 10; 1 Pet 5:5–6, 8–11; 1 John 1:9, 3:16–20)

74. Stopping to Think

WE, AS CHRISTIANS, NEED time to think in a busy world of pressing needs and urgent agendas. We will have to stop the roller coaster, let the vibrations fade, take our spiritual pulse, and think about where we have been, what has happened, and where we really need to go. Often, these days, people pride themselves on being multitaskers. Our cultural emphasis on achievement requires a great deal of accomplishment for us to feel good about ourselves, achieve social approval, or attain the coveted identity of a "successful" person. We can't rest until everything is checked off the "to-do" list. But it has not always been this way, nor is it this way today in those cultures where life is savored and meditation on the meaning of life is valued. In the biblical days of David and Solomon, wisdom and poetry were highly valued, and though being willing to work hard was a virtue, meditation was an inclination of the heart.

We would do well to seek some stillness, reflect on God's ways, and notice the themes of our desires and the assumptions of our hearts in the present moment. Before all the days of our lives are gone, it is good to stop and reflect on what God has done and why it mattered—to think about what we have learned and journal our walk with God. We might then help another person ponder what God has accomplished in their life even when they were too busy to notice, too distracted to pay attention to him. Western people are doers. But getting things done should not be the only motive for our day-to-day lives. There must be time for being and becoming as well as doing. (Josh 1:8; Pss 1:1–3, 16:1–11, 27:1, 37:3–6, 23–24, 66:16–20, 73:21–28, 90:12, 14, 17, 119:46–48; Prov 10:4, 19:15, 26:14–16; Isa 30:15, 32:17, 66:2b; Mic 6:8; Matt 6:33; Eph 5:20; Phil 2:3–4, 4:4–9; Col 3:1–4; 1 Thess 4:11–12 with 2 Thess 3:10–13)

75. Wounded

OUR BEHAVIOR IS DEVELOPED and patterned in our early years by the socialization we experience, which can sometimes be dysfunctional and even abusive. No one is a perfect parent; no one had a perfect childhood. When dysfunctional, our poor socialization causes us to try to cope with the emotional pain or compensate for what was lacking. As children, we seek to defend ourselves against further emotional distress or loss and fill the void with whatever seems to help. The patterns and rituals, the emotional defenses, become habitual and can shape our behavior for a lifetime unless God is allowed in, unless we allow ourselves to trust him and his way for us completely.

You are not an accident. God's providence has brought you into this world and to this moment in your life to read these words, to know about his grace, to trust him, to see his will for you in the Bible. He is not a father with the weaknesses and failures of earthly fathers. And nothing in our lives can prevent us from experiencing his grace and becoming his sons and daughters today. He knows the pain sin has brought into the world and wants us to find relief and peace in our relationship with him while we wait for the door to our perfect existence with him to be opened. He delays this final act so more people in this broken world can come to him. In the meantime, if we trust him, nothing will prevent him from using us as part of his work in the world. (Pss 119:70-72, 139:1-18; Isa 43:1; Matt 6:31-34; John 1:10-14, 14:27 with 15:9 and 20:19-20, 17:15-19; 1 Cor 2:8-10; Phil 4:4-9; Col 3:12-17; Jas 1:2-8; 1 Pet 1:3-9, 5:6; 2 Pet 3:9; Rev 7:16-17, 21:1-5)

76. Culture's Way

PEOPLE ARE PRODUCTS OF the culture in which they grow up. They are socialized according to existing values, beliefs, understandings, and assumptions of their context without their choice. These, in the end, drive their behavior and attitudes. The deepest assumptions are seldom questioned, and the values and beliefs are powerful influences on the members of the society to the point of overwhelming their judgment. These understandings take root in the minds of children, and by the time they are in their early teens, their worldview is in place as a foundation for the rest of their lives. They are threatened with social exclusion if this perception of the world does not shape their behavior. In their honor and shame culture, Jewish people in the Bible were socially rejected if they appeared to step outside the traditions and moral code of the oral Torah. They became impure in the eyes of their social group, untouchables.

Perhaps no one knew this ostracism more than Mary and Joseph when they followed God's leading at the time of the birth of Jesus. Their culture had shaped them to do life one way, and then God changed their world completely. In many ways, he turned it upside down. They started out with good standings in the community. Joseph had honor, and Mary had purity in the eyes of their community. But they ended up at the bottom of the social hierarchy among their friends and family. God was making the last first and the first last in every event of the birth of Jesus.

We may need to expect something similar. When we become Christians later in life, we are already shaped by cultural influences. We can see the glaring contradictions but do not readily recognize the more subtle conflicts these influences have with our new faith. As a survival system, we have trusted our culture as the way to go about life and achieve mental, social, and physical survival. It is not easy to redirect that trust and loyalty. But we have a new leader in Christ and must turn our allegiance to him. We must be relevant in our culture but no longer prisoners of its influence.

(Matt 6:33, 7:21–23, 12:50; Mark 10:31; John 8:31–32 with 36; Rom 12:1–2; 2 Cor 5:15–18; Gal 5:13; Phil 1:9–11, 3:12–14; Col 3:1–4; 1 Pet 2:16; 1 John 2:15–17, 4:4–6)

77. Self-Awareness in Christ

CHRISTIANS ARE NOT EXEMPT from the temptation to lean on their own efforts to satisfy their preferences or achieve their "success." We can easily drift back into concerns for the recognition of our efforts for feelings of self-esteem and worth in our individualist society. Self-interest is always just around the corner for us individualists, waiting to pounce on us. We hardly notice its subtle influence if we do not regularly check our spiritual pulse against human inclinations. Even in our best moments, it is in the wings waiting to jump on stage where only Christ belongs. Pride, greed, self-assertion, or control of others must not characterize our new role in the story God is writing.

In addition to this need for recognition and "success," careless habits and self-centered addictions triggered by emotional pain or anxiety must be exchanged for trust in the One who cares for us, our creator and savior. They can keep creeping in and distract us from our desire to serve God. But we are never beyond God's help and grace, never. He knows the pain we feel. We must recognize these habits for what they are. Satan uses them against us, and we may need the help of a pastor or Christian counselor to see our way out of them. These people are God's gifts to the body of Christ to help us appropriate his love and forgiveness and know his grace going forward. He can and will use them to shape us for his purposes as they use his word to show us his way.

We would like to have it both ways—the benefits of both the narrow and the broad roads. Syncretism always seems to be our first choice. But compromise cannot be endured long by those whose salvation is in Christ. We must return our loyalty to God. It is a human and cultural deception of an intensity that requires early detection and decisive action to return to trusting him for all things. Allowed to continue, divided loyalty is spiritually crippling, preventing us from the peace of trusting him. (Prov 3:5–7, 26:12, 27:2; Jer 17:9; John 14:27; Rom 6:8–14, 8:5–17; 1 Cor 3:18; 2 Cor 5:15–18;

Gal 2:20; Eph 4:11–13; Phil 1:20–21 with 27, 4:6–7; 1 Pet 1:13–21, 3:18, 4:1–2, 5:6–7)

78. Ungratefulness

It is the nature of the human heart without Christ to take the good things God gives without gratitude and blame him for the evil in the world. How blind the eyes and mind of the unbelieving. How much of what they have do they deserve? What have they achieved of eternal value on their own? What does true justice say about their selfish and irrational thoughts and actions? They must come to realize that they deserve nothing at all, if not misery, for their rejection of the creator. It does not go unnoticed. Though all seems quiet in the shadow of the judgment of God, it is not that he overlooks sinful hearts; it is because he waits. He is just outside the lives of men and women with patient love to offer grace undeserved the moment they look his way and realize Christ is the way, the truth, and the life. But he will not wait forever. They are in the eye of the storm. Their time will come—for each outside of Christ a summons to judgment decreed by the creator of the universe. Satan's deception runs deep, and his spell is cast far and wide; the minds of men and women are blinded, their turning to God difficult. Ungrateful are the creatures he created until they humble themselves to know and accept their Creator's grace. Without this humility, it is impossible to be saved; without gratefulness, it is impossible to worship God.

    We who know God through his grace must hold out this message to those lost in the world. God has given each of us a part in his plan for doing that. Through our talents and skills, our unique backgrounds, and our particular concerns and burdens, we can show the gospel to those around us, not just in words but in our actions, so they might see that grace at work in us and our gratefulness for it. (Jer 17:9; Matt 18:1–4; Mark 10:17–31; John 3:16–21 with Rom 3:23–24 and 1 John 1:9; 2 Cor 4:4, 11:14–15; Eph 4:17–18 with 22–24, 5:15–18; 2 Thess 1:5–10; Heb 9:8–15 with 23–28; Jas 2:14–17, 4:10; 1 Pet 5:6; 2 Pet 3:1–15; 1 John 3:18)

79. Social Recognition

MANY PEOPLE IN OUR individualist culture are attached intensely to others' opinions of them: their reputation in a social circle for achievement, importance in the group, physical attractiveness, and even the recognition of their good works. Unfortunately, it is so even among many Christians, among whom we can add that some are attached to the desire to be seen as spiritual. The danger is that they may get that recognition, and it will push God's grace from their hearts and fill them with self-admiration. The question is, Are we among them? There is a part of the old person in us that is really quite vain, but we must not allow it to push us around. Who and what we are in Christ is the lifeboat that can save us from the sinking ship of self-fixation. For sink it will. We are talking about one of the most central issues of being a Christian: dying to self and trusting God for his way in our lives. He wants our hearts and will work in our lives to have them. His ways of bringing us to him from self-attachment may be uncomfortable. But the pain that brings awareness of our pride, bitter as it may be, is a welcome medicine if we will endure the whole course, take the last drop. Not all the damage can be repaired here on Earth, but we will know his grace, the way ahead will be clear of old debris, and we will be grateful people. Our God is good, but he intends to have our hearts. (Pss 94:12–13a, 119:75–77; Prov 3:11–12, 11:28, 28:26; 2 Cor 5:15–17; Heb 12:1–6; Jas 1:2–12; 1 Pet 4:12–19)

80. The Anxiety of Doubt

ONE OF THE MOST challenging enemies of the Christian is the occasional doubt that disturbs the soul. For some, it may be doubt about God's existence, but for most, it will be about his attention to us. Whether it concerns God's provision of resources, relationships, the resolution of some problem or conflict, health, or the courage to face some adversity, doubt is Satan's sharpest weapon against us. It worked for him in the garden of Eden; if we let it, its razor edge can cut deep into our well-being in Christ. When we notice doubt creeping into our outlook on the problematic events and upsetting circumstances of our lives, we must beware. We may be tempted toward a dishonest or unfair solution. Yes, we Christians are not immune to scheming and plotting our way out of problems. As individualists, we are naturally inclined toward self-assertion, but we must recall God's promises instead.

Abraham had no indication that Isaac would live when God sent him to the mountain to sacrifice his son. Yet he obeyed without understanding the purpose or knowing the outcome. God had promised he would make a nation of him through Isaac. He trusted God's way to that end, as impossible as it seemed. We, too, are to give him our anxieties, and he promises peace. We are told to change our thinking and allow the God of peace to care for us. When we allow his word to transform our minds, we can rest in him for the things we do not know or cannot do on our own, for what we cannot change in our circumstances. But it demands trust on our part. Do not allow anyone to lead you to think you cannot do it. Abraham did it, and God gives us his example for today. We can and must trust God, too, whatever our situation, though it is easier said than done.

It is not a call to a life without problems and difficulties but one of peace and confidence in the midst of them. Paul's many imprisonments, beatings, and shipwrecks are an example. We are to rest in Christ's work for us and in the hands of our loving Father, who will give us peace. Let his providence prove itself. No weapon of Satan's can be effective when we know God is our rock, our strong defense, our loving Father full of grace. Nothing can remove us from his hand. The seed of the woman has bruised the head of the serpent. Though he has not long to continue his deception, in his wild desperation, Satan continues to spread his influence in the hearts of men and women. We may stumble, but we will not fall. The storm of his assault on our little boat will not succeed. In the quietness and confidence of our trust in God, we will prevail, for he is our strength. What God said to Israel, he says to us who are in Christ: "You are mine." (Gen 3:14–15, 15:4–6, 22:1–18; 2 Chr 32:7–8; Pss 20:7, 33:16–22, 34:4–8, 37:1–11, 23–24, 28, 84:10–12, 91:1–4, 115:11, 146:3–6; Prov 3:5–7, 16:9, 24:16; Isa 30:15, 32:17, 43:1; Matt 11:28–30; Luke 8:22–25; John 6:35–40, 10:28–30, 14:27, 16:33; Rom 1:17, 12:1–2; 2 Cor 11:1–4, 24–29; Phil 4:4–9; Heb 4:9–11, 11:1 and 6; Jas 1:5–8; 1 Pet 1:6–7)

81. Doing the Right Thing

ALWAYS DOING THE RIGHT thing or never doing the wrong thing sounds like it would be ideal for us as Christians, but if this is the emphasis of a person's life, it can be the very opposite. The motive may be devastating, leading to the coldness of heart that accompanies legalism. To do or not do is not the essence of the Christian life. It is much more about being than doing; the doing follows naturally. It comes slowly at first, but eventually, it will become more habitual and characterize our lives. A heart given to God first in loyalty and trust—a love and commitment to him will motivate our behavior. Obedience coming from this kind of heart brings freedom, not legalism.

This relationship with him and the guidance of his word give us a way of judging the value of this or that behavior. This is the beginning of wisdom. We will know what honors him and experience freedom and contentment in Christ. As we trust him, we grow in this wisdom, are dissatisfied with superficial gains, and grow deeper in our loyalties to God. There is still much to be done after this trust takes hold, first in the way of good works that cultivate the ground and then in planting the seeds for making disciples. All are evidence of our faith and loyalty to our God, who is at work in us. (Ps 90:12; Prov 1:7, 4:5–9, 21:2–3; Matt 13:8–9 with 28:18–20; John 8:31–32 with 36; Rom 12:2; Gal 6:9–10; Eph 1:15–21; Phil 1:6, 9–11, 2:13; Col 2:16–23; 1 Tim 6:18; Titus 2:7, 11–15, 3:1, 8, 14; Heb 13:15–16; Jas 1:22–25; 1 Pet 3:13–17)

82. Truth

TRUTH ALONE CANNOT ACCOMPLISH God's will. As important as it is, it cannot stand alone for the Christian. Truth did not come to us alone in Christ; it came with grace. Both must be fully embraced. Too much emphasis on truth will lead to cold, harsh legalism. Too much stress on grace will lead to romantic sentimentalism. Neither result came with Christ. The law came through Moses, but grace *and* truth came through Jesus Christ. It takes more trust in God to allow grace to be part of the truth and more loyalty to him to stand on truth in the face of cultural expectations and pressures or the self-deception of pride and vanity.

Many unbelieving people have information about God, as inaccurate as much of it is. But they have not seen a good example of the effects God intends for that information to have in our lives. They have not seen that which would encourage them to seek answers. Unfortunately, they may have had many bad examples that work, like a vaccine, against wanting to look into Christianity. Grace must lead the way and prepare their hearts for truth. We must become people of grace and truth to represent God to the world around us. Satan has blinded their minds to it, but grace is the answer that gives light so they can see. When combined with truth, it turns people from a journey for self to a relationship with God. (Matt 18:21–35; Luke 7:36–50; John 1:15–18; 2 Cor 4:4–6; Eph 1:3–8, 2:1–10, 4:32; Col 3:13–14; 1 Tim 1:12–17; Titus 3:3–8; Heb 4:14–16; Jas 1:22–25, 2:18–19; 1 Pet 3:18; 2 Pet 3:18)

83. Nations under God

GOD ALLOWS NATIONS TO exist. Under human management, they take their course, and we find human vices at work keeping them from the ideals God created in Eden. Positions of status and wealth alongside poverty and injustice fill every nation. The flourishing or decay, freedom or bondage, peace or civil war result from human choices. The lust for power, wealth, and recognition—choices to control people and resources for selfish interests—usually lead to the self-destruction of a nation from the inside out. The most significant losses for any nation are the privileges, freedoms, and unity the people lose because of the lack of a virtuous society. The appetites of political leaders do not allow virtue to succeed. The love of power, status, and money, the gods of their lives, brings corruption.

Christians of any nation may lose their freedoms under human leaders, but they will not lose the security God provides. He endures for all time. Though the men and women who govern us may come to despise him and his people, he remains; his justice is not done away. He waits. We must be patient, realizing God does not sleep; he is at work. He watches over us as he did Israel and will be exalted among the nations.

We must consider, too, that some of our losses, even as Christians, may be of our own making. We may grow weak in our faith, and our light may dim. But he remains strong. We must renew our trust in him and our loyalty to his cause. Love and grace must abound more alongside truth in our lives and churches. The world must know we have a message of God's grace that matters. They must know that we care about them and God waits for them. We are salt and light in this world and can show the way. If loss brings that about, it is not entirely loss but also gain. Some of us will endure a great deal more than others to serve God in this world. But he has his hand on all of us in his plan and prepares a better place for us. (Pss 37:7–11, 46:1–11, 121:1–8; Isa 44:9; Matt 5:13–16, 38–48, 6:19–21, 22:15–22, 26:22, 50–54;

John 14:1–4, 6, 16:33, 18:10–11 with 36; Rom 13:1–7; Phil 1:20–30, 3:7–9; Titus 3:1; Jas 1:12; 1 Peter 2:13–14, 3:10–17, 4:12–17)

84. God's Words

GOD'S WORDS ARE INTENTIONAL, powerful, and final. In Genesis, God spoke the universe and humankind into existence. The Hebrew word for "word" carries the idea of activity; words accomplish something. God never fails to do what he says. In John chapter 1, that word becomes flesh in Jesus, and he accomplishes God's purpose in his life, death, and resurrection. Our Western use of words today is superficial compared to God's. We do not always mean what we say, say what we mean, or get all the meaning of someone else speaking to us. We are not good listeners, being easily distracted by our surroundings and self-concerns, and we may bring these habits with us when we read God's word. We give him about half our attention, are easily distracted, and soon forget what he said. But his words endure forever, accomplishing their intended purpose.

There is also the problem of our experience giving us associations for the meaning of words in communication. God carefully wraps his message of himself and his purposes for us in words. The vocabulary of any language carries only the speaker's meaning for the ideas and concepts to which it refers. The speaker or author depends on the listener's cultural frame of reference and personal experience to accurately interpret his or her ideas. Even when people belong to the same culture, personal experience gives each one concrete and emotional associations with the words used for communication that are not in the words themselves. So, meaning is in people as the words are shaped by the speaker and understood by the listener through associations from their experience. Obviously, the better we know the listener—their culture and experience—the more successful we are at creating an understanding of our intended meaning. A communication expert depends on the culture and experience of his audience, using their situational frame of reference to his advantage in creating intended meaning. Salespeople rely on it (and often get more of our attention than God does). But God does not speak to us in a vacuum, either. He knows all this about us. It is our pride, self-interests, fear of failure, negative associations with words, etc., that often keep his words from penetrating our hearts—keep him from accomplishing his purposes in our lives.

In the last paragraph, the negative associations mentioned are often unconscious. What is serious to one person may be hilarious to another. What is important or reassuring to one may be mundane and meaningless to another. A negative experience in one church may give a person negative meaning when they hear someone talk about the wonderful fellowship in another church. Calling God our Father is assuring to some but may not be to others because of personal experiences in their family. The vocabulary has different meanings for each person. So, communication between humans is often imprecise. We might ask ourselves what we allow to color God's words; when are we allowing our experience to keep his intended message at a distance? His is the most important communication in our lives.

We must let him speak for himself and use his meanings, not ours. His words are the wisdom that leads to life. Any humanly shaped meaning for them leads us in the wrong direction. But missing his meaning in the words will not change his intention. The words of God are life to those who listen and follow his way. He will always do what he says. (Ps 119:103 with 105; Prov 4:1–13 with 20–27, 8:6–21, 14:12; Isa 40:8, 55:8–11; Jer 15:16, 17:9; Heb 4:12–13; Jas 1:22–25; 1 Pet 1:24–25; 1 John 1:5–7)

85. Divine Communication

GOD KNOWS EVERYTHING ABOUT US: our emotions and experiences, the pressures of cultural expectations on us, and the true loyalties of our hearts. When he speaks to us in his word, he meets us where we are. And when he listens, he considers our intentions, motives, desires, and circumstances, not just our actions. He understands the stress and anxiety behind our words when we come to him. But all this does not mean he will show or give us what we expect or want him to. We must pay special attention to his message. In his word, he intends to reveal himself as he is, not as we would like him to be or how we might twist his words to make him. He tells us that he is more interested in our being something for him than in what we say or do or have. What we express in our words and actions and how we possess what he has given us must come from a changed heart. It may take some time for us to let him be God in our lives, and we may find that his blessings lie in some other direction than we imagined. We may disagree with him for now, but his good intentions and purposes for us, we can never question. (1 Sam 16:6–7; Pss 33:11, 18–19, 103:10–14, 119:71, 103, 105, 138:6–8; Prov 16:2, 20:27, 21:2; Matt 6:33, 7:24–27, 15:7–20; Luke 6:46–49, 7:11–17; Jas 1:22–25; 1 John 3:18)

86. Knowledge

Information can deceive. Knowledge alone is not God's intention in his word. In giving us this revelation of himself, his purpose is that we become something, a different kind of person than our human culture or personal achievement can produce. He intends that we become his sons and daughters in a relationship that goes beyond information to trust and intimacy. He would have us step out of what the world and our experience have made of us into what he would make of us as we trust him wholly. To see God's word as intending anything else will take us to an end outside his purposes.

The Bible is not solely a book of information to be bound in volumes and stacked on shelves. It is intended to give us a new perspective on life and reveal the true nature of reality in him, his works, and his purposes for our lives. It brings forgiveness, freedom, grace, wisdom, love, and compassion into our existence. Life on Earth can be miserable without it, and the afterlife a catastrophic tragedy. Trusting God's intended message does not mean we will never have difficulties or trouble in life but that we face them with hope, wisdom, grace, and peace from him. (Ps 51:6, 16–17; Prov 1:7, 9:9, 16:2, 25, 21:2; Hos 6:6; Mic 6:8; Matt 6:1–8, 7:15–23; John 12:24–26, 16:33 with 14:27; 1 Tim 1:3–7; Heb 4:12–13; Jas 1:22–25)

87. Conversion Takes Humility

RECEIVING CHRIST IS AT once his providence in our lives, our response to him in humility and faith opening the door to his grace, and his entering our lives. These events are difficult, if not impossible, to separate, and all must work together. We cannot bring about our conversion alone, and he refuses to do it alone. He never barges in. As we open our lives to him, they are filled with meaning and transformation by his entering and ongoing work in us. We turn the latch; he fills the house room by room as we allow him. He has not removed our freedom to choose by entering on his own and occupying. We are forgiven, but we can resist his guidance and choose against his way, even as Christians.

    He is patient with us and always accepts our return to his purposes. But we must be vigilant. He has the answers, but we must choose them at each turn in life until it becomes our habit to do so, our lifestyle, as we become more fully his. In choosing his way, there must be no legalism or selfish pride, only a relationship of trust and freedom in Christ. It will take effort on our part to keep it that way. It is not a religion of ritual behavior but knowing God and his grace, a growing desire to be loyal to him, a turning around in our loyalty and allegiance, and humble gratefulness for his part in our lives. Without faith, it is impossible to please him, but without humility, there is no faith. (Pss 18:27, 51:16–17, 100:5, 103:9–14, 145:18–19; Prov 15:33, 18:12, 22:4; Isa 66:2b; Mic 6:8; Matt 5:3 and 8, 18:1–4; Luke 15:11–31, 18:9–14; 2 Cor 3:17, 5:15–17; Eph 2:1–10; Heb 11:6; Jas 4:10; 1 Pet 3:18, 5:6–11)

88. Freedom from Fear

SIN CAN BE A willful rejection of God's ways. But Christians, too, often experience a distance from God. Not all distance from God comes from an intentional refusal of him. We may know a lot about God but fear to trust anything but our personal and cultural defenses of self for survival. Other times, it is simply a preoccupation with self. Sometimes, the letdown and discouragement we feel in a local church disturb our relationship with God and replace freedom with fear. He has given us ample reason to trust him, but we are not all helped by local expressions of traditional Christianity to that end. The institutionalized church may push us in a different direction. It, too, is made up of people who may call him "Lord," but their hearts can be a distance from his. We are all imperfect examples of God's grace in our lives and must look at ourselves before criticizing others. We do not know their hearts, but we can know our own. Nonetheless, some who lead Christians lead them in the wrong direction.

Legalism, for example, increases that fear rather than relieves it. These teachers emphasize works to earn approval rather than the truth, married to grace and consummated by trust in a dynamic relationship with God. They disparage our freedom in Christ based on this relationship with God and his people. People caught in legalism are not in God's will for their lives. It may not be a willful and knowing rejection of God's way for these followers, but they are still distant and deceived.

We can also resist trusting him out of our fear or emotional pain experienced in the past. This is not what he wants for us either. He will become the protection and security we seek for survival if we let him. We may never forget, but we can and must let go of pain and fear to trust him. It is a process that has to be intentional on our part and will mean practicing this trust over time. In him, we have his help and care in the pains and discouragements of life. There is freedom and contentment in Christ that many have yet to discover. (Pss 9:9–10, 26:12 with 28:7, 27:1, 34:1–22, 40:1–4, 46:1–3 with 7a and 10a, 91:1–2, 121:1–8; Prov 3:5–7, 26:12, 28:26; Matt 7:15–23, 13:24–30, 14:28–32; John 8:32 and 36 with 16:33; Phil 4:5–7; Jas 1:22–25; 1 Pet 5:6–7)

89. Materialism and Asceticism

MATERIALISM IS AN EXTREME, as is asceticism. Neither loving the world nor rejecting it entirely are biblical ways of life in the present. With a proper view of God's creation as good, we can enjoy his blessings without reservation. There must be discretion, but there need not be fear. To love the world or our selfish inclinations more than God himself, however, is spiritual adultery. To see our enjoyment of his creation as a right instead of a privilege is arrogance. To take advantage of someone else in his creation for personal satisfaction is cruelty and willful defiance of love, but to say what God has given us is evil is to make him a liar. The greed of materialism and the legalism of asceticism are unbiblical. As with many biblical truths, there is a path outside these two extremes that God blesses. To enjoy all God has created for us is a blessing from him in which to delight with gratefulness. We shall not know it through self-assertion or self-denial, only through humility, gratefulness, and love for him and others. These are the boundaries of our freedom in Christ. (Gen 1:31; Prov 30:7–9; Eccl 5:11–12; Hos 4:1 with 12 and 6:6; Acts 10:15; 1 Cor 6:12, 10:23—11:1; 1 Tim 4:4–5; Titus 1:15; Jas 1:16–18, 3:13–18; 1 John 2:15–17)

90. Spiritual Life Lived in the World

LIFE FOR THE CHRISTIAN is not only spiritual; it is also highly physical and intricately social. God intended this from the beginning, giving Adam and Eve a beautiful garden, delicious fruit of the trees to eat, a relationship without selfishness, and oneness without inhibitions or shame. Our spiritual values are to be lived out in this physical world, in the human context. That context is now tainted heavily by sin and under the shadow of the lies of Satan. Yet, we must embrace life in this world so unbelievers can see God's will incarnated in our behavior in the same concrete context with them. Jesus engaged with people in their human and physical context. He communicated with them using their cultural and social frames of reference.

Yes, as the saying goes, we can be so heavenly-minded we are of no earthly good. God gave us the earth, all of the physical creation, as the situation in which to live for him, honor him, glorify him, and be witnesses to his grace in what is now, a broken world. Though we are not perfect at it, spiritual commitment must come to life in our day-to-day experiences, on the streets of our communities, and in our homes. The world has had enough of professional Christianity and needs an authentic expression of our faith to see God's will in everyday life in terms they can understand. That does not mean the response will always be welcoming; many will turn away and try to stop us from influencing others away from the many lies. But we are not to lose heart. The natural man or woman does not have a sensitivity toward God. Many have worked hard to eliminate it altogether. We must be salt and light in a lost world, bringing hope and showing the way to God. (Gen 1:1–31; Eccl 7:20; Matt 5:13–16, 28:18–20; John 16:33, 17:13–19; 1 Cor 2:14–16; 2 Cor 4:4, 12:7–10, especially 9; Col 1:3–6; 1 Thess 3:11–12; Titus 3:1–2, 8, and 14; Heb 6:10; 1 Pet 2:11–17; 1 John 1:1–5)

91. Passion and Loyalty

AS SURPRISING AS IT may seem to some, the emphasis of the New Testament is not on the worship of God or the evangelism of others. These are, of course, present and very important, but the main emphasis is on trusting God, his grace in our redemption, our freedom in Christ, and living out the gospel in our day-to-day situation. This is walking worthy of the gospel. Our lives are to be lived out in a wholehearted relationship with God characterized by our loyalty to him and gratefulness for his grace. In our weakest moments, it will be what helps us the most. Our lives must come under his leadership, which includes enjoying all he has given us with gratefulness for his blessings. It may sound strange to some, but killing our passions in this endeavor is as dangerous as fulfilling them wantonly. Passion must, instead, be ruled by loyalty.

We must be passionate about the One we love and trust for survival here and hereafter. God's causes, as well as his blessings, must be ours. Passion for him allows us to order our own desires within his boundaries rather than destroy them with legalism, gluttony, or greed. Though it takes time, it makes way for faithfulness to become our natural inclination. It makes us want the law of love he has given us to bind our every action and embrace all of life in ways that honor his purposes. We must be careful not to throw out passion as bad but temper it with loyalty and allegiance to our great God of grace. It leads to virtuous action, which some of us know too little of. Loyalty, allegiance, and passion are a part of biblical love. We will fail to always be perfect in our loyalty, but though we stumble, we will not fall. In his forgiveness and love, he is faithful to us with a grace that will never fail. It should encourage us to renew our loyalty, strengthen our allegiance, and direct our passion to his purposes for us. (Pss 37:23–24, 55:22, 78:8 with 35–37, 147:11; Prov 24:16; Matt 22:34–40; Luke 19:1–10; John 13:5–9, 34–35 with 14:15 and 15:9–13; Rom 12:9–13; 1 Cor 13:7; Gal 5:13–14; Eph 2:1–10, 3:12, 4:1–3; Phil 1:27, 2:1–4; Col 2:21–23)

92. In Love with Self

THERE ARE TWO EXTREMES in our thinking about the self: complete self-denial and conceited admiration of our achievements and self-improvement. The self, indeed, needs a good deal of attention when we become Christians. But, as usual, these extremes do not represent God's desires for us. We must end the love affair with self or self-denial and focus our loyalties on God himself. Though some denial and improvement are needed, our primary goal is to assess our thoughts and emotions and to calibrate them daily within the boundaries of God's love and the guidance of his word. We must look beyond self as we become preoccupied with God and his plan. Though we need spiritual disciplines to develop our thinking and behavior in our relationship with him, the self should always be seen in the light of his grace, resulting in humility. As we mature in Christ, the weakness of self shows us God's strength and his patient, untiring grace. Though it is his greatest gift to be created in his image, the self must be under constant supervision. We must learn to monitor our emotions, attractions, and inclinations to seek to honor God in them.

In our old concerns for ourselves, we were sometimes afraid, and it seemed like we might miss what we wanted in life, but his way meets every real need beyond our expectations. In him is where true freedom and contentment are found. But these things are in the big picture, the long view of our lives. Our culture of immediate gratification and instant results works against us. Discontent must be met with patience, faith, and trust in his providence and grace. We must cultivate a long-term orientation in our lives as Christians. This is the attainment of wisdom in God's design for us. (Pss 37:1–8, 90:10–12; 130:5–6; Prov 3:5–7, 4:6–9, 8:10–21, 20:22, 26:12, 28:26; Isa 40:31; Matt 6:31–34; Eph 2:8–10; Heb 11:6; Jas 1:1–8, 12)

93. Hardship or Riches

A LIFE OF HARDSHIP and sacrifice caused by legalism or a bitter spirit is a life of suffering. But demanding a life of material and physical blessing based on a prosperity gospel message also ends in misery. Neither extreme is biblical. The life God intends for his own is a matter of freedom and truth together, seasoned with grace and bounded by love. Embracing the blessings and finding grace for the hardships in life are ways of knowing and opportunities to trust God, serve him, and make his grace known.

Jesus tells us to expect trouble, but he also promises peace. Often, what we consider hardship or a demanding situation turns out, in his providence, to be the best thing for us. We must trust him. To desire only good and see difficulties only as evil is not in the Book. We live in a broken world. It is not how God wanted it, but he gave humankind freedom to choose, and the first man and woman chose not to trust him. We live with the results but not without his blessing and grace. And it will not be long now. He is soon to remake it all and give us a place in the new creation we cannot imagine now. The limitations of time and space of this physical universe will be removed; the brokenness, suffering, hardships, and struggle will be over. It is the eve of his coming. (Job 2:9–10; Pss 37:1–11 with 34, 119:71; Prov 3:5–7, 16:9; Matt 5:3–12; John 1:17 with 8:31–32, 14:27, 15:18–21; 16:33, 17:15–19; 1 Thess 3:11–12; Jas 1:2–12, 4:10; 1 Pet 4:12–16)

94. Reality

MOST WESTERN CHRISTIANS HAVE a hard time shaking their dichotomist worldview of the concrete, scientific aspects of the universe on the one hand and the realities of the spiritual universe on the other. We are linear thinkers controlled by our dualism. We live with secular and sacred categories of life that inhibit an understanding of God's intentions. The true nature of reality is that we live in a spiritual universe in which God has placed temporal fixtures and given us free will for objective decisions about them. If we believe this is reality, we must talk about it accordingly. The words we use matter. You don't say you believe in gravity, but you say you believe in God. Gravity is as temporary as the world, and God is forever, but we use the word *believe* for God. Both are real, but the spiritual universe is permanent.

In the English language, there is a difference between believing and knowing. Whether by authority or by experience, we know many things. Yet, we leave God in the category of belief when we have both his authority in the Bible and our experience of his grace to shape our understanding of reality. We also have many examples of his purposes, power, faithfulness, and providence in the lives of his people in the biblical account. What we say we "believe" we actually know to be the true nature of reality. We know it in the same way we know gravity exists: by authority, experience, and examples.

When people are outside of Christ, they correctly say they do not believe in God or are uncertain if God exists. They distrust the authority and do not have the experience or have had negative experiences concerning Christianity. They discount any examples they are given. These things are spiritually discerned, and those outside of Christ will not know the spiritual universe exists unless they take a step of faith, however small, and trust God's grace for them in Christ. Otherwise, they will not know until it is too late that they are indeed part of an actual spiritual universe. As it is, they do

94. REALITY

not have the Holy Spirit, and Satan has blinded their minds. For them, it remains a matter of fairy tale belief or "educated" and, often, proud disbelief.

But once you have trusted God and experienced his grace, you not only know that he exists, but you know him. A relationship is not based on belief but on trust. We must be more careful how we talk about our knowledge of him. Our culture has had the upper hand in shaping our thinking within physical limitations and emotional domains, but there is more, and it is more important. When we believed God and accepted the work of Christ for us, we made our first step outside the boundaries of our human culture and the dark powers that rule it into the domain of his kingdom of light. As we grow in Christ, we rise above those limitations and seek to live in human culture as an incarnation of his ways and purposes. We are sojourners here who realize the mountains are still full of horses and chariots of fire. (2 Kgs 6:15–17; Matt 6:10 with 31–34; Luke 16:19–31; John 8:12; Acts 26:15–18; 1 Cor 2:14–16 with 2 Cor 4:4–7; Eph 2:1–2, 6:10–18; Col 1:13–14; Heb 11:1–3 and 6; Jas 1:5–8; 1 John 2:15–17)

95. Barriers to Our Search for God's Will

THE PRIMARY BATTLES OF our Christian lives seem to be fought on the three hills of cultural expectations, theological systems, and personal inclinations in areas of need and desire. The outcomes of these battles can come between God and us and can be powerful barriers to knowing his will and growth in our relationship with him. We expect God to be and act as our Western cultural values and beliefs say he should—that he should follow our logic, our notion of efficiency, and our need for the social recognition of our achievements. We accept human theological systems as if they were the final word. Sometimes, they add legalistic barriers to the freedom he has granted us, and often, these systems define him in ways that do not allow for all he has said or his prerogative to be God in his actions. Then, we sometimes find what we expect or need to see in his word, not allowing God to speak for himself.

Patience, humility, and wonder are left behind in our search for the God of our cultural, theological, and personal preferences. We use these filters to strain out what we do not want to be true of God's will. We seek what we think should be in his word, not what is actually there. It is a disastrous mentality many have embraced. We are locked out of God's will while holding the key. Our expectations cannot come near the realities of his wisdom, grace, and goodness. We should have a healthy skepticism of human certainties and let God be God. He will care for the rest. (Pss 27:13–14, 37:1–11, 130:5–6; Prov 3:5–7, 20:22, 21:2, 26:12; Isa 55:8–9; Matt 6:33, 7:15–23; Luke 11:52; John 15:5–8; Rom 11:33–36; Phil 3:17—4:1; 2 Tim 4:1–4)

96. Popular Christians

THIS IS A BROAD category of people who like Christianity. They may be superficial, seeking social approval or affirmation. They may be legalistic, trying to establish approval from God through works and emphasizing rituals and rules more than relationships with God and his people. They may have mystical tendencies to seek miracles as emotional confirmation of God's love and promises. They may have tried to syncretize their passion for the world with their "love" for God. They may be simply unaware of the deeper themes of godliness and need biblical and incarnational instruction. They may be stuck on the informational level and know things about God without really knowing him. Distracted by their personal inclinations, preferences, and expectations, they are generally consumer-oriented to what seems helpful to them on their level. Led astray by their culture and, perhaps, their theology, they have fallen in love with Christianity, the church building, their position of status in the church, or their ability to influence others. There is a gap between God and their Christianity—they are not in love with him.

Popular Christians will struggle more than others when the going gets rough. Their loyalty to God will not rise up against their self-centered human inclinations. We must move from being popular Christians to biblical Christians, beyond loving Christianity to knowing God as he revealed himself. In the everyday, mundane things of life, our thoughts must turn to the purposes of the Creator-God of the universe, his love for us, and his particular desire for us to know him and be part of his plan by his grace. We have our human weaknesses, but ultimately, we must grow to trust him and his providence and grace in all things. (Pss 78:35–39, 91:1 with 9 and 14–16; Prov 3:5–7; Isa 66:1–6; Jer 9:24–25; Ezek 33:30–33; Mal 2:1–2; Matt 7:13–14, 21–23, 15:8–9; Col 2:20—3:4; 1 Tim 1:3–7, 6:3–6; 2 Tim 3:1–5, 7; Titus 1:15–16; 2 Pet 3:3)

97. Sacred Calling

It seems we should be way beyond it, but many Christians still think some vocations are more spiritual than others. Many people in churches carry guilt because they did not become a missionary when they felt they should have but chose some other vocation instead. They heard a missionary speaker, and he or she made them feel guilty that they did not respond to "the call." Notice the emphasis on feelings here. Yes, we have a sacred calling. It is to love God with all our hearts, to be faithful to him in our everyday vocations and responsibilities, and, through this incarnation of his will for us, to make disciples. This is intended to be done in our day-to-day lives with those around us. Some may be accountants or mechanics, others bankers or welders, piano tuners or plumbers, surgeons or dentists, and some are pastors. Each is gifted and trained in different ways, but all are called. They are all full-time in their task of incarnating God's will as Christians wherever they are, whatever they are doing. These are witnesses to God's grace in Jerusalem, Judea, and Samaria.

Yes, some will become missionaries, sent out with the gospel beyond their nation's borders, not because their calling is higher, but because their aptitudes, skill set, training, and personality are more adapted to crossing cultures. (For people to go outside their culture for ministry without these abilities has results similar to a plumber who does not know how to do plumbing. He leaves leaky pipes all along his way.) They, too, must incarnate God's will, but in a different culture. Making this vocation the "highest" or "most sacred" calling of God on a person's life has caused a great deal of harm to ministry in other cultures, mainly by people going with the wrong motives, without training, or lacking the aptitudes necessary.

There is no secular domain. No matter your history, if you are a Christian today, you are called, and that calling is sacred. It is to full-time living for Christ that others might see in you God's grace and forgiveness and your experience of freedom in Christ as a result of the gospel in your life. It is a calling for anywhere and everywhere you go. (Prov 21:3; Hos 6:6; Mic 6:8; Matt 5:16, 28:18–20; Luke 5:8–11; Acts 1:8; Rom 8:28–30; 1 Cor 7:17 with 20–24; Eph 4:1–7 with 11–16; Phil 3:13–14; 1 Thess 4:11–12; 1 Tim 1:18–19; 2 Tim 1:8–9; 1 Pet 2:12)

98. Biblical Christians

BIBLICAL CHRISTIANS DESIRE GOD'S will more than their own, but they are not flawless in living it out; they are not super-spiritual. There is no such category among us. But there is a difference between those who love Christianity (popular Christians) and those who love God. Biblical Christians seek to love and trust God, to be loyal to his purposes, whether they are leaders in a denomination or members of a church or not. Few of them are well-known, fewer, if any, are celebrities. But they experience freedom in their day-to-day lives and have peace concerning the future, which is in God's hands. They are not easily sidetracked by cultural preferences, selfish expectations, or bad theology. Their faith is simple and enduring—they trust God and his grace for them in the work of Christ. They are growing in wisdom and understanding of God, learning to incarnate God's purposes in the world. They are not perfect, and they know it. But they are on the right road; God's grace humbles them, and their gratefulness knows no boundaries. (Rom 1:17, 14:5–8 with 22 and 15:5; 1 Cor 9:19, 10:23–24; 2 Cor 3:7 with 4:7; Gal 5:1 with 6b; Phil 3:13–14, 4:4–13; Col 3:12–17; 1 Tim 4:4–8; Titus 1:15; Heb 12:28–29; Jas 3:13–18, 4:10; 1 Pet 2:16–17, 5:6–7)

99. Knowing God's Will

IT CREATES UNEASINESS, IF not anxiety, among Christians, when someone in the group constantly talks about knowing God's will for their life, having found the secret to an "abundant life," or is always mentioning their spiritual gift. Sometimes, they talk about a special, personal revelation from God in a passage of the Bible that no one else can see or a sign God gave them that no one else can experience. It may come from insecurities they are compensating for—the need to be recognized as a "spiritual" person—but their point is that certain special people can "discover" God's specific will for their lives, and they have found it.

This special knowledge of God's will approach, unconscious and thoughtless for some and intentional for others, makes those around them feel very ordinary and unable to achieve this special status with God. So, in the end, it is a way to control the thoughts and opinions of people around them in their favor. It is most unbiblical when it is a tactic to gain attention as one who knows—an elite among the unremarkable, garden-variety Christians around them. Competitive, self-interested, brazen declarations of being that "special" person destroy the humility and faithfulness God seeks in the hearts of his own. Gratefulness for God's grace should make us want to encourage, not compete with one another, to serve rather than to be recognized as more spiritual than the rest.

God is not mystical about making his will known. It is not a matter of secrets, discoveries, or "special" people. It is not something hidden that only a few can find. It is before us every day in God's word and the opportunities to serve him and incarnate his love and grace that are ours. God's calling and will for each of us is that we become a certain kind of person: one who trusts his love and providence, is loyal to his purposes, is considerate of others' needs, and wants the best for those around us. Though his will is the same for everyone, each will express it in a way unique to them in their circumstances and in their service for him. The emphasis is on being more than doing because that must come first.

The doing will come more naturally and is only worthwhile as a result of these motives. The doing will be more characterized by good works than preaching the gospel. Good works plow the ground so that it might welcome the seed of God's grace when the gospel is shared with others. Neither mysticism nor legalism opens up God's will to us; humility before him, loyalty to his purposes, love for those around us, and trust in his providence are his priorities. (Pss 32:8–10, 37:1–8 with 23–24 and 34a; Prov 3:5–7 with Ps 37:23–24 and 28, Prov 5:21, 16:2; Isa 30:19–22, 32:17; Hos 6:6; Mic 6:8; Rom 12:1–8; Gal 6:9–10; Eph 2:10, 4:1–3, 5:15–17; Phil 1:9–11, 27, 2:1–4, 3:12—4:1; Col 1:9–14 with 4:12; 1 Tim 6:18–19; Heb 13:15–16; Jas 1:5–8, 3:13–18; 1 Pet 3:13–17; 2 Pet 1:3–11)

100. Missional People

EACH CHRISTIAN WHO COMES to the Bible and examines the mission of God in creation comes to a conclusion. They will see it as God's work in the world and turn the page or decide to become part of it all, become missional with him in the world. Being missional means becoming part of God's plan rather than letting him be part of our plan for life. Being missional also involves our motives and goals. God's priority is on what we are rather than what we do. We must respect his power, majesty, and mystery and be grateful, humble, and loyal to his purposes while passionate about our part in his plan and our place on his team. We must seek to become useful, resourceful people in his hands, incarnating his grace and being salt and light in the world. That is being missional. Most of the time, it is in our day-to-day activities and circumstances. That is where God's mission becomes authentic in us. Sometimes, we take on a more public role in ministry or even a cross-cultural one. But it is all about being responsibly faithful to him with the abilities he has given us wherever we are and whatever we do. We are then part of his purposes for the redemption of humankind in the world and the culmination of all things. (Ps 33:11; Matt 5:14–16, 28:18–20; John 3:16, 13:34–35 with 17:20–23; John 17:15–19, Eph 2:8–10, 5:8–10; Col 1:9–12, 4:5–6; 1 Thess 4:11–12; 1 Tim 2:1–6; Titus 2:11–12, 3:14; Heb 6:12, 12:28–29; 1 Pet 5:6; 2 Pet 1:3–11, 3:8–14; 1 John 2:15–17; Rev 21:1–5)

101. The Nature of the Church

ACCORDING TO PAUL IN his letters to the churches, though there is diversity in the body of Christ, the church should be a body of grace-covered, like-minded people who seek to worship God, learn from his word, and encourage each other in every way. Jesus emphasizes the love believers must have for one another and the unity that must characterize their relationships. It doesn't seem there are many churches quite like this. Yet, it is the expectation of the New Testament. Though it is intended to be the norm, and there are some examples of it in the New Testament, churches are made up of people who do not always value this love (*agape*) and unity.

Even in the early days, biblical authors spent a lot of time addressing deviations from this norm. The church at Corinth is, of course, the first example we think of, and by the end of the first century, many churches were struggling in various ways. Seven of them were addressed by God through John in the book of Revelation. The goal of growing strong in our trust in God, loyalty to his purposes, grateful humility for his grace, and consideration for one another is not easily attained. But that does not weaken the goal of God for the church. His purpose is that we become motivated, missional people in our lives, showing unity, reaching out to our communities with God's love, and encouraging others to do the same. Anything we add to this purpose for the church must be scrutinized carefully for its purpose and function. Whatever adds to the institutionalization of the church should be suspect.

The church must be culturally relevant but not a prisoner of cultural norms. An individualist culture presents a number of challenges to relevancy without syncretism. As a system for survival, Western culture teaches its members to seek survival on their own through self-assertion, competition, and achievement. But that is incompatible with God's will for the body of Christ. It works against the very purpose and work of God's word in our lives. We must be relevant in our world, but we must live above the demands of our culture in these things. By this and not its buildings, numbers, or denominations, the church must be known. (John 13:34–35, 17:20–23; Rom 12:9–16, 15:5; 1 Cor 12:24b–27; 2 Cor 12:20–21; Gal 5:13–15; Eph 4:11–13; Phil 1:3–11, 27, 2:1–4 and 12–16a with 3:15; 1 Thess 1:2–7; 1 Tim 1:3–7, especially 5; Jas 3:13–18; Rev 2:1—3:22)

102. Spiritual Gifts

AN EMPHASIS ON DISCOVERING our spiritual gifts of a miraculous kind works against us in the church. The verses in the Bible that deal with these spiritual gifts were not written to tell us how to discover them but to correct the abuses. The New Testament does not make knowledge of one's spiritual gifts a qualification for service, even for leadership in the church. In such a case, we must approach the topic with caution and reserve. God's choice to use miracles and signs is just that, his choice. And his choice to use them seems quite limited to introducing new events of his movement in the world. What we know of these gifts is that they were not typical in the early churches, and they showed up in troubled churches such as Corinth. Instructions to young pastors in other churches emphasize teaching self-control and good works without mentioning spiritual gifts. They are not required for the churches.

The Bible tells us to become loyal to God's purposes, walk worthy of the gospel, and get busy with ministry using whatever abilities he has given us. Nowhere are we told to seek special revelation or signs from God or recognition of our spiritual maturity from other Christians. Though God used them to affirm his sending of the Holy Spirit, nowhere are we told of their need to prove his acceptance of us or his work in our lives.

It does not apply to all situations, but, as with most good gifts from God, there are often false teachers and terrible abuses. Using Christianity or the local church for personal advancement is the same sin we see in the merchants and the money changers Jesus drove from the temple. Comparing ourselves to other Christians to feel better about ourselves is similar to the story of the Pharisee and the tax collector in the temple. We already know what God wants. In addition to his other counsel, Paul's instructions to his disciples Timothy and Titus set the stage for churches that honor God and help Christians mature in Christ. The trouble is that we do not always like or choose this model for the church because it does not bring us the social affirmation, recognition, massive expansion, or material benefits we are looking for. We must not seek spiritual gifts to feel special or get what we want from the church but, instead, serve God with whatever talents and abilities we have in humility, to the encouragement and edification of believers, and in helping people to follow Christ in our broken world. (Mic 6:8; Luke 18:9–14; John 2:12–16; 1 Cor 12:4–11 and 27–31 with 13:1–13; Gal 5:16–26; Phil 2:1–8; 1 Thess 4:11–12, 5:4–8; 1 Tim 1:5–7, 3:2, 4:1–16; 2 Tim 4:5; Titus 1:1—3:15; 1 Pet 4:7–11, 5:6)

103. Special Guidance

WE HAVE MANY EXAMPLES in the Bible of God giving people unique guidance or miraculous direction for his purposes. But these were quite exceptional cases for key people in his plan. The vast majority of believers in the Old or New Testaments did not receive this supernatural direction. God's roles for them were to be faithful, honor him with their lives, and be loyal to his purposes. They were to live peaceful, quiet, faithful, and productive lives as a testimony to the truth of the gospel. Some people get exceptional guidance from God even in our day, but they are in particular circumstances. It is not the norm for us, and we are not told to seek it.

We are told to trust God and that his providence is at work in our lives. We already have what we need to know in his word. And, on those rare occasions of special guidance for some, he does not give them more revelation about himself but rather practical guidance to help them find or follow what he has already given them. Persistent attention to the familiar truths of his word will make our way clear to us. (Ps 37:1–9; Prov 3:5–7, 27–28, 16:9; Matt 5:13–16; Rom 8:32; 2 Cor 9:8; Phil 2:12–16; Col 1:9–14; 1 Thess 4:11–12; 1 Tim 2:1–4; Titus 2:11–12, 3:1–2, 8, 14; Heb 11:1, 6, and 13, 13:15; 1 Pet 2:11–17; 2 Pet 1:3–11; 1 John 3:16–20)

104. Hope

THOUGH A FOOL'S HOPE comes to nothing, for those who trust him, hope in God gives contentment and well-being in the good and bad circumstances of life. The essence of hope is knowing that the seemingly random events in this life are not outside the awareness and power of God's good providence. Even in suffering and loss, though he knows the stress of their weight on us, he tells us not to despair, for he bears it with us in this broken world and can use even our suffering for his purposes. We can expect his grace in our circumstances and have the assurance of his activity on our behalf. The psalmist suffers intensely, then returns to his trust in the God of his salvation—the God of living hope, powerful providence, and everlasting lovingkindness. Hope gives us the patience to wait on the Lord and long for his will to be done. He does not remove the pain, suffering, and loss sin causes in the world, nor us from that world until our time comes. But his grace is sufficient, his love everlasting, and his providence at work for his purposes and to meet our needs, even when our hope wanes. For nothing can stop his work in us from being accomplished.

At the same time, he is at work for the consummation of all things in the world. He will set things right once again. The righteous judge will bring justice and vindication, but while we wait for him, he is the God of grace to those who trust him. Hope is not primarily emotional; it is the assurance of objective truth. It goes on forever unless we drift from it or allow cultural or social expectations to steal it from us. But if we let it, it will cause our faith and love to flourish as we look for its fulfillment. (Pss 27:13–14, 37:1–7, 44:23–26 with 42:5 then 46:1–3, 10 and 62:1–2 and 5–7 and 73:21–28, 71:14–18, 130:5–6, 146:5–10; Prov 11:7, 16:9; Isa 40:31; Lam 3:25–26; Matt 12:15–21; John 3:16, 16:33, 17:15; Rom 8:24, 28–39, 15:13; 1 Cor 15:12–19; 2 Cor 12:7–10; Col 1:3–6; Heb 11:1 with 11–16; Jas 5:7–11; 1 Pet 4:19, 5:10–11; Rev 21:1–4)

105. The God We Know

THERE IS A KNOWING of God that goes beyond the popular notion of knowing things about him to experience him. It is a stillness before him that brings calm and wonder, a settled awareness of his greatness and grace, a particular respect for his power and mystery, and a deep gratefulness for his uninterrupted care for us. It is the full breadth of the fear of the Lord throughout the Old Testament and the deep theme of a trusting relationship with him in the New Testament. We know that we are those upon whom he sets his eye, the objects of his providential love. If we let him, he will respond to us in our stress and suffering with grace and goodness. He is alert to our every need. We may not recognize his hand in our situation because our minds are clouded by what we want or expect him to do, the limitations of our cultural frame of reference, or our desperation and anxiety. But he wants our good more than we do.

Though the world may seem out of control, he is aware, attentive to our situation, and awaits our trust. He is not changing the world's brokenness for us but changing us to live in that world with a message of hope and life. His ways are past finding out, but we can see the results of his care looking back. He has always been there for us when we least expected it, even when we caused our own suffering. Be still; this is the God we know, the creator of the universe and the lover of our souls. (Pss 28:7, 34:4–10, 37:5–9, 46:1–11, 91:14–16, 121:1–8, 124:1–8, 145:13b–14, 18–19, 146:5–10, 147:11; Prov 1:7 and 9:10 with 14:26–27 and 15:33; Isa 26:8–9, 30:15 with 32:17; Jer 17:7–8; Luke 15:11–24; John 17:3, 13–19; Rom 11:33–36; Phil 2:12–13, 3:7–11)

106. Kindness

Kindness is in your power. You can choose to bless another with it at any time. God has been kind to you; you must spread his grace with the same. The need for kindness in the world is without limits. Everywhere, there is an enormous need to do good, showing our expression of his patience, love, and compassion. Through our consideration for others, the soil of their hearts can be tilled to receive the seed of God's grace. We are to be salt and light in a broken world, beginning with the good we can do. Making disciples depends on trust in a relationship. Trust is born of kindness. Your good works can be used by God to soften hearts to him who has given you all you need in himself. No one has been more kind to us than God. We cannot keep that to ourselves.

As important as it is, kindness has never been prolific in our culture of self-assertion, even among Christians, and it is becoming increasingly rare in our times. A kind person may not be known for outstanding personal achievements. They may be somewhat countercultural as a soft-spoken person, alert to the needs of those around them but not intruding into their lives. On the other hand, they always seem to have time for others. Secure in their understanding of God's ways for us, they are seldom defensive, even around other Christians, and are thoughtful of their words and opinions. They move through life with quiet confidence. Queen Elizabeth used to say, "Never complain, never explain."

This kindness is often noticed by those outside Christ, where it is strikingly unlike other Christians they have seen. It softens the ground of people's lives to receive the seeds of the gospel. Notice that good works are mentioned repeatedly in Paul's short letter to the young pastor Titus, reminding him to teach his people to be kind. It was an important message for the early church and should be more a part of our lives today. (Ps 16:1–11; Prov 12:25, 16:24; Matt 5:13–16; Luke 10:25–37; 2 Cor 9:8; Gal 6:9–10; Eph 2:10, 4:32; Phil 2:3–4; Col 3:12; 1 Tim 6:18–19; 2 Tim 3:16–17; Titus

2:1—3:14 [notice the opposite in 1:13–16]; Heb 6:18–19, 10:24, 13:15–16; Jas 3:13; 1 Pet 2:11–12 with 15, 3:13–17)

107. Syncretism

SYNCRETISM IS THE MIXTURE of two divergent ways of understanding or accomplishing something. The end product differs from either of the ways that were brought together. Regrettably, it is often allowed in a negative way among Christians. We try to mix freedom in Christ with legalism, truth with romantic feelings, biblical absolutes with cultural absolutes, or the true nature of reality with mystical imaginations of what we want it to be. As striking as these pairs of opposites may seem, their mixtures are usually quite subtle. We are at home with our culture, and its influence is very persuasive. It gives us familiar ways of achieving personal worth and identity among those around us as our individualist needs are pressing in on us. But there is no shortcut to knowing God as he is and seeking his solutions to our problems, his purposes for our lives. Culture's solutions will have to be left behind.

We must not be caught in the trap of solutions for survival our culture offers us that sidestep God's way. It will contaminate his ways with ours. We are to have a culturally relevant expression of the truth of our faith, freedom in Christ, biblical absolutes, and the true nature of reality that puts God at the center of all things. We must not let anyone take this from us or strap us down with faulty and weak interpretations and syncretized expressions. But we are limited on our own, and syncretism can creep slowly in between God and us. We often don't notice it until it has settled in and had some effect. The unbiblical expression or view does not look like it is from the dark side. It appears inviting, innovative, trendy, and desirable and, therefore, seems highly appropriate without question. But we must be on our guard.

Relativism and relevance are not the same. Cultural relativism approves of biblical truth only when it agrees with our culture's values. Biblical relevance speaks to the true needs of our culture in understandable ways. This contextualization is authenticated by love and is illustrated by our incarnation of the truth of our message in daily life. We are strong and free in

Christ and need to show people the relevancy of God in a dark world. (Gen 3:6; Pss 20:7 with 146:3–6, 27:13–14, 33:16–22, 37:5–7a, 84:1–12; Luke 9:23–25; John 12:23–26, 13:6–10, 17:15–19; 2 Cor 3:17, 11:13–15; Jas 4:1–7; 1 Pet 5:8–11; 1 John 2:15–17, 4:4–6)

108. Allegiance

FALSE ALLEGIANCE IS COMMON in our day. Our true loyalties show through and guide our lives no matter what we say, for loyalty is more than words. If our allegiance is to self, there will be pride and defensiveness, the assertion of our ways, and perhaps the controlling of others to enhance our feelings of self-worth and achievement. We will covet power to make things the way we want and tie our identity to success. If allegiance is to the world, there will be grasping and hoarding, an appetite never satisfied even when we have more than we need. It may seem strange to find false allegiances among Christians, but veiled as they may be, they are more frequent than we think. They eat away at the image of God that should be incarnated in the church and in each of us. They keep his will from being accomplished among us and do not go unnoticed. Our allegiance must be ruled by God alone. Though we will not be perfect at it and realize it the older we get, our attachment must be to the purposes and values of his kingdom. Self, culture, and social expectations are short-lived and lethal substitutes. (Josh 24:14–15; Pss 37:3–6, 40:4, 52:8–9, 56:3–4, 11; Prov 11:28, 26:12, 28:26; Jer 9:23–24; Matt 6:19–21 with 33, 7:24–27; Luke 9:23–25; John 14:6, 15:5; Acts 4:12; Phil 4:12–13; Jas 4:1–5; 1 John 2:15–17)

109. Loving God

We have used the English word *love* for too long in our Bible translations to describe our relationship with God. The term is too weak and too romanticized to adequately describe what our relationship with God should be. This connotation does not fit our relationship with God and is not very helpful in other relationships. Our use of the term has a great deal to do with feelings, which are simply not the point, even though they often accompany relationships. They are not good indicators of the true value of love. They can be beautiful and gratifying, but they can also be deceptive, and when we depend on them in our relationship with God, they can lead us astray from guidance, truth, and wisdom.

People may think God has lost interest in them when the feelings are gone. Others deal with guilt when they don't feel affection for God. Yet others spend a great deal of time and effort trying to generate and maintain feelings of love for him. To love God is about being and doing based on the truth he gives us. It's more about loyalty, commitment, willingness, and honor than affection and inclination. Feelings follow. Overwhelming gratefulness for his grace, peaceful contentment in his providence, and confidence in Christ follow our allegiance to him and the freedom he gives us in Christ. (Job 2:9–10; Pss 23:4, 42:5–8; Dan 3:16–18; John 8:31–32, 14:15, 21, 15:9–14; 1 Cor 13:6–7; Eph 3:12; Heb 4:14–16; Jas 1:22–25; 1 John 1:3–6, 3:18)

110. Empathy

EMPATHY IS A CORE consideration in good relationships within the family, church, and community. It is knowing and giving attention to how another person feels about something that results in some action on their behalf. It is understanding, respect, and disinterested help for others but is not necessarily attached to feelings of affection for them. Empathy is central to *agape* love, a desire for the highest good of the other, whether attractive or not, whether there is benefit in it for us or not, and whether we feel like it or not. This is a matter of loyalty to God and a commitment to another's welfare. It is a central theme in collective cultures. However, in our individualist culture, empathy is not often displayed or returned. But it is where wisdom and goodness come together in action and is the strongest indication of the truth of our faith among those outside Christ. (Prov 3:27–28; John 13:34, 15:12; Rom 12:9–19; 1 Cor 10:23–24; Eph 5:1–2; Phil 2:3–4; Col 3:12–14; Jas 3:13 with 17; 1 John 3:16–20, 4:9–11)

111. Choosing the Best

Though many would say that a person cannot make choices to do good, that only God can do that through us, decision-making is a fundamental, necessary, and powerful attribute of freedom God has given to men and women. We can and do choose good or evil. Because of this, we look back with gratitude or regret and live this present moment with purpose and wisdom, selfish ambition, or even laziness. We can choose to look to the future with anxiety or hope and trust in God's providence. Knowing that we constantly make choices makes self-awareness essential for the Christian. We grow in wisdom as we become aware of our desires, attitudes, and motives and redirect them to honor our God and King.

Maturing in Christ helps us see and choose between good, better, and best in our lives in response to God's word. Some may take issue with this, believing that God's word only gives us good and evil, and our choice lies between these. But though there are clear directives on many things in God's word, the Christian life, on the whole, is not as black and white as we might want or expect. A good deal depends on our hearts' intentions in our outward actions. We learn to choose between options within the boundaries of his will, choices that must be made with wisdom. This creates ambiguity for the legalist who prefers everything to be objectively clear, but there is freedom in Christ if we allow God to speak for himself. God's word not only allows for but expects and speaks to the diversity of behavior among honest Christians. Though none of them is perfect, each is using the talents and burdens God has given them to follow his way. Each seeks to honor God in the responsibilities he has given them and, by his grace and forgiveness, has a conscience clear of guilt. To know this is to know God's will.

Our decisions must follow biblical principles, be tempered by the situation, and be restrained by what is best for the people in our lives at the time. But we are not under the law and must not return to its cold authority in our lives. We are now directed by love for God, sensitivity to others, understanding of the situation, and commitment to the truth that sets us free. Yes, this freedom to choose is God's choice for us, and it demands wisdom steeped in God's word. (Josh 24:14–15; Prov 1:5, 28–33, 2:5–6, 10:13, 15:14, 17:24; Hos 14:9; John 8:32 with 36; Rom 12:1–21, 14:13–23; 1 Cor 1:26–31; 2 Cor 3:17; Gal 5:13–14; Eph 1:17–19a, 3:12; Phil 1:9–11; 2 Tim 4:9–10; Jas 1:22–25, 2:12, 3:13–18; 1 Pet 2:16–17)

112. Hidden Treasure in a World of Woe

CULTURAL VALUES, PERSONAL NEEDS, and previous experiences motivate behavior in our lives. A cultural frame of reference gives us a human system for mental, emotional, physical, and social survival. Our individualist society encourages self-centered courses of action condoned by the overpowering needs for independence, personal identity, self-worth, and pleasure. We say things like "survival of the fittest" and "if you are going to be nice, you'll have to pay the price," "first-come, first-served," or "truth is what is true for me." Self-assertion is often the way to success. In our decaying culture, competition and manipulation for the survival of self and its appetites are the stakes, the battle for which is fought on the hills of class, race, and gender, using the weapons of injustice, bullying, deception, violence, blackmail, and corruption. Individualists who say "Be true to yourself" are blind to what we have made of ourselves in our culture and have lost sight of God's ideals for us. It's true we should not let cultural values and people's expectations push us around. But without God, we are not a very good standard to live up to. Selfishness is not the goal.

Ultimately, these human values are self-destructive and destroy society as it disintegrates into camps of blood-thirsty, warring tribes. Those who see these values for what they really are find themselves at odds and out of sync with that culture. They are considered weak, the "losers" regarding success and achievement of human pleasure and power. But things are not what they seem. In Christ, we are not under culture's human ways and limitations. Our loyalties are above and beyond it to the One outside this universe. The world no longer shapes our motives for behavior, and, to a great degree, we become countercultural. The world is neither our friend nor our adversary but the context within which we live out our faith and seek to win the hearts of others for Christ.

Seeing the world this way gives meaning and contentment. These qualities of life are not found in self or culture but outside them in the

112. HIDDEN TREASURE IN A WORLD OF WOE

Creator-God of the universe. Though our loyalties are not to the world, we must make the message of contentment and freedom in Christ relevant in that world, bringing light into the darkness. We show the way to the rare jewel among the plain pebbles, the salvation of God to those who seek it. It brings meaning, purpose, forgiveness, contentment, and peace to life in this world and leads to joy in the next. (John 9:4–5 with Matt 5:13–16, John 3:16–17, 13:44–46; 14:27, 15:19, 16:33 17:13–19 with 1 John 2:15–17; 1 Cor 1:20–31; Eph 3:12; Heb 12:1–3 with Phil 3:7–11 and Luke 9:23–25; 2 Pet 3:3–15a; 1 John 4:1–6)

113. Loyalty to One Lord

GOD'S WORD CALLS FOR complete loyalty to him, leading to loyalty to our families and his people, the body of Christ. It is not primarily a question of what you do but what you are. We cannot be loyal to ourselves and loyal to God. Divided loyalty is not loyalty at all. Allegiance to God leads to a desire to honor him. It is characterized by honesty, humility, faithfulness, and trust in his providence. But loyalty is not characterized by perfection. It is, rather, a result of continual repentance and unconditional forgiveness. This is walking in the Spirit.

Loyalty is the central theme of *agape* love, making it more robust than the English word *love*. When used to refer to our relationship with God, our English word is inadequate. *Agape* does not carry romantic ideas with it. It is not about feelings but being, which results in doing what honors him. It is a term of steadfast loyalty, and we must allow it to decide our course of action in each life event more and more. (Exod 20:1–6; Josh 24:14–15; Pss 78:8, 35–37, 139:1–12; Isa 50:10–11; Matt 6:24, 18:1–4; John 1:3 with 10–11 and 3:19–21, 8:12, 14:6; Acts 4:12; 1 Cor 8:5–6; Gal 5:22–25; Eph 4:1–7, 5:17–18; Phil 2:5–11; 1 Tim 2:1–6)

114. Resting in God

JESUS PROMISES REST, BUT we often find ourselves struggling for survival. Even pastors and missionaries in ministry know a good deal of stress. At every turn, they are either wrestling for survival in a busy schedule, balancing the expectations of those in their ministries, or dealing with people fighting for their survival. Our culture of achievement and competition plays on our insecurities, and we become anxious and stressed out. We have allowed popular Christianity to become a pressure cooker, building up steam and risking the peace we should have in Christ. The institution we have made of the church adds complexity and strain to our lives when it should be a refuge. It becomes difficult to trust God for our social and personal well-being when there are such poor examples around us, even in our churches. Our need for a spiritual reputation, for our achievement and success to be recognized, and for material security tends to take over. But these are cultural absolutes barging in and smothering the biblical absolutes we are given. We see only risk in trusting God wholly, but from his side, it is the only way to know rest.

The great paradox is that we must die to ourselves to truly live. We cannot measure resting and trusting in God by our culture's norms, preferences, and demands. His purposes for us are not limited by these temporary human standards. Biblical Christianity takes us beyond popular Christianity into the rest he has for those who trust him. Though we will not know it perfectly in this life, we can taste it and know its permanence is our future. Many who have gone before us tasted and knew the rest God offers now and that which awaits us when we leave this earth, even though they knew suffering in this life. We can, too. (Pss 20:7, 33:11 with 16–22, 34:1–22, 37:23–24, 62:5–8, 146:5–6; Isa 26:3–4, 40:28–31 with 41:10; Matt 6:25–34, 11:28–30; Luke 10:38–42, 12:13–21; John 14:1–4 with 27 and 16:33; Phil 4:4–9; Heb 11:1–39, 13:7–8 with 15–16; 1 Pet 5:6–7; Rev 21:1–4)

115. The Old World

IF WE APPLY OUR logic, our linear thinking, our cultural values, our personal preferences, and the influence of our experience to our thinking about God, we will limit him to our human situation. We will bring him down to our level and see only a distorted God of our own making. If we let God be God and speak for himself in his word, we will find him quite different from what our human expectations allow. Yes, there is mystery. The paradox of the first being last and the last first is a strong theme. The principle that only death leads to life is found throughout the Gospels. Double meanings in prophecy are common. We will have both trouble and peace in our Christian lives. And God looks at the heart, not at the outward appearance.

These are not the values of our culture nor the ways we organize our world. But God is above and beyond our human thoughts and experience. We will have to open new compartments in our minds, use new wineskins, transform our minds, be born again, and start over. We must re-enter the world with a new understanding of the nature of reality. Sprinkling more Bible verses over the old worldview will do no good. The old wineskin cannot be trusted. We must leave a good deal of the old world's values and expectations behind. We walk with God as new people in the old context, no longer controlled by its norms and standards. (1 Sam 2:7, 16:7; Prov 3:5–7; Isa 26:3–4, 55:8–9; Matt 9:16–17, 19:29–30, 20:16, 25–28; Mark 9:33–37, 10:29–31; Luke 9:23–25 with Matt 11:28–30; John 3:16–17, 5:24, 12:24–26, 16:33; Rom 11:33–36, 12:1–2; 1 Cor 6:12 with 19–20; 2 Cor 5:15–17; Phil 3:13–14; Col 3:1–17; 1 John 2:15–17)

116. Obedience Is a Choice

OBEDIENCE TO GOD DOES not exist without the possibility of a choice not to obey. We nurture our intentions and choose our actions. God does not do that for us. The power he gives us to follow him is in the form of showing us more of himself, his grace, truth, and providence. He does not barge in and override our decisions, making us obedient. Though he is at work to shape our lives by his providence, it is still a choice for us to trust him and follow his way or choose our own way, just as our ancestors did in the garden.

He can use our past mistakes for his purposes when we give our lives to him. But we still choose to be loyal to him or to ourselves. This responsibility is one of his gifts to us. Our mind and our senses at work in our bodies that he created in his image give us at once great freedom and great responsibility. When we pray for help in temptation, it is most likely to come in the form of reminding us of his faithfulness and love, his power in providence, his lordship over all, and his infinite grace. We will, in the end, still choose our course of action. God is not asking for perfection, but that our hearts be in the right place, desiring to honor him and be obedient. (Ps 103:10-18; Prov 19:9; John 15:1-10; Rom 6:8-14; 2 Cor 12:7-10; Col 3:1-17; 2 Thess 3:6-15; Jas 1:13-25; 1 Pet 1:13—2:3; 2 Pet 1:3-11)

117. Gifts of God

GOD HAS ENDOWED PEOPLE with many gifts, having created us in his image. A heart of trust values this deeply. Our minds can reason and appreciate, analyze and evaluate, choose or reject. Our physical senses are also gifts from him. Sight and hearing, taste, touch, and smell guide us in our days here and bring great enjoyment to the sensitive soul. But when we choose our own way, we use these same gifts for ourselves in ways outside God's intentions. It is hard to believe that the same gifts that are blessings to his created beings can be used to reject the giver. To know that God gave these to all people, along with the freedom to use them as they choose, to be able to trust the Creator or refuse him, is to know something about the mystery and paradox of God's ways, but also something about God's grace. He gave us our life; we have it on loan from him, and we are responsible for choosing what we do with it. He only gives it once here on Earth. Like a candle, it is burning down, and we have only so many days to honor the giver in our choices and activities. (Gen 1:26–27 with 31; Pss 8:3–9, 90:4, 10–12, 14, 17; 102:11–12, 103:6–18, 139:13–16a; Rom 6:11–14, 12:1; 1 Cor 6:19–20; Jas 3:9–12, 4:13–17; 1 Pet 1:22–25)

118. Experience

UNLESS WE ENTER THE reality of who God is, what he has done, and what he will do, we do not yet have truth. Unless truth about him is converted into an experience of his faithfulness and providence in our lives, we do not yet have the beginning of wisdom. Only a trusting relationship with the God of the truth we know leads to the security and rest we need. Truth about God is information, but information about him must become a reality in our lives. God himself is the reality about whom that information speaks.

We can talk about truth, but we must experience reality. Information about God is intended to take us into that reality. It is not an end in itself. The Gospels are full of stories about reaching that reality in people's everyday lives. We see there that it is not usually the wealthy, worldly wise, influential, or powerful who come to the truth and experience its reality. It is generally the poor, the little-known, those without influence, the ordinary people of the times. These are the poor in spirit who know their need and seek the treasure of knowing God. "Theirs is the kingdom of heaven."

Wisdom is experiencing the effects of the realities of God in life. Only with time and more experience of God's providence and lovingkindness, more trust in his goodness in difficulties and uncertainties, and more gratefulness for his grace do we become wise. It is a lifetime pursuit. Yet this wisdom is to be sought at any cost, and its rewards are beyond measure. (Pss 90:12, 111:10; Prov 3:5–7, 13–18, 4:5–7; Luke 14:15–24; John 14:21–23, 15:1–8, 17:3 and 20–23; 1 Cor 1:20–31; Eph 5:15–20; Col 2:3; Jas 3:13–18)

119. Culture and Conversion

We are blind to our dependence on culture. It interprets our experience and influences our thoughts and actions far more than we realize. Even as Christians, our values about what is important or significant and our beliefs about what is true or possible are more often from the powerful influence of our Western culture than God's word. This cultural frame of reference contaminates our understanding of God. Our values and beliefs are built on theories, assumptions, and interpretations this worldview gives us. It is our human idea of the nature of reality, while God wants us to be transformed by the true nature of reality and to pour our new understandings into this new wineskin, not try to make them fit the old one.

Being born again begins with this change in worldview, that is, with our understanding of the reality of God and the spiritual nature of the universe that we have always thought of as only physical. But, as humans, many of us are still struggling with our old worldview. It continues to conflict with our new one in our reading of the Bible and trusting God in our experience. For many of us, the gospel message was not about regeneration at that deep level but dealt mainly with beliefs and feelings of guilt. But our knowing God must go beyond information and emotions to embrace his perspective and purposes in the world. Our beliefs and values must grow out of that new allegiance. Jesus said we have to start over, be born again, enculturated by God's word instead of the human system around us. The gospel message must penetrate our core and, starting there, change every area of life.

We must continue living in the world but no longer submit to its secular understandings and theories or be in love with its ways. We are now aware of this spiritual universe, and we must go beyond *knowing* something about God to *being* something for him: a product of his goodness, grace, and truth. Free from the influences and expectations of our human culture, we can walk the often difficult path of our lives in this world with confidence and freedom as we trust his providence in each twist and turn of the way.

119. CULTURE AND CONVERSION

When it leads through pain or desert places, when we are upset, discouraged, or anxious, we must not return to the old ways of survival our culture gave us. In his love and wisdom, he wants us to trust him as he brings about his purposes in our lives. If we do, though we may not understand all that is happening, we will not regret our choice. We will enter into his rest. (2 Kgs 6:15–17; Matt 9:16–17; John 1:10–13, 3:1–21, 8:12 with 12:35–36 and 3:19; Rom 12:1–2; Gal 6:14; Phil 1:9–11; Col 3:1–4 with 16a; Heb 4:9–11 with Matt 11:28–30; 2 Pet 1:3–11; 1 John 2:15–17, 4:1–6)

120. Love Your Enemies

WHEN WE READ THE psalmist's pleas for God to destroy his enemies, we may be tempted to skip over those verses as having no purpose for us. They seem foreign, hostile, and not at all what one should ask God to do. So why are they in God's word? It has helped me to see these enemies mentioned in the Bible by distinguishing three categories of people. Some hated God and sought to lead his people away from him, such as the nations surrounding Israel in the Old Testament. They knew what they were doing. These sought the life of the psalmist, and he correctly saw them as enemies of God.

There were also people who said they knew and served God but prevented others from seeing his true intentions, keeping them in a prison of legalism as they sought money and glory for themselves. Like the Pharisees or money changers in the temple in the New Testament, these knew what they were doing, and for most of them, their pride and love for themselves kept them from God's grace. Today, some lead those of simple faith away from God. But God's love for his own is unconditional, his grace on their behalf infinite, his commitment to their welfare unbending. When people go against those who belong to God, they go against God himself. Jesus put these in their place as those rejecting God's grace and abusing his people. He will always be against those who lead his children away from that love and grace. "Better a millstone be tied around their neck, and they be thrown into the sea." This generalization sets people like Nicodemus and Paul in high relief. They were exceptions as they turned from the ways of the Pharisees to trust God in Christ.

Then, there were those in that day who abused or offended Christians out of sheer ignorance. They continue in our day, and we are to turn the other cheek when offended. Jesus asked God to forgive the soldiers at the cross because they did not know what they were doing. These people can be hard on us but may not be beyond God's love and grace. For them, we pray. God waits for these to come to him, but he will not wait forever, and we may be the only examples they will see of his grace toward them. (Pss 21:8–9, 92:9–15; Isa 43:1; Matt 5:10–12, 38–48, 7:21–23, 13:36–43, 23:1–15; Luke 6:35–38, 17:1–2; John 2:13–17; Rom 16:17–19; 2 Tim 4:14–15; 1 John 3:11–13)

121. God in the World

WE LIVE IN A day of arrogant self-assertion and injustice, hatred without foundation, and corrupt, even antisocial, use of power. The world around us is being reduced to materialism, hedonism, power, and social recognition—the gods hewn by human hands. Morality and virtue have been demoted to personal preferences, people to political pawns. But, highly in contrast to this, the true nature of the universe is spiritual at its core. Just as Elisha's servant was shown the mountains to be full of horses and chariots of fire in response to the Aramean military threatening Elisha, God oversees his creation and everyone in it.

In his sovereignty and omnipotence, God's hand is on the course of human history, bringing about forgiveness by grace and his purposes for the faithful, beauty in a world where sin has brought destruction and suffering. Evil will not prevail. Unstoppable, an unrelenting movement of God's Spirit continually offers his way to all humankind, bringing those who are willing to himself. It is part of his grand and unrelenting movement toward the redemption of the entire universe, the big picture of God at work in the world. The horses and chariots of fire are still there. He moves in history in his own way and for his own purposes. No one can frustrate his intentions; no resistance alter his course.

Human efforts cannot thwart God's plan for the redemption of the world and those who believe. We who know him always have his attention and are part of his plan. We must want his purposes more than our own and allow him to write the part for each of us as characters in his grand story. It may not always be what we want or expect, but we must trust the God of the universe and his providence in our lives. (Gen 50:19–21; 2 Kgs 6:8–23; Pss 11:4, 14:2, 33:6–22; 37:1–9, 115:3, 139:1–4; Eccl 7:8–9; Isa 43:1–3a, 10–13, 44:9, 46:10; Dan 3:15–18; Mic 4:5; Luke 6:46–49, 9:23–24; John 12:23–26; Eph 1:7–14; Phil 1:12–14)

122. Defending the Faith

DEFENSE OF THE FAITH has its place, but it can also be information empty of the most important factor, the meaning of that information for our lives. It can even carry an element of pride in the display of knowledge. Any Bible teaching has this potential for the teacher. Paul talks about those who preached Christ out of selfish ambition. The defense of the faith must, however, be undertaken with humility, for we speak, as Paul, only by God's grace. In our day, being in Christian leadership is glamorized, a coveted position to be sought. Humility is often left behind. It is serious business to represent God in the world or in the church. We must remember that we are products of that grace, and that the most important thing is a faithful life, trusting his providence at every turn.

Being one of his is more than knowing about him. There is a great deal we, in our human, limited state, cannot know. What we do know is overwhelming and makes us small in its presence. Gratefulness, humility, and awe must be ours as those who speak for him in any capacity. Any defense of our faith must be bathed in these attitudes and seen as a service to our great God in light of his grace. Living his message is first, and defending it is second. Generally, the incarnation of the message is more convincing of its truth than propositional arguments. It is essential that reasoning about God is planted in tilled and fertile soil in the hearts of people. The incarnation of the truth of God, with his help, prepares the soil of people's hearts for its seeds. (Matt 5:13-16, 7:15-23, 18:1-9; 1 Cor 15:10a; 2 Cor 4:4-7; Eph 4:11-13; Phil 1:15-17 with 2:3-8; Jas 3:1-2 with 13-18; 1 Pet 3:14-18)

123. The Process of Conversion

TO OPEN OUR LIVES to Christ is to begin a process of relearning all we know about the world and ourselves. It is aptly called rebirth. We cannot stop short. Discipleship must be a process of helping another dig up the old foundations to construct a new temple from the ground up. The old life is past and over now that we have been made new. Today, life is lived in the light of God's grace and providence. We may have had many bad experiences in the past. It did not seem so at the time and may not look like it is possible now, but God is at work in us and can use even those experiences for his present purposes in us. He can and will use even the bad things that come our way today—the difficulties and hurts we have and may continue to endure—to shape us to serve him.

We are each a new creation now and cannot patch up the perceptions of our old life with a few Bible verses. And the new temple must not be built on faulty ground. We may have doubts along the way as we grow in our faith and trust in God, but we should never want to return to the old life after being introduced to God's grace—not like the children of Israel who wanted to return to the leeks and garlic of Egypt, who wanted meat instead of manna from God. We must become people who trust God. But we must also realize that becoming people who walk worthy of the gospel is a process rather than an event.

Our hearts should want to honor God, and though we are not perfect, we short-circuit the process if we lose sight of his sacrifice and grace on our behalf. It should begin to produce loyalty, love, humility, and honesty in our lives on day one. Our desire for him should become an all-or-nothing commitment, but we are in a process, and when we fall short in our faithfulness, he is "faithful and just" to forgive us. But words alone are not enough. To say we are Christians without any fruit of that commitment in our day-to-day lives will produce something worse than before we heard the gospel. Some become those of a popular Christianity that turns others away from

123. THE PROCESS OF CONVERSION

God instead of toward him. True conversion is different. It starts with a humble acceptance of God's grace and allows the process of his work in us to change everything in our lives from that point on. (Num 11:4-6; Eccl 7:20; Matt 7:13-14 with 24-29, 18:1-4; Luke 5:37-38; John 3:7; Rom 12:1-2; 1 Cor 3:16-17; 2 Cor 5:15-17; Phil 1:6 with 2:12-13; 1 Thess 5:23-24; Heb 3:12-13; 2 Pet 2:20-22; 1 John 2:15-17)

124. False Teaching

WE READ OF FALSE teachers in the New Testament. These mixed other teachings with the gospel and sought a following. Teaching God's word with conjecture is not much different. It is easy to make the Bible say what we prefer and convince ourselves and others that it is God's way. For some, there is a reputation to build and money to be made if they can convince others they know secrets in the Bible hidden from others. Just so, the proponents of the prosperity gospel convince naïve supporters they will be wealthy, and legalism makes followers believe they can earn God's approval. We are not obliged to say everything we know in every situation, but we are duty-bound not to say what we do not know as the final word in biblical interpretation. Humility must replace speculation; a certain theological modesty must precede our interpretive efforts. God's revealing of his greatness is better seen from that vantage point. We must let him speak for himself and not bend what he says to fit our theological system, personal preferences, or cultural trends. We must approach the mystery in him and the paradox in his ways with trust. For the last will indeed be first and the first last.

The Jewish leaders of the Old Testament and in Jesus' day simply rejected that gentiles would ever be welcomed into the kingdom or that the Messiah would not come to deliver the Jews from the Romans but from their sins. They hated the gentiles and preferred prophecy to say otherwise. When anyone's interpretation of God's word is seen as inspired, it is a cause for caution. We must accept the original message and trust God for what he has not told us if we are to let God speak for himself. (Matt 7:15–23, 13:24–30 with 36–43, 24:4–5 with 10–12 and 23–24; Luke 18:9–14; Acts 20:28–31; 2 Cor 11:13–15; 1 Tim 1:3–7; 2 Tim 4:1–4; Titus 1:15–16; 2 Pet 2:1–3 with 19; 1 John 4:1–6)

125. Salvation

IN OUR CULTURE, COMING to Christ is sometimes considered salvation from hell, from punishment for the guilt of our sin. But, though he does forgive us and prepares to receive us into his presence for eternity, Christ steps into our lives for something even more significant, for which forgiveness is only the beginning. He brings salvation from our rejection of God and our infatuation with self so that we might personally know the creator of the universe, the God of all grace. This is the heart of the gospel. Salvation is not just about avoiding punishment but, based on righteousness in Christ given to us before God, it makes a relationship with God possible that changes everything. Though we may feel with Paul that we are the worst of sinners, God opens himself up to us through our faith in Christ; he makes his home with us. We were dead but are made alive in Christ now and forever. The contrast could not be sharper. He struck down the powers and authorities of darkness over us who were keeping us in fear and captivity. Now, guilt is gone, and so much more is here. A never-ending relationship with God full of grace, forgiveness, and freedom is ours.

God's grace in saving us is not something our logic can figure out or our propositions define. He is not looking for the best and brightest for his plan; he is looking for you; he is looking for me. We are his plan. The father received his wayward, prodigal son with joy. The vineyard owner paid full wages to those who came last and only worked an hour. The woman at the well and another caught in adultery received what they really needed, not what they deserved. Jesus forgave Peter for his denial. The Samaritan helped his sworn enemy, crippled on the road to Jericho. When we humble our hearts and come to him in trust, God's grace is poured out on us beyond measure. We do not receive what we deserve but what we really need in him.

We then become those who follow him out of love and gratefulness, those who worship him in spirit and truth, instead of those who obey out of legalistic fear of his anger and punishment, hoping to gain his approval. We are not perfect in ourselves, and in this life, there will be suffering and pain, rejection and injustice, but in him, we have all we need and grace beyond measure. That is our peace, and that is our message to the world. Grace in salvation wipes out legalism. The legal matters have been cared for. We who have been saved by grace must live by it and the freedom it gives us. (Ps 103:10–14; Eccl 7:20; Matt 5:3–10, 11:25–30, 20:9–15; Luke 10:25–37, 15:11–24; John 1:10–12, 4:7–26, 5:24, 8:12, 31–36, 10:10, 14:21 and 23, 27, 15:5–8, 17:3 with 20–23; 1 Cor 1:26–31; Eph 2:1–10, 3:12, 5:25–27; Phil 1:6; Col 2:13–15; 1 Tim 1:12–17; 1 Pet 3:18a; 2 Pet 1:3; 1 John 2:3–6, 4:18–19)

126. Complexity in Knowing God

VOLUMES OF THEOLOGY AND technical commentaries may make Christians without formal training feel overwhelmed. They may despair of ever understanding the seemingly endless complexity of information about the Bible. Of course, though much of it is excellent research and very helpful, some of that to which theologians give elaborate labels is outside human boundaries of understanding and experience. God is beyond the limitations of our human minds, but he does not give us complexity for our faith and how to live our lives. There is a lot we can know, and studying the Bible is rewarding and enriching as it reveals God's heart and ways, his plan for the world, his path for a flourishing life, and his relationship with us. But there is danger in adding complexity and density to a level only professionals can understand and explain. Complexity may be wondered at, but it is grace that is profound, and it is quite straightforward in the gospel. We were blind, and now we see; we were dead, but now we are alive; we walked in darkness but now walk in the light, though we have done nothing to deserve it.

We must admit there is mystery in learning more about God because he has not told us everything we may wish to know. There are also the paradox and irony of his ways that we must become comfortable with. If it were necessary, he would have told us more. But he intended that only those with eyes of faith will see and know him as he is. Though much has been given to know about him and his ways, we must not create complexity where simplicity is God's purpose. We must not theologize about what we do not know. Wisdom, trust, loyalty, and humility must rule our hearts. (Pss 1:1–6, 15:1–5, 24:1–6, 37:3–6; Prov 22:4; Isa 66:2; Mic 6:8; John 1:12, 3:16, 5:24, 8:12, 9:1–41; 2 Cor 4:6–7; Gal 5:1–6; Eph 2:8–10; Col 2:6–10, 16–23; Heb 11:1 and 6)

127. Judging Others

SINCE THE DAYS OF Jesus, his followers often find themselves questioning the behavior or conscience of someone else in the body of Christ. In our Western culture, we are highly competitive. Pushed by our democratic capitalism, we individualists learn to earn personal value through achievement. Our culture tells us we must achieve more than those around us—and be known for it—to make progress. But that is not the way for those whose identity is now in Christ. We must be concerned about our own lives before God and allow other Christians to do the same. He is not more impressed with an extrovert than an introvert, a well-published author more than a plumber, or the pastor of a large church or a missionary more than a groundskeeper, secretary, or nurse if they are loyal to him. He works with each person differently to shape them for his purposes. Each has their responsibilities before him. Each must live in loyalty to God and trust him for their lives.

The freedoms another has in Christ may not be the same for us. The truths of God's word, our loyalty to him, and the humility and gratitude that must rule our hearts are minimums for all of us, but the expressions of our faith are for each person to work out. We must each look into the mirror of God's word for what it tells us. We do not know all his purposes for others, but we can prepare ourselves for his purposes in our lives. (Matt 7:1–5; Luke 6:31 with 37–38; John 21:17–22; Rom 2:1–11, 12:9–13, 14:1–22; 1 Cor 10:23–31; Gal 5:1–6; Phil 1:6 with 2:1–4, 12–13; Jas 1:22–25, 4:10–12; 1 John 3:18)

128. The Worship and Love of God

Some have given us a God who coldly demands worship of himself, but it cannot be. He did not create us to demand we indulge and gratify some need of his for our worship. He alone is worthy of worship, but worship commanded is not worship. It must be voluntary. Throughout the Old Testament, God sought willing hearts to follow the many laws for worship. Moreover, worshiping the gods of this world must be redirected. For God to tell us he is the only God and, therefore, our hearts must be directed toward him is a matter of his love and correction, for it is the difference between life and death for the worshiper. Consequently, he has the good of the worshiper in mind, though worshiping him is still a choice from the heart made in spirit and truth.

Loving God is part of worship, but the word is closer to loyalty and allegiance than our emotional ideas of love and attraction in modern English. It was not the other loves of the Greek language: *eros* (passion), *philia* (true friendship, used occasionally by Jesus of God's love for him, John 5:20), or *storge* (family affection), but *agape* (an interactive love of commitment to loyalty and purposeful service to another) that is used of our love for God. Expressing this loyalty is part of worship, and living it out glorifies God (makes him known and reveals his goodness, power, grace, and providence). Emotional love cannot be commanded from others, but loyalty can because it does not require emotion. It is a volitional choice, and the One requiring it knows its outcome in our favor. We must not depend on our affectionate feelings toward God, for we cannot manufacture them, and he does not demand them. We must, instead, check on our loyalty to his purposes in moments of doubt or confusion. We can choose loyalty to the right master. It is then that our activities called for by that loyalty become evident, though they may differ from those of other Christians. (Pss 15:1–5, 24:3–6, 40:6–8, 51:16–17, 145:18–19; Prov 21:2–3, 22:4; Isa 29:13, 66:2; Ezek 33:29–33; Mic 6:8; Mal 1:10–14; Matt 15:7–11; John 4:23–24, 14:15–24)

129. Legalism versus Relationship

THEOLOGIES FULL OF LEGALISM give us a callous God who talks about grace and forgiveness but expresses neither in his relationship with us—one whose approval must be constantly earned. This legalism is made up of interpretations added to God's intentions. It only reminds us of our sins and holds us in the prison of guilt, for we can never be good enough. As Isaiah said of Israel, we can have the right words in our mouths while our hearts are far from understanding his ways. Legalism is not God but Satan keeping us from God's grace, forgiveness, and freedom in Christ. He reminds us of our failures and those of others we needed to trust in our past. He repeats the harsh words of legalistic sermons in our minds, sowing doubt where God's intentions of grace could not be more explicit.

Legalism, mysticism, and syncretism are marks of popular Christianity, but we must be biblical Christians. The truth shall set you free, not hold you in bondage. We are not near perfect, but we are forgiven, and God keeps it that way as we come to him. Grace and guilt do not mix. Acknowledgment of our sins and his unconditional forgiveness are the ways of God, and his grace covers all. Feelings of guilt have no place in those who are forgiven and redeemed. We must no longer walk in darkness, but in the light he gives us. We are no longer lost but found; now, we belong to him. Loyalty to his purposes becomes our desire in such a relationship. (Ps 103:10–14; Isa 29:13, 43:1; Ezek 33:30–33; John 1:1–5, 16–18, 8:12, 31–36; Rom 3:21–28, 14:1–23, especially 5 and 22; 2 Cor 3:17; Gal 5:1–9 with 13–14; Eph 2:4–10, 3:12; Col 2:16–23; 1 Tim 1:3–7; Titus 3:3–8; Heb 9:11–14; Jas 1:22–25; 1 John 1:8–10)

130. Conscience

WITH THE KNOWLEDGE OF good and evil came conscience. When conditioned by God's word, conscience is a gift he uses to help us. But it can be a prison of guilt and pain when regulated by legalism, cultural demands, faulty human standards, or childhood experiences. It can also be controlled by our imagination or inaccurate perspective on some Bible verse that disregards the rest of God's word for us. Though God is suspected of causing all our feelings of guilt, as we can see, they come from many different sources. As such, they are not only unhelpful but can drain our emotional resources and make us legalistic in our battle against them. Thus, they can keep us from the good things God has created for us to enjoy in our lives of commitment to him.

Accepted standards may come from the family, the society, and even the church, but human standards are often not of God. People in every culture have a human conscience, and Christians frequently try to retain this social conscience and a biblical conscience together in their lives. A conscience conditioned by God in his word will sometimes enhance but more often override that of human society. To allow both to rule is to have difficulty satisfying either. It is usually to fail to fully know God's purposes for us. A culturally shaped "Christian" conscience will syncretize human traditions and man's desires with God's design, bending and twisting his intentions for us.

A culturally relevant Christian conscience based on God's word, without legalistic additions, is our goal and will be our peace. It will be balanced with freedom in Christ, embrace God's grace and forgiveness, and relieve us of false guilt. (2 Sam 24:10; Prov 3:27–28; John 3:17; Rom 14:1 with 5 and 22; 1 Cor 8:1–13, 10:23—11:1; Phil 2:12–13; 1 Tim 1:5, 19 with 4:2; Titus 1:15; 1 Pet 3:8–17; 1 John 3:16–24)

131. Judgment of Believers

THE BIBLE TELLS US that Christ will judge believers in the future. But there is also the fact that there is no condemnation for those forgiven in Christ. This confuses many Christians. Indeed, we will never answer for any sins already forgiven by God's grace at the judgment seat of Christ. Then why a judgment of believers? Because not all who call themselves Christians know God. Others say they know him but are not faithful to his words and use their position for self-advancement.

Those who know God's grace are painfully sensitive to how often they fall short of his desires for them. Many of us feel like we will never be done confessing our sins. But many others go through their "Christian" lives with unrestrained self-assertion, pride, greed, or envy that is never acknowledged, though they condemn it in others. This may show up in controlling others for their advancement, legalism, false teaching, building their own kingdom in search of affirmation and recognition, and generally using Christianity for their own ends. Many are the sins these rationalize and condone in their lives, unwilling to humble themselves before the grace of God, though they say they "know" the truth of his word. Some people like this are weeds in the wheat field, goats who will be placed on the left of Christ. Others are Christians whose attitudes and works will be assessed at the judgment seat of Christ.

But for those imperfect but faithful to him, those walking with him in repentance and humble gratefulness for their forgiveness, there is no fear. Their loyalty is evident, their sin forgiven, and their guilt removed as far as the east is from the west. God looks at the heart and is at work in their lives; they are an ongoing project. They may need their feet washed from their journey in this broken world, but though they stumble, they do not fall. They are clean. There is no condemnation for those loyal to Christ. (1 Chr 29:17a and 18b; 2 Chr 7:14; Pss 34:22, 37:23–24, 51:16–17, 103:10–14; Prov 16:2, 21:2–3, 24:16, 28:26; Isa 42:1–3; Matt 7:15–23, 13:24–30 with

36–43, 15:7–9, 18:6; Luke 5:22–26, 11:52, 17:1–2; John 3:17–18, 36, 5:24, 13:8–10; Acts 20:28–31; Rom 3:21–24, 4:7–8, 8:31–35; 1 Cor 3:10–15; 2 Cor 5:15–18a; Phil 1:6, 2:12–13; Col 1:13–14 with 21–22; 1 Thess 5:9–11; Titus 1:15–16; Heb 9:23–28; 1 Pet 3:18; 1 John 1:8–10)

132. Superficial Christianity

WHETHER A LAY PERSON or a Christian leader, to love one's church or Christianity itself more than God is but popular Christianity. The love of one's own Bible teaching or ministry more than God is a desire for personal achievement and reputation. God may use our efforts despite us, but we are far from truly knowing and selflessly serving him. There is no true repentance until one understands one's motives and agenda and how terribly short we can fall from God's way. Seeking to serve both God and self, one does not serve God at all. There is no relationship. It will take humility and trust, and the self-asserting individualist pursuing social survival will find that hard.

It seems harsh, a kind of high treason to mention this to a popular Christian. Yet, we must surrender our self-asserted "freedom" to have true freedom in Christ. The great paradox of the gospel is that we must lose our life to find the true life. The importance of humility has been removed from the message of the gospel, and the emphasis is put on believing what Jesus did for us. This makes the gospel only a cognitive issue for Western individualists. True faith is not possible without humility. People who give only mental assent to the message of God's grace start off on their Christian journey at a grave disadvantage for following Christ. The selfish ambition of individualism is still in control with a new sugar coating by which it is condoned in the church. We are still trusting our culture's solutions for mental, social, and material survival.

It is spiritual adultery. We have married Christ and offer a good deal of lip service to our Christian commitments, but we have a mistress, a secret lover on the side where our true loyalties lie. This is syncretism: sprinkling the new message over the old worldview. The two ways become tangled in the person's life, and the mixture hardens. These are worse off than before they heard the gospel. They have put the new wine into an old wineskin, and the results are disastrous. They have deceived themselves and are inoculated

132. SUPERFICIAL CHRISTIANITY

against the true purposes of God in their lives. If these become leaders in our churches, they will claim to help and serve others in ministry, but they are only building bigger barns for themselves. It must not be. Only faith born of humility brings salvation. (Matt 6:24, 9:16–17, 18:1–4; Luke 9:23–25, 11:23, 12:13–21, 16:13–15; John 8:31–32, 12:24–26; 15:1–11; Phil 2:1–4; Col 2:13–23; Titus 1:15–16; Jas 4:7–10; 1 Pet 5:1–11; 2 Pet 2:19–22)

133. Perfection

WHEN THE BIBLE SAYS to be holy, it means to be set apart from the normal. God is not demanding that we be perfect in our ordinary English sense of the word. He wants us, instead, to be consistent in our acknowledgment of him, humble in receiving his grace, resilient in trusting his word and providence, and honest in realizing our dependence on him. The attitudes God asks of us in our day are countercultural. He wants us to become mature in our faith, established in our relationship with him, and fair and loving in our relationships with others. But our culture demands self-assertion to seek our own survival. What God wants for us is not the norm; it is quite different from our society's standards—a life deviating from cultural demands. This is the meaning of holy for us.

Becoming what God wants us to be this way is a process, a journey. The important thing is that we love him enough—are loyal enough to his purposes—to make progress. We become better people along the way, some faster than others, as we acknowledge him in all we do. The examples of faithful men and women in the Bible do not show us perfection but his grace and providence at work in their lives as they were faithful. Paul desired it deeply and strained to see God's purposes achieved in his life and ministry. But perfection is yet to be had. Though God does not expect it here in our every moment, he has plans for it soon. (Pss 91:1 with 14–16, 103:10–18; Prov 3:5–7, 16:9; Mic 6:6–8; Luke 18:9–14; Eph 4:11–16; Phil 3:13–14; Col 3:1–4 with 10 and 17; Heb 11:1–13; 1 Pet 1:13—2:3; 1 John 3:1–3)

134. Good Works

BEING PEOPLE SAVED BY grace and realizing its value, we often forget how important good works are in God's plan. We may even feel that emphasizing good works is disregarding his grace or causing dependence on them for the right standing with God. But we are saved by grace to do good works. God's word is given to us so that it might result in good works in our lives. These good works are evidence of true faith and are God's will for us. They are our sign to the world, and as the end draws near, we must increase in them. As Paul's young disciple and pastor, Titus, is told, they are central to our lives in Christ. God will never forget them.

Words alone are not enough. Information about God or his will by itself does not meet God's desire for us. The words of truth must find their way into our daily walk. Whether we know little or much, we must become people of good works who honor him with our lives. Those who know little, who are simple in their faith but express it in their works, are greater than the professional theologian who has collected volumes of information but does not see its meaning for our day-to-day lives. (Prov 21:2–3; Mic 6:8; Matt 3:8, 5:14–16, 7:15–20; Gal 6:9–10; Eph 2:8–10; 1 Tim 6:18–19; 2 Tim 3:16–17; Titus 2:7, 14, 3:1, 8, 14; Heb 6:10, 13:15–16; Jas 2:7; 1 Pet 2:15, 3:13–17; 2 Pet 3:10–14; 1 John 3:16–18)

135. Painful Events

MOST PEOPLE HAVE HAD painful experiences; for some, these have been traumatic. We regret these times terribly and can see their toll on our lives. But to think we were or are outside God's grace is to forget who he is. The events were hurtful and damaging, but God is good. How can he allow these things in our lives? We may never know all, but we can be sure these things do not and cannot change his purpose for us. He never wanted us to know evil in this way. We live with the choice made in Eden that bears its many terrible results today. And we continue to commit that sin of not trusting God ourselves. But when we come to Christ in faith, the pain we have known and may still carry with us shapes us to honor God more than we could without it. We may have never turned to him except for some hurt, some love withheld, some tragic event. We look at these as ruinous in our perspective of life. But God has other plans, and Jesus asks him not to take us out of this broken world. We're bound to have some scars, but God has a purpose for our being here.

    Contrary to what our culture tells us, painful experiences as Christians can be times to grow in wisdom, endurance, and trust in God's love, grace, and providence. We must face life's difficulties with grace, honor his name, and live in his purposes through them. It may seem long and difficult to us, but life is short, and we can live it to honor him despite the pain, trusting his purposes in our lives, or we can be bitter or dwell on the past and waste this chance to know more of his way of grace and show it to others. The choice to know good and evil was made in the garden. We are not the only ones to know suffering and pain as a result, but having God's grace, we can help others who are hurting find the peace he gives. This life is lived on the porch; we have not yet entered the mansion prepared for us where all is well, but we will. (Gen 50:19–21; Pss 25:1–21, 34:4–7, 17–19, 73:21–28, 138:6–8, 139:1–12; Prov 3:5–6; John 14:1–4, 17:15; Phil 1:6, 12–14, 2:13,

4:4–7; 1 Thess 5:23–24; 1 Tim 4:3–10; Heb 12:1–3; Jas 1:2–12; 1 Pet 1:3–12, 5:6–11; 1 John 3:1–3)

136. Patience and Gratefulness

WE MAY NOT HAVE been born with a high measure of intelligence, or a magnetic personality, or come into a lot of money, or have our culture's idea of physical beauty, but God is not only aware of that; his hand is at work to bring about his purpose in our lives just as we are, lacking these traits. Though we may be painfully aware of what we feel are shortcomings, we have no idea of the human inclinations toward self-absorption and arrogance these characteristics rouse and the temptations they bring for others.

Jesus would teach us something different in the Beatitudes. The traits he values are countercultural regarding physical, intellectual, or material advantages. They do not depend on personality but on the condition of the heart. Lacking traits valued by our culture may give us attitudes and preferences that go against these biblical values, so we miss his purposes for us. We can live in resentment or wait on God and his way for us with an openness to his providence that has brought us to where we are with the qualities and talents we do have. The rewards of God far outweigh the praise, status, and feelings of self-worth our culture offers.

Our perspective is limited to our culture's superficial trends and shallow values; our opinions are but human, our outlook finite. God has an eternal perspective and intends to accomplish a work of art in us toward his good purposes for us in the world. What he has promised he will do. We may prefer our culture's definition of happiness now for ourselves. But he intends to bestow uninterrupted happiness on all who would choose him forever. Patience. Do not long for and seek what God has not seen fit to furnish you. Seek first his kingdom and realize the deep gratitude you should have for the blessings of his grace. Never doubt you matter to him just as you are; there are no mistakes. God has given you all you need to do his will. As you allow him, he will bring about in you his purposes for his work in the world. You will find your identity in Christ as you share his righteousness and the gift of his peace.

136. PATIENCE AND GRATEFULNESS

God's loyalty to us is fierce, his mercy unyielding, his patience unending. We can be part of his working toward his purpose for us or pursue immediate gratification and temporary fulfillment. But if we go his way, it will take patience, for though there are joys along the way, his goal of complete happiness for us is unbending, and he may use adversity out of love toward his objective. What may seem to you unhappiness now may result in the happiness of many forever if we allow him to be God in our lives. It will certainly lead to yours. Once again, God leaves the choice before us. So, wait on the Lord. Allow the full weight of his grace and love wrapped around his purpose for you to influence that choice. (Pss 25:4-5 with 8-9, 27:13-14, 33:11, 34:4-10 with 17-22, 37:3-11 with 34a, 42:11, 105:4, 127:1-2, 130:5-6, 138:8; Lam 3:22-24; Matt 5:1-10, 6:33 with 5:16; Rom 8:28, 12:9-13; 1 Cor 1:26—2:5, 13:4-7; 2 Cor 4:6-7, 12:7-10; Eph 4:1-3; Phil 1:6, 2:12-13, 4:10-13; 1 Thess 5:12-15, 24; Jas 1:5-8, 12, 5:7-8; 2 Pet 1:3-9)

137. His Way

God did not choose a grand entrance for his Son at the incarnation. At that time, the proud, "knowledgeable" Jewish leaders did not look in his direction for the Messiah; the "powerful" government did not notice except to seek to destroy a potential irritation. If anyone deserved the world's recognition, it was the Creator when he visited his creation, but that is not God's way. A smelly animal stall, a worn feeding trough, and a few dirty shepherds marked the coming of the God of the universe to his own creation. Later, he was recognized by pagans while Jewish leaders were blind, and Herod sought to destroy him. It is one of the paradoxes of God that he uses the unexpected to reveal eternal truth, common things to reveal the uncommon, simple things to reveal the profound nature of his dealings with the universe. A drink of water, a few fish, a cup of wine, a piece of bread, a lost coin, a wayward lamb, all point to his work in the world.

It is the same with people. He lifts up the humble and puts down the proud. He makes the first last and the last first. He did not intend that his purposes be accomplished by the influential, the wealthy, or the recognized, but that his church would show his grace and love to the world through the weak, the pure in heart, the unknown, and the unassertive who are not recognized by the world. So, as from a small and inconsequential mustard seed comes the plant that overarches the garden, God uses the least expected people in the most important undertaking of the universe: making him known to the world. The proud, the wealthy, the powerful, and the socially influential will have to come down from their self-importance to meet God. He receives no one else.

There are no Christian celebrities, and only a few celebrities who are Christian. If our goal is to make the church respected by the world, we have the wrong objective in mind. If the church becomes popular in our present age, it may be because it is syncretized with its surrounding culture, off the rails God laid for it. The day is coming when the meek will inherit the earth, the faithful rule the world, and the pure in heart see God. The powerful and influential, as the world sees them, will be gone. (1 Sam 2:3–9; Ps 37:3–11; Prov 16:19; Isa 66:2b; Jer 9:23–24; Matt 5:3–10, 19:23–30, 20:16 with 20–28; Mark 10:29–31; Luke 1:46–55; John 21:17 with 20–22; 1 Cor 1:20–31, 12:10; 2 Tim 3:1–5; Jas 1:9–11, 2:1–9, 4:10; 1 Pet 5:6)

138. The Great Change

WHEN WE ENCOUNTER THE gospel, we must realize its truth and see God for who he is and ourselves as we are. He is ultimately good, all-powerful, and absolutely just. The supreme authority. Before we know God, we may think we are okay, even better than most, and highly achieved in the world's eyes, but if we think so, we are like those at Laodicea: hopelessly deceived, sinful, weak, and desperate. But when we meet Christ, we know. Instead of golden decanters, we are clay pots and cracked ones at that. And we know that he knows, and we are accountable in his presence. We can do nothing about our situation on our own. The sentence has already been pronounced, and we can only plead for mercy. Counting the cost, we must willingly hand ourselves over to God and allow his justice and grace through Christ to make us new.

Understanding the truth and coming to him will take humility and repentance. But, as the gospel tells us, we will find God's unconditional love and powerful grace that overcomes all. It results in overwhelming gratefulness. We will see we were wrong, and he is right; our most outstanding achievements will be unimportant; we will put our reputation in his hands. He will be everything. We will begin to see meaning in what he has created and what he has done in our lives. As we go along, our worldview will begin to be renovated, our value system will be turned on its head, and what is true or possible will be changed in our minds forever. We will come to know him as we have known no one else, and our goal will be to trust him without question.

Now, with the help of his Spirit and his word, we must face a battle. We have responded to God's invitation to accept the sacrifice of Christ on our behalf. We now stand in his righteousness before God. We have a new master. But we must be ready for battle as self-assertion, our culture's values, and Satan himself seek to undo our faith in him and discourage our every move. However, God has not stopped being God; we have in him every reason to trust and none to doubt his work on our behalf. We must put on the armor of God and abide in Christ for the days ahead. (Isa 6:5; Matt 9:16–17, 18:1–4, 25:31–33; Luke 5:8–9, 18:9–14; John 15:1–8; Rom 10:1–4, 12:1–2; 2 Cor 4:4–7, 11:13–15; Eph 2:1–10, 6:10–18; Phil 1:9–11, 2:12–13, 3:7–9; Col 3:1–4; 1 Pet 5:8–9; 2 Pet 1:3–9; Rev 3:17)

139. "Good" Christians

MANY THINGS MAY ACCOMPANY a person's claim to be a believer. They may be the love of wealth, the longing for recognition, the satisfaction of achievement, or the sense of security from controlling others. If so, they are cancers as yet undetected and, if unattended, will be lethal in the body of Christ. Though becoming what God intends each of us to be is a process, there is no middle ground. A person is or is not pursuing God's way, moving toward him or, though seemingly close, moving away. Movement away from Christ is the description of an unbeliever.

Words are not enough. Someone who says they are a Christian must show their faith through their works. We must use discernment, for the weeds in the wheat field look very much like the wheat. We may be impressed as Samuel was with Eliab, but God looks at the heart. The truth is buried in people's motives where we cannot see, but it inevitably surfaces in the fruit it will ultimately bear. Finding that someone has a true heart for God usually happens among the more mundane activities of life outside the church. Natural behavior is always more telling than ritual behavior. (1 Sam 16:6–7; Pss 33:18, 34:15, 52:7–9, Prov 3:5–7, 27–28, 16:2, 17:3, 20:27, 27:19, 28:26; Isa 66:1–6; Jer 9:23–24; Matt 7:15–23, 13:24–30 with 36–43; Titus 1:16; Jas 1:22–25, 2:14–16, 3:13–18; 1 John 3:18)

140. Trust and Love

IN THEIR MORE SUBSTANTIAL meaning, trust and love are among the most important virtues among human beings. God created all things good, and, in his wisdom, he gave the crown of his creation, men and women, free will. This made trust and love possible between human beings and between humans and God.

God's creation was perfect, but he did not put Adam and Eve in a perfect universe. The enemy was already afoot with evil intentions toward God. We do not know all, but Satan craved loyalty and allegiance to himself instead of to his Creator and decided to serve himself, desiring to be like God. He would try to turn the hearts of all men and women against God. Adam and Eve would be given the same chance to choose. And they did. All humankind would come to know the evil of mistrusting God and abusing his good gifts. All would choose between God or self for their love and loyalty. There was no other way. For trust, love, and loyalty do not exist without choice.

Trust and love cannot be forced or legislated. They are evident because people choose to give that trust or express that love to someone. Of course, being so central and powerful, these very virtues are abused by those seeking self-satisfaction. The greatest gifts may be used as deceptive weapons to betray or blackmail others. But God is never deceived. Men and women may choose good or evil, but he knows their hearts. It was a risk he was willing to take so that real love, trust, and loyalty might always be possible. It gives us some idea of how important these virtues are, even though the freedom of choice also allows for evil and suffering. Our trust and love of God must be what we lean on in that sort of world, where there are troubles and deceptions, or it is not trust and love at all.

For the virtues of trust and love to become real in a person's life, another element is required. The person must humble himself or herself before their Creator-God. Every person must choose self over God or God over self. They must admit their desperate need for him and accept his grace in the sacrifice of Christ on their behalf, making peace with God. Our proud hearts do not want to accept it, but Jesus truly is "the way, the truth, and the life." No one comes to the Father except through him. There is no other mediator between God and humankind, no other way to the love and trust of a relationship with the Creator. The proud must lay down their weapons, for they cannot know God any other way. (Gen 1:26 with 31 and 2:15–16 and 3:1–7; Josh 24:14–15; Pss 34:1–22, 37:1–7; Prov 15:3 with 8–9 and 11; Isa 5:20–23; Jer 17:9–10; Amos 5:14–15; Matt 19:16–22, 22:34–40; John 14:1, 27, 16:33; Acts 4:12; Rom 1:18–22a; 1 Cor 3:11–15; Phil 3:17–21; 1 Tim 2:5; 1 Pet 3:8–12; 1 John 3:16)

141. From God?

NOT EVERYTHING IS FROM God. Much in the world is against his will for creation, against his desire for us. He very much regrets the absence of goodness, justice, and humility in the hearts of the people he created. He laments their rejection of his grace. Most did not recognize their creator when he came to his creation, and most continue to refuse his way today. Just as cold is the absence of heat, and darkness the absence of light, many evil conditions and the suffering around us are caused by the rejection of God's way, the refusal of his grace, and, therefore, his goodness. The temporary rewards of evil may be striking, and the outcomes of his grace may seem subtle, but in the end, one is destroyed while the other flourishes and lasts for eternity. Once again, people choose.

    He is at work in the lives of his people, and no evil can stop him. He offers himself to those not yet his people, hoping they may turn in his direction. We who are his are secure in his hands while we live among the effects of evil, for it is the chosen path of humankind and has contaminated the perfect world God created. But we have a relationship with the God of the universe in the context of this temporary world and an eternal perspective of our salvation. We are part of his plan. His eye is upon us, his love envelopes us, his grace covers us. We trust his providence in our lives and remain in the world as witnesses to his goodness. Everything really good can come only from the Father. (Gen 2:15–17; 2 Chr 7:14; Job 42:1–2; Pss 32:10, 33:11, 37:4, 16, 115:3, 135:6; Isa 43:10–14; Jer 17:11; Dan 4:35; Mic 6:8; Luke 19:41–44; John 1:1–5 with 10–12, 3:16–21 with 36, 10:28–30, 12:43; Rom 1:18–23; Phil 3:17–21; Jas 1:17–18; 2 Pet 3:9)

142. Decisions

TO MAKE GOOD DECISIONS as a Christian is a matter of wisdom. Floundering in indecision can waste a great deal of time and energy and keep us from important things God has for us in life. Resting in Christ and seeing the big picture of God's work in the world moves us ahead, giving us perspective in making decisions and confidence in his plan. Often, there is not one single person, object, or way that is his will for us but a range of choices bounded by love for him and those around us. One Christian may choose one thing, and another decide on something else in the same bounded area, and both be in the center of God's will. Other mature Christians may help us better understand what is best among these choices, but our primary guidance after praying for wisdom, comes from his word, a pure heart, and our desire to honor him. That is wisdom at work. (Ps 37:4 with 23; Prov 2:1–11, 3:5–6, 24:3; Rom 12:1–2; Eph 5:15–18; Phil 1:9–11; Col 1:9–12, 4:12; Jas 1:5–6, 3:13–18)

143. Self-Worth

IN AN INDIVIDUALIST SOCIETY, there is a high value on establishing one's identity and rank among others and a need for affirmation and approval for feelings of self-worth. Often spoiled by their inability to gain the approval of their parents while young, a person's identity becomes closely attached to their ability to achieve approval later in life. Their intent is self-survival. Many men are still trying to prove their masculinity, and many women their beauty. Yet others in our day are trying to establish their identity by abolishing moral standards they feel are judgmental of them. They want to be free to follow their inclinations and be recognized as those who do so without inhibition. Gender, racism, and freedom have all been weaponized against social and especially biblical boundaries. Everyone wants to stand out to others in a unique way. In Western culture today, it is taken to an extreme. Though a person's identity is important, for many, it is all they have, and it is central to their survival. In such a situation, survival will inevitably depend upon destroying the opposition. Anyone differing from their ideology or not adding value to their status is utterly wrong, even criminal, and must be silenced. Freedom becomes the tool to destroy the freedom of others.

It is very difficult for people in this condition to realize that, in relinquishing self-importance or status by surrendering to God, a new self is found. In the humble trust of God, one can be secure in their gender, race, and personhood, love people from any ethnic background, and feel genuine worth in their position in Christ, and, therefore, before God. If the creator of the universe has given you a right standing before himself, what can you or other people add to your status? If you are his, who can add to your worth? Gaining the whole world's approval does not compare. The acknowledgment of God is clearly the most important decision of a lifetime, and fear of the Lord truly the beginning of wisdom. (Pss 14:1a, 111:10, 139:1–12; Prov 3:5–7, 13–18, 4:5–9, 9:10; Isa 55:6–7, 66:2b; Mic 6:8; Matt 6:25–34,

7:13–14, 13:44–46, 16:24–26; Luke 9:23–25; John 12:24–26; Gal 2:20–21; Phil 3:7–19)

144. Good Fortune

MANY THINK THEIR SOLUTION to survival, their good fortune or success, is just around the next corner, that something good will happen to get them out of their difficulties and put them on Easy Street. Maybe the sweepstakes will be the answer. They keep looking expectantly for it in the mail, but it never comes. Others seem to get it. Maybe tomorrow. They want their barns to be filled with plenty. But what they need is not to be found here, where the treasures are only temporary if they are to be had at all. Waiting for our luck to change is a terribly discouraging place to be.

It's not about luck. Lasting treasures are found in God himself, in his lavish grace, unconditional love, and good providence. They are sure, and all one will ever need or want once they have them. While we are here, the difficulties in life go on. There will be suffering, heartbreak, and loss, but we can have confidence in his care and providence in carrying out his purposes for us in his plan. He knows and carries our burdens with us. We must remember his love for us, for while we were enemies and among the walking dead, he sent Jesus for us. Nowhere else is this grace to be found. Remember, he is still at work for our good when we least feel like it. Our future here is in his hands, but this life is only the beginning, the waiting room. We stand before the door to eternity that will soon open to him and the real life we were made for. Nothing is left to chance. (Pss 34:19, 37:23–24; Prov 8:17–21, 11:28; Matt 6:19–21 with 25–34, 13:44–46; Luke 12:15; John 1:14 with 16–18, 14:27 with 16:33; Rom 5:6–11, 8:31–32; Eph 1:3–8, 2:1–10; Phil 1:6, 2:13; Col 2:1–3; Heb 10:32–38; Jas 1:16–17; 1 Pet 1:3–9, 5:10–11; 2 Pet 1:3–11)

145. God's Care in Adversity

CHRISTIANS OFTEN MENTION EXTRAORDINARY things and events in life as God's providence, but even in the most mundane things, his providence is active, and the miracles of life are operational. The abilities to see, hear, feel, taste, smell, and reason are miraculous gifts from him that have become commonplace, normal, to us. But in the smallest use of these gifts, in the ordinary things of life, we can honor him. In his providence, he has blessed us, even in our adversities, whether we recognize it at the time or not. On our worst days, we can only think about bad events using the miracle of reasoning he gave to us. Our emotions may be flat, but the gifts of God are still there if we choose to use them; his blessings still surround us. We must use these gifts from God to encourage others in their adversity.

When God granted humankind free will to choose good or evil, sin spoiled a perfect creation and made life difficult. But God is not absent in the situation humanity has chosen to endure. He knew the outcome of freedom for men and women, but there was no other way to make love and loyalty possible. In our situation, he never ceases to care for us, and we must care for others—showing kindness and genuine concern for them in the throes and perplexities of life. In this way, we can reflect God's grace toward all his creatures.

Kindness would not mean anything in life if we did not also know adversity. There would be no compassion, empathy, or encouragement, no love or trust, no need to care. As it is, however, adversity is an opportunity to trust God or show concern for others. Empathy and compassion are great needs in our world. Just as he is concerned and caring for us, so we must be to others. We are to be lights on God in a dark world. Kindness in adversity is part of showing the way to him. (Pss 91:14–16, 95:6–7; Prov 3:27–28, 16:9, 21:13; Matt 5:13–16, 25:34–40; John 13:34–35; Rom 12:3 with 9–21; 1 Cor 13:1–13; Eph 2:10, 5:8–10; Phil 2:1–4, 4:4–9; Col 1:21–23; Jas 1:22–25; 1 Pet 1:3–7, 2:11–12, 5:7; 1 John 3:1–3, 18)

146. Judging Others

WE MAY THINK WE understand the motive of another person; some demonstrate theirs such that it cannot be missed. But we need to take care, or we will attribute the wrong intentions and desires to people, perhaps the ones we might have ourselves in such a situation. Jesus has told us that the measure we use to judge others will be used to measure us, that we do well to get the log out of our own eye to see clearly to help another with the speck in their eye.

Our individualist culture does not give us much training in empathy. We are more concerned about competing to come out on top, comparing ourselves and trying to look better than someone else, or practicing skills to assert our opinion. We must win. Our self-help training seminars are often about controlling our environment. We are not trained in humility and kindness, and there are few examples in our lives, so we don't have much to go on. But God's word gives us his way of grace with people, his understanding, compassion, and patience with us when we are at our worst. He empathizes with us in our weaknesses, temptations, and inclinations to serve ourselves. He knows we are but human, but loves us and has purposes he continues to work toward in us. We are projects, each of us, in the hands of the Potter, and he is not finished yet.

Empathy slows down self-assertion and our rush to judge another and gives us a chance to show consideration. Though we must be wise in our relationships with others, it is better to err on the side of compassion with caution than on the side of coldness and rejection. That is not to say it is good to be gullible in our day of shams, scams, and phishing. God makes it clear we should avoid evil people. Caution and reserve, as well as compassion, come with wisdom and will serve us well. (Pss 1:1–3, 103:6–18, 139:1–12; Prov 6:12–19, 11:15, 13:20, 22:24–27, 26:23–28; Matt 7:1–6 with 12, 10:16; 18:21–35, 25:31–46; Luke 6:37–38; 1 Cor 16:17–20; Eph 2:1–5, 4:32—5:1;

Phil 1:6, 2:1–4, 12–13; Col 1:13, 2:13—3:4; 1 Tim 1:12–17; Heb 4:14–16; Jas 1:19–20; 2 Pet 3:9; 1 John 3:1–3)

147. Men and Women in Marriage

THE TEMPERAMENT AND ROLE of the husband and those of the wife are indispensable to the success and balance of the family. Each is quite different from the other in disposition and preferences, not to mention personality, but the relationship is intended to be complementary, not competitive. It must maintain a balance central to God's purposes for each person and family. Together, spouses complete each other and bring wholeness to the family. Each must value the other's needs in terms of a trusting relationship, emotional security, physical intimacy, material provision, vocational demands, and child-rearing. It means taking on part of the other person's values and preferences and being more flexible with your own. In this sense, it is not unlike adapting to a new culture.

Every marriage is different, and we cannot compare ours to others. Each has differences in adversities and difficulties, in peaceful times of warmth, understanding, and encouragement, and in intensities of romance and reasoning. Men tend to be more monochronic and low-context in relations than women, and women tend to be more polychronic and high-context. A good marriage recognizes these general differences but differs from any other marriage.

Though neither person in a marriage is perfect, most of us far from it, God intends each marriage to honor him. The husband and wife must seek to understand each other but not give up their differences, usurp the other's role entirely, or ignore the other's viewpoint. God's plan is at stake, as well as their peace and that of the family, though they may not think so. There is no better example for children than parents who love each other and trust God in the ups and downs of life. (Gen 2:24; Ps 33:11; Prov 5:15–23, 12:4, 18:22, 31:10; Mark 10:6–9; 1 Cor 7:1–5; Eph 5:22–33; Phil 2:3; Heb 13:4; 1 Pet 3:1–7)

148. Forgiveness and Dirty Feet

GOD REMOVES OUR SINS entirely when we come to him in humility and faith. In his grace, he forgives us, having paid for our transgressions by his Son. However, he reminds us that we need that grace continuously. We will not go on in life sinless after we are in Christ. We must often confess our sins to him and seek his forgiveness. And though they will never be held against us again, we must never forget what it has taken to forgive us, to give us a standing of righteousness in his presence: the sacrifice of his perfect Son. His grace is not cheap, even though it is given to us freely.

So, though we are fully capable of falling into sin again after the grace of God has been lavished on us, we cannot escape his love, with which he continues to cover us, and he continues to work in us to bring us to maturity in Christ. Walking in this world damaged by sin leaves its residue on the best of us. Jesus would not leave Peter until he allowed him to wash his feet. And he will not leave us alone until we come to him to wash our feet again and renew our fellowship with him. We must accept that grace in every area of our lives, forgive ourselves, and, letting go of the past, realize every regret is covered by that grace.

Humility is central to the Christian in every aspect of life. Walking in the Spirit is practicing awareness of our thoughts and behavior and confessing our sins as soon as we realize them. Though our feet get dirty along the way, we are overwhelmed with gratefulness for his grace that always forgives and welcomes us. Interestingly, Jesus did not wait for the disciples to confess their proud attitudes about who was the greatest among them or their refusal to wash each other's feet upon entering the upper room. He washed their feet before they admitted their need. Then, they realized their pride. Humility grows with every application of his grace in our lives, as does our intention of loyalty. He wants our hearts, and he washes our feet to get them. (Pss 40:1–4, 103:10–14, 139:7–10; Mic 6:8; Luke 22:14–27; John

5:24, 11:25–26 with 13:6–10; Rom 3:21–24, 4:6–8, 5:6–11; Eph 1:7–8 with 2:6–7, 5:18; Phil 3:12–14; 1 Pet 5:5b–6; 1 John 1:5–10, 3:1–3)

149. Trusting God

TRUSTING GOD MAY SEEM like a terrible risk to those outside his grace. Unfortunately, some may have seen only the worst examples of people who call themselves Christians and are put off. What will God ask of them? What of all their progress toward the things they want in life? Will God take all of this away and make them cold legalists like those they have seen? Is God always angry? How unhappy will he force them to be? Their questions must be many.

But we who are inside, who know God's goodness, may also find it hard to trust him for certain things that come up in life. It seems an unreasonable weakness. After all, he gave us his Son out of his love for us, and we have seen his faithful providence in our lives; how can we still hesitate in our faith? It's a good question, but not so easily answered. Our culture and experience have shaped us to such an extent that we often do not know why we feel a certain way, have certain inclinations, or take a particular course of action. It is not easy to prevent these ongoing influences of individualism, social competition, and self-survival. We need to practice an awareness that includes our position in Christ, his unreserved grace, unconditional loving care, and determined providence in our lives. Jesus refers to this as abiding or remaining in him. In Christ, we are free of guilt and the power of the past over us. We will find rest if we trust him each day, in each event, with each relationship and responsibility in our lives. It is an ongoing effort to trust him in all things. But nothing is more essential for resting and abiding in Christ than "simple" and straightforward trust in God's hand on our lives. We are his, and he cares for us. If we don't trust God with our lives, nothing else really matters. (Pss 4:5–8, 20:7, 21:7, 34:8, 37:3–6, 91:1–16, 112:6–8a, 139:1–12; Prov 3:5–7, 11:28, 16:9, 28:26, 29:25; Isa 30:15, 43:1; Matt 11:28–30, 16:26; John 15:1–11, 17:20–23; Rom 8:28–32, 9:33; Phil 1:6, 4:6–7; Heb 4:9–11; 1 Pet 5:6–7)

150. Life and Death

THINGS WERE SO DIFFERENT on the other side when we were dead in our sin. Now we are alive. It is the difference between darkness and light. We were blind, and now we see. We are changed for all eternity. The old system of self-centered values our culture gave us is no longer needed for social and personal survival, and we must resist letting it interfere in our new lives. Achievement and recognition no longer provide our identity and worth. They are found in his love and the sacrifice he made so that we might stand before God in the righteousness of Christ. All that is needed is given to us in Jesus, the way, the truth, and the life, as we go about our lives seeking to honor him.

When Satan sows doubts about our new life, we must recall the enormous work of grace on our behalf. His ruses are not true, for all things are different when we allow God's way in our lives. We have freedom in Christ after being in a prison of self and culture. Sin and guilt are gone, the past truly over with his forgiveness. Satan's accusations fall flat. Inner peace takes their place. We must live in that new freedom. Legalism, syncretism, and mysticism must not come near, for they are shadows of that death we have left behind. But we must never forget what it was like to be dead, for the people around us still are, and we must reach out to them with understanding. (Gen 3:1–5; John 3:5–7 with 16–17 and 36, 8:12, 14:6; Rom 8:31–32, 16:20; 2 Cor 3:17, 4:4–6, 5:17, 9:8–9, 11:13–15; Eph 2:1–10; Col 1:13–14 with 2:13–15 and 3:1–4; 2 Thess 2:16–17; 1 Pet 2:21–25, 3:18, 5:8–9; 2 Pet 1:3–11; Rev 12:7–10)

151. Our Attention

WE ARE OFTEN TOO busy to notice, but everyday life has beauty and wonder. It is unfortunate that we miss so much. The things we see each day can become common; we look past them to what meets our needs, fits our goals, draws our interest, or distracts us. But all that God's hand has touched retains the trace of his wisdom, power, and care, even for what we might consider insignificant. Though tainted by humankind, the creation around us is extraordinary, and all of it was given to us to enjoy.

The most remarkable and crowning act of creation is man and woman. Though spoiled by sin, men and women are redeemed as they come to him, and the beauty of his image becomes more evident in them. The beauty of relationships realizes its potential as self is set aside for God's ways—friends, spouses, children, all gifts from God, become deeper blessings, more meaningful to our lives and God's purposes for us. All creation has been tainted to some degree by the free choice of humans, but there is still beauty when we allow his light to shine on it and on us. If we stop insisting on our way, our task, our goal, our opinion, we will see it. Take time to notice what God has done and what he has given us. It will restore your perspective, deepen your gratitude, and sharpen your thinking about life. He intended it to bless our lives along our way in this world. Decide not to miss it. (Gen 1:1–27; Pss 19:1–14, 118:19–27a, 148:1–14; Prov 30:21–31; Matt 6:25–33; 1 Cor 10:31; Eph 5:8–33; Col 1:16; 1 Tim 4:4; 1 Pet 3:1–7)

152. Another Day, Another Choice

ANOTHER DAY IS NOT just another day. Each is new and bathed in peace and contentment, preoccupied with worry, or consumed with selfish anger and resentment by our choice. In poverty or plenty, in pain or good health, in stressful or peaceful relationships, we make this choice. This world will have physical and emotional tensions and strains for us, but we choose our attitude. It does not mean there will never be dark days. It means we do not have to walk in that valley alone. God's grace is always fresh if we will notice. His promises are full of hope. His word is truth and encouragement in dark times. While the world carves its idols to worship, God is at work, and nothing can change his purposes. His attention is turned toward us. We have another day, a renewed opportunity to love and serve. Clean and forgiven, we start it in the shelter of his lovingkindness, under the shadow of his strength, and there, we can remain through its ups and downs if we choose.

We carry the cross, but he strengthens us to do so. We work for him in the world, but we also rest in him. We are his children and can bask in the care and concern of our loving Father each and every day. When we trust him, there remains little room for anger, resentment, envy, anxiety, or selfish ambition in our hearts. Beyond the needs of our souls, trusting him adds wellbeing to every other area of our lives. We will be ready for each new challenge to our peace, our new wineskin full of the new wine of trust. All of this is a choice we make.

Though we have to keep reminding ourselves of it, there is no fear in love when we trust God. We cannot bring about any good for anyone, especially ourselves, with petty, self-centered attitudes bred by fear for our survival, anxious about the next event, the next moment. When we start the day with a "What's in it for me?" attitude, we forfeit peace with God. It is wisdom to let go of selfish emotions and place ourselves in his hands. There, we find "rest for our souls" for each new day. (Pss 1:1–3, 5:3, 23:1–6, 33:11,

34:4 with 17–19, 37:23–24 with 28, 40:3, 42:5, 91:1, 14–16, 115:1–8; Prov 3:5–8, 13–18, 17:24; Isa 40:28–31, 41:10; Matt 11:29; John 14:6; 2 Cor 5:17; Eph 4:22–24; Phil 2:3–4; Jas 1:19–20, 3:13–18; 1 John 4:13–21)

153. Rare and Fleeting Moments

WHAT IS RARE, SUCH as gold or diamonds, is costly and treasured. We value owning these rare commodities. What is extraordinary but fleeting, like a sunset or rainbow, is considered beautiful, and we long to see it again. The moments of our lives are both rare and fleeting. They are rare in that only those alive to them notice them. Each has never come before, nor will it come again. They are brief, like the smoke of an extinguished candle, soon over and gone but, for those who are aware, leaving the scent of God's presence in the air. Each is a gift that cannot be earned, an undeserved blessing of God for we who know him, transient but followed by the enduring shadow of his providence. But for those who do not trust God, each moment is filled with inevitable cultural demands for survival, of living only for oneself. The world of the individualist carries the danger of this curse as we are trained to look out for the self and accomplish its survival by our own efforts, by whatever means possible.

Better the man or woman who has nothing of the world's praise or wealth but sees each moment as a blessing of God than the one who has everything but is desperate for their survival, fears the loss of their achievements, or dreads facing another day. The poor in spirit "receive the kingdom of God"; the meek "inherit the earth"; the pure in heart "will see God." Yet others wake up each day with worry and anxiety. They wonder how they will get through another day. Even the basic needs of life are unpredictable. They feel they have no one to help them manage the pain and difficulties along the way.

But there is one who will help them. God has already provided for their deepest needs if they will but notice. He has secured their forgiveness, opened the way to himself, and set aside the powers of darkness for them. When they turn to him, he will begin to make them over. He will turn their suffering into gratefulness, their hollow feelings into contentment. The requirement for it all is in "the way, the truth, and the life" found in Christ.

In him, we can trust in God's grace, providence, and purposes. There, we will find grace, hope, and freedom for each rare and fleeting moment. (Pss 34:4–8, 37:3–6, 16–17, 63:1–8, 90:12 with 14 and 17, 91:1–2; Prov 3:5–7, 13:7, 14:12, 15:16–17, 16:19, 28:6; Eccl 5:10–15; Matt 5:3–10, 6:19–21, 25–34; Rom 8:31–32; Phil 4:4–7; Jas 4:13–17; 1 Pet 5:6–7)

154. Always Busy Doing Something

OUR WESTERN SOCIETY WORSHIPS doing. We often ask our neighbors how it's going, and they typically comment about how busy they are. It is so common in our communities we don't usually notice the values behind the comments. It has become part of a thoughtless greeting, revealing the mindset of a virtue and a curse. If you had a good day, it is usually because you accomplished everything on your list. People around you will notice how positive you are. You go to bed feeling good about yourself. If you did not get much done, the people around you will know it by your nagging comments about it, and your mind will be cluttered with negative self-talk. Your self-esteem takes a hit because life has become all about doing, and you have not done enough.

God has purposed that we all do an honest day's work, not that we stress about our feelings of achievement. God made the vocation for man, not man for the vocation. We must see other things as necessary and important as well, often more important. He intended that we also have times of rest and quietness, times to reflect on life and think about him, times to help and encourage the needy, times with family and friends, and, at all times, to be grateful. From these kinds of deeds to honor God and help, encourage, and enjoy others, we can emerge feeling calm about our lives and go to bed with a peaceful heart even if our list of things to do is not finished. We must not let our culture have the upper hand with its performance expectations; the list may not be as long as we think. We live by a higher standard. (Ps 1:1–3; Prov 17:1; Matt 6:25–34, 7:24–27, 11:28–30; Luke 10:38–42, 12:15–21; Eph 2:10; 1 Thess 4:11; 2 Thess 3:6–13; 1 Tim 2:1–4; 2 Tim 3:16–17; Titus 3:14)

155. Individualism and Success

THE WORLD OF THE individualist is full of self-interest, for that is what Western culture demands for survival. It is the root of such ideas as "conquering the West," "the survival of the fittest," and "first come, first served." The egalitarian sense that we all have an equal chance in our pursuit of happiness and the value of achievement accompanying Western culture's competitiveness are its symptoms. Success is the goal of life that our society expects. Failure to achieve it is shameful by the same cultural frame of reference. That for which achievement cannot be quantified is avoided for objectives that can be completed, accumulated, and counted. There are consequences in this force of culture for the Christian. It blinds us to much that God has not given us in objective data. Growth in grace, love, humility, and trusting God can be difficult to measure and maintain. They are qualitative, while we are programmed to prefer quantitative elements and avoid uncertainty and ambiguity.

Western culture also blinds us to the emotional aspects of the needs of others, making empathy foreign to our natural way of going about life. We can even become unable to love and adore God himself, wonder at his mystery and greatness, or understand the measure of his grace poured out on us. Every human culture has its traps. This one is ours. We Christians who are products of Western culture must realize that its individualism need not hold us in the grip of its cold talons, blackmailing us at every turn. As long as they last, we must use our Western freedoms to be salt and light in the broken world. But our loyalty belongs to God, and our love for one another comes before our allegiance to the human ideals of our culture. (Prov 3:27–28; Luke 18:9–14; John 13:34–35; Rom 11:33–36, 12:9–21; Eph 1:3–10; Phil 1:9–11, 27, 2:1–4; Jas 3:13–14; 1 Pet 5:6–9; 1 John 2:15–17, 3:16–24)

156. Necessary Avoidance

AVOIDING THE LEGALISTS, WHO desire influence, control, and position, or those who syncretize cultural values with biblical teaching for popularity, or yet those who seek success in the world's eyes to get God's attention can be difficult if we are not aware of our own self-seeking. They seek to achieve God's approval by their works and discard his grace. They seek their own glory. But we must turn away. Their influence must not be allowed to touch the soul that is free in Christ and taint the lives of those who want to live for him, even if they are influential in the church. They do not have what the mature in Christ need and cannot help the faith of the weak. They trample the very truths that lead to life, leaving death in their wake for anyone who would be overtaken. Yes, they must be avoided.

In reaction to legalism, however, we must not go to the opposite extreme by saying that the Christian life is all from God; he gives it to us and does it for us, so "let go and let God." No, he has washed us by his grace, lavished it on us so that we might live for him in response to it. Now that we know his grace, we are "created in Christ Jesus to do good works," to glorify him with our lives, and "walk worthy of the Gospel." He gave us his word that we might be "thoroughly equipped for every good work." And he has given us everything we need for it.

These tendencies toward legalism, self-seeking, and syncretism are not of God. We must learn from teachers who are pure in heart, who are loyal to God, and who let him speak for himself. In God's word, we will find both truth and grace; he will give us what is good and perfect. In Christ, we have freedom. We must not allow these uses of Christianity to bind us in their chains. (Ps 1:1–3; Prov 16:25, 22:24; Matt 7:15–23, 23:1–7 with 12–13; John 1:17, 8:31–36; Acts 20:28–31; Rom 12:1–2, 16:17; Gal 2:14, 21, 5:1–6 with 13; Eph 2:8–10, 4:1; Phil 1:15–17, 27; Col 1:10–12; 2 Tim 3:16–17; Titus 1:15–16; Jas 1:17, 3:13–18; 2 Pet 1:3–11, 2:2; 1 John 4:1–3)

157. Simple Faith

IT HAS ALWAYS BEEN God's way to use the simple to confound the wise, the weak to overcome the strong, those people and things most unlikely to bring about his purposes in the world. Those humble and without public talent will outdo the self-assertive and over-confident when God is allowed his way, but it may never be known in this life. It is the irony of God to turn human expectations around and always do things in a way that demands faith. The Jews would never have expected the Messiah of Israel, the King of the Jews, to be born in an animal stall, bring a kingdom of spirit and truth without violence, and die a criminal's death. Their theology and pride said differently; they twisted the prophecies and filtered out the truth.

There was no notoriety or social rewards for becoming a follower of the sort of teacher Jesus was. Only those with eyes of faith would know he was the King. God still seeks the humble in our day. Simple faith, not stardom, is the sign of his people. The New Testament vibrates with the news that he is coming again, this time through the front door. The proud and powerful will be overwhelmed. Those of simple but enduring faith will be overjoyed.

As our society becomes more emotionally fragile, more neurotic, and out of control, those with eyes to see and ears to hear will wait patiently for the Creator-God of the universe to act. Those Jesus talks about in the beatitudes of Matthew chapter 5 await the fulfillment of the promises. They know the way, the truth, and the life, though the world tries to tell them otherwise. Simple but courageous faith overcomes the world's ways. The humble will inherit the earth and own the kingdom. (2 Chr 7:14; Pss 37:1–11, 40:3; Prov 16:18–19; Isa 52:13—53:12; Matt 5:1–10, 11:25–26, 18:1–4; Luke 1:51–52, 18:9–14; John 14:6; 1 Cor 1:20–31, 2:6–10 with 16; 2 Pet 3:1–9; 1 John 4:4–6, 5:1–5; Rev 19:11–16)

158. God Calls People to Himself

GOD CALLS ALL PEOPLE to himself; he is not willing that anyone should perish. He loves his creation. No human doctrine can undo his longing that all people come to know him. Some hear and follow him, believing what he says of himself. By his grace, they awake and begin to walk in the light at his side. Others have not yet heard or have turned away. They have a choice to accept or reject his call, but God earnestly desires that they open their eyes to the truth. They who refuse him walk in darkness by choice. They allow their minds to be blinded by the enemy; their lives are full of distractions and the noise of the world. Their love is for other things; they have chosen the broad road.

    Perhaps worse than rejecting God outright is the case of those who hear and are not satisfied with the message of God. They put words in his mouth and worship a God of their own making, teaching others to do the same. They act out of fear and seek his approval through ritual behavior, obeying sterile rules like a modern-day oral Torah. Others see Christianity as an opportunity to finally be known for "success," to be accepted, even respected, and eventually be a leader with prestige, able to influence or control others. But God speaks of grace, forgiveness, humility, and freedom, to all of which they are blind. He seeks trust in the heart born of faith. We must listen and let him speak for himself—let God be God. Only those who do can truly know him. They are among those who have followed and are called sons and daughters of God. They are elected to an eternity with him. (Matt 7:13–14, 15–27, 19:16–24; Luke 8:4–15; John 3:16–17, 8:12, 9:26, 14:6 with 21–24, 17:3; 2 Cor 4:4–6; Eph 5:14; 1 Tim 2:1–6; 2 Tim 1:8–10, 4:1–4; Titus 2:11; Jas 1:22–25; 2 Pet 3:9, 15)

159. Worn Out Words

MANY ESSENTIAL TRUTHS OF the Bible become worn out with abuse and misuse until they are clichés that get ignored. Eventually, many lives of those using those words no longer give credibility to their truth. So, the world looks the other way. They can't understand: "How can these things be true and untrue at the same time? God is love? God is good? Prayer works? We must be born again?" "There is so much suffering in the world! Surely a God of love, goodness, power, and justice would not allow it."

Nonetheless, these words are true no matter how they come to be seen by the world. Suffering in God's perfect world was the choice of a man and woman, a decision to doubt God's words and reject his way. They are blind, those who blame God for the destruction and suffering humans have wrought in the world by their selfishness, for whom these words have become an offensive noise. Those who know them to be accurate and whose lives reveal it know him. They may indeed suffer in making these truths known in a world of rejection. But the old accounts vibrate with reality for those with ears to hear. They are worth any risk to follow. To know the truth brings freedom and marks us as sons and daughters of God. (Gen 3:6–7; Pss 34:8, 86:5; Prov 19:3; Matt 19:16–24; John 1:12, 3:7 and 16, 8:31–32; Rom 3:21–24; 2 Cor 4:4; Eph 2:8–10; 1 Tim 1:15–17; Jas 1:16–18; 1 Pet 2:23–25, 4:12–19 with 5:10–11; 1 John 1:9, 4:7–8)

160. Right Thinking

GOD CREATED US WITH the amazing ability to reason. We can think about ourselves, others, the creation, and God himself. We can plan our day and put our lives on a course. But we often let our thinking run wild, letting it rest on the most unhelpful notions, useless things, deranged values accompanied by the most hopeless feelings, and perhaps, on bad experiences or their residue in our hearts. These negative and hurtful thoughts, being controlled by regrets, condemning ourselves, others, or even God, are an abuse of God's gift. His purpose was that our minds would be filled with positive thoughts full of confidence in the Creator's love and providence, his control of the universe, his grace each day in our lives. But a good deal of that is up to us. We must choose to allow his word to "transform and renew our minds" and "forgetting what is behind," move ahead in his grace with our new identity in Christ.

He gave us our minds so we might be constructive and helpful, insightful of his ways, and encouraging to others. Evil is never more than a thought away, so we must protect the boundaries God has given us for our minds. We must intentionally care for our thoughts, renew our minds, and set them on things above. Reason will go its own way if we do not take care. It is a treasure that can be abused and misused by simply letting it have its way. Guard your heart. (Job 38:36; Prov 4:20–27; Isa 26:3–4; Rom 8:5–8, 12:1–3; 2 Cor 4:4, 10:5; Eph 4:20–24; Phil 3:12–16, 4:6–8; Col 3:1–4; 1 Pet 1:13–21; 2 Pet 1:3–9)

161. Religion

RELIGIOUS PEOPLE ARE NOT necessarily closer to God than irreligious. They can often be further away. Knowing God is not about religion; it is about a relationship. It is revealed (incarnated) by natural, everyday behavior, not ritual behavior. We have its example in Jesus, and though we may do many things religious people do, we who know God often do them for different reasons. What we do must be done in spirit and in truth—with a pure heart. It is what God wanted of his people in the Old Testament who were under the law. He did not want the religion of their empty obedience; he wanted their hearts. Religion can actually be a dangerous and worse enemy than willful sin because it cloaks itself in symbols of spirituality that may be hiding hypocrisy or deceiving the innocent. Legalism brings death. The body is engaged, but not the heart.

This gap between God and religion can be sensed by nonbelievers. We must set them straight if they are ever to listen to the gospel of God's love. It is not easy. We have made quite a mess of things, sometimes with the best intentions. Religions around the world are full of well-meaning people looking for a way to resolve the problems of suffering, the meaning of life, and life after death. But they look in the wrong direction. If Christianity is made into a legalistic religion—if I do this for God, he must do that for me—it is among them, another human effort to achieve salvation and approval. It may seem right, but sincerity alone is not an indicator of truth. The truth is that we are all lost without the grace of God in our lives. Both grace and truth came through Jesus Christ, and we will have to start there to truly know God.

A true follower of Christ desires to trust him. This trust leads to loyalty that seeks to follow his teachings because of who he is, not to achieve acceptance or approval by what they can do. He forgives us through Christ and enters into us and, putting self aside, we into him. Human though we are, we remain in an unbreakable relationship with the God of creation and re-creation. However, we may not look religious to others. Our relationship with God is a matter of the heart. Though we regret our weaknesses, he makes us clean by his grace. He accomplishes his plan through us, as imperfect as we are, and if we allow him, for we stand before him in the perfection of Christ. (Ps 91:14–16; Prov 16:25, 21:3; Jer 9:23–24; Hos 6:6; Mic 6:8; Matt 5:8, 6:1–8, 8:5–13; 15:8–9, 18:1–6; John 3:1–21, 36, 4:23–24, 8:32, 36, 10:28–30, 13:8–10, 14:21–24, 15:1–11; Rom 3:21–24, 7:14–25; 2 Cor 5:17, 12:7–10; Titus 1:15; Jas 1:26–27; 1 John 1:8–10)

162. Medicine for the Soul

AMONG THE THINGS GOD gave us in creation is humor. We can enjoy seeing our own silliness, the backward way we seek to move forward, funny, unexpected results, and sometimes, just plain nonsense. It is part of enjoying all he is and has given us. Kindness also brings a smile and lightens another's load. We can give others the gifts of kindness and laughter as medicine for the soul. They can bring healing and relieve the tensions that are naturally a part of our lives in a broken world. But we enjoy life too little and take many everyday events too seriously. Encumbered with worry and anxiety for ourselves, we turn inward. We must let go of the petty and insignificant cares in this life and enjoy our freedom in Christ, trusting him for what we cannot change. Kindness is always needed, and he did not create laughter for nothing. (Pss 95:1–7, 100:1–5; Prov 3:3–4, 12:18, 25, 15:13, 15, 16:24, 17:22, 19:22; John 15:11; Gal 5:1; Col 3:12–17; 1 Thess 5:15–18; 1 Pet 1:3–9)

163. Knowing God's Will Is Not Complicated

A GREAT DEAL OF mystery has been added to knowing God's will for our lives. But it was not intended by God to be a difficult spiritual achievement. There have been attempts to straighten us out on the matter and put it in the simplest of terms: "Do what you know and trust him for what you don't know," "Love God and do what you want," "Make a list of the things you don't want to do and then, don't do them." But that seems too simple to us. We have questions, and life is not so black and white. There appears to be an endless number of shades of gray. And we always feel our situation is different, that life is more complicated for us than other Christians recognize and appreciate. That may be true, but the complexity we add to "finding" God's will for us does not come from the Bible or make us more spiritual. God is more aware of our situation than we are and cares much more than we realize. He wants us to know him and his ways. He is not hiding them. But his plan for us is different from what we think, and ours tends to get in the way.

Our cultural values and self-centered "needs," mixed with God's word, cloud our understanding and keep us from trusting him entirely. God's word makes it more straightforward than we expect and maybe more than we want. We hope for special signs from God, but they are hardly ever necessary, and we are not encouraged to seek them. What we need to know about his will is already before us. Sometimes, the difficulty is that we think we have to be a Christian superhero, a celebrity for Christ. But that is not at all the goal. Or, we are looking for happiness in the wrong places and do not realize it is, first of all, to humble ourselves and trust him—to place ourselves squarely in his hands.

Our culture tells us it is up to us to make something of ourselves, to achieve an identity and a reputation. But to walk in God's will for our lives will take that simple trust and humble heart so unconventional, so countercultural in our context, so contrary to our desires for personal achievement and its recognition. It is to be faithful to what we know of him, loyal to his purposes, trusting his providence, and loving those he has put in our lives. We will still be human and aware of our weaknesses, but his grace is sufficient and helps us move ahead. Personal happiness is a result, not a pursuit. (Pss 22:3–5, 25:8–10, 33:11 with 20–22, 33:16–19 with 20:7, 37:3–7a; Prov 3:5–10; Mic 6:8; Mal 3:10; Matt 6:19–21 with 33, 16:1–4, 19:29–30; John 15:1–8; Rom 12:1–2; 1 Cor 10:26–31; 2 Cor 12:7–10; Phil 1:9–11, 3:12—4:1; Jas 1:17)

164. Choosing Good

EVIL AND THE SUFFERING it brings were neither created nor desired by God for his creation. But that he gave us the freedom to choose good or evil—to trust him or not—is actually a gift of the Father of heavenly lights. His gifts, always good, can always be abused. Unless we could equally choose evil, there would be no choice of good. The good at stake in Eden and constantly at risk today is choosing to trust God over selfish ambition, inclinations, and indulgence—our own pursuit of happiness. That choice is now affected by the pain and suffering from all that Adam and Eve set in motion.

The belief that God cursed mankind that day so they could only choose evil and never good puts a grave motive in God's intentions. Though he told them they would know both good and evil, most humans continue to choose darkness instead of light, to trust their own way instead of God's, but we must not let our theology lead us astray. There is no such thing as the *total* depravity of those created in God's image. Though at times there has been so much evil on earth that it seems so, and not even one person is perfect, humankind can and does choose good or evil each day. People choose loyalty to God or to self as the theme and purpose of their existence. The fact that we are inclined more to evil than to good is not the result of a curse from God; it is the result of freedom combined with selfishness—an unrelenting pursuit of personal achievement and gratification.

The decision of our parents in Eden changed the world in which we live. They opened the door to sickness, suffering, and death for all. The decision to trust God may be harder today than it was for them in their perfect world. It is a courageous decision. It is more difficult to trust him and lean into his grace in a broken world where suffering abounds, and it is countercultural to do so. He does not remove us from that world when we trust him. He wants us there as light in the darkness. But the benefits and blessings of belonging to God while in it surround the pure in heart, while the rejection of God eventually brings misery to those in its way. There were times in the Old Testament when God found his people's rejection of him overwhelming and dealt severely with them. Those times are lessons for us today. For a day is ahead when he will come with that severity again—when he will judge humankind for its choice between self or Savior, and many will be put on his left.

The fulfillment of our senses to enjoy the pleasures God intended is quickly turned to selfish gain at the expense of all those around us unless we choose otherwise. Its result is always suffering and pain in the end. It is also true that when people who say they know God act selfishly, they too will know pain, but the grace of God is abundant for those of faith, however weak it may be. Though he may use the pain as a reminder that we are straying from his way, his patience does not tire. The curse is about the inevitable results of choosing against God in the world. We live for him in that broken world. But it will not always be so. (Gen 3:1–24; Josh 24:14–15; Prov 16:25; Matt 7:13–14, 19:16–24, 23:37–39; John 3:19–21, 36, 16:33 with 17:13–19; Eph 2:8–10; 1 Thess 5:9–11, 21–22; 1 Tim 4:4 with 1 Cor 10:23–24 and 31–33; 2 Tim 3:16–17; Heb 3:12–15 with 10:6 and 11; Jas 1:13–18; Rev 22:1–6)

165. Pretending to Be Wise

THE BOOK OF PROVERBS talks about the fool, the simple, and the lazy. When people pretend to be something or someone they are not, even the most intellectual of them fit the category of the fool. Regrettably, our culture encourages competition rather than wisdom. People feel they must know more, achieve more than others, or at least look like it to feel a sense of worth and well-being. They have never faced who they really are or their need for God's grace. His way is before them, but they seek their own, and they find it. It never ends well for them.

God, in his careful providence, made each of us as we are. He shaped us in the womb, and then, through our experiences in life, severe as some of them have been, he gave and continues to give us opportunities to trust him. But we are slow to do so, and many of us are hurt and damaged along the way. However, he welcomes us as we are when we turn to him. He forgives our sin but does not erase our experiences. He uses them to shape us into the kind of person he wants to use for his purposes. The choice is before each of us to see ourselves as his workmanship, given to him and his purposes, or try to be someone else of our own making.

He gave us each a mind to think and reason, to choose good over evil, wisdom over foolishness. We can use our minds to defend what we have made of ourselves or choose wisdom and humble ourselves before the Creator-God of the universe. There is a way that seems right to a man, but the end of it is death. We must not be like the fool, the simple, or the lazy. We must choose God's way with discernment and trust his work for us and in us. It is not the way of the world, and we will look like fools and weaklings to those outside of Christ, but we will know him, who is the wisdom and power of God. (Pss 14:1a, 52:7 with 53:1, 139:14–16; Prov 1:7, 12:16 with 14:8–12, 15 and 16:2, 9, 17:24, 19:3, 15, 20:27, 26:12, 28:26; Eccl 10:18; Luke 12:13–21, 16:19–31; Rom 1:21–22, 12:3; 1 Cor 1:23–29; Gal 6:3–5; Eph 2:10; Phil 2:12–13)

166. Desires and Needs

EVERYONE HAS NATURAL NEEDS. Hunger and thirst are natural, and we turn to nourishment. An itch is unavoidable, and we find a way to scratch it. Tiredness from a day's work calls for rest. Income from honest work is necessary for life. We need a home, clothing, and tools for our work. The desire to be accepted and loved is also natural. God intends and provides for these needs to be fulfilled in our lives as we trust him. But we may seek to fulfill many of our needs selfishly without loving others, without loving God. That does not mean the desire or need is bad, but we can choose selfish and disastrous ways to satisfy legitimate needs. We can act out of self-interested motives that exclude the needs and desires of others. This does not mean we should not fulfill our natural needs as God intended and fully enjoy what he has given us with gratitude. But we must not make bad from selfish motives what he has created and called good. What he calls good is good indeed. (Gen 1:31; Pss 40:4, 103:1–5; Prov 11:28; Jer 9:23–24; Matt 6:25–34; Rom 14:16–18; 1 Cor 10:23–24; Phil 2:1–4; 1 Thess 3:11–12; 2 Thess 3:6–10; 1 Tim 4:4; 2 Tim 2:1–6; Titus 1:15, 3:14; Jas 1:16–18; 1 Pet 2:1–3)

167. Church Membership

ONE OF THE MORE confusing aspects of the church is the institution of membership. To be a corporation of members and officers in good standing, staying ahead of a budget, and having multiple paid staff are all part of the institution. It might not be too complex if it stopped there, but then our cultural values come in the door, and many unwittingly give them the upper hand. Their expectations cause competition for the budget, give people levels of status in their positions, cause a need to grow in numbers to support it, encourage professionalism, and attract like-minded people while judging and repelling those who are different. Introverts are often seen as those who dampen the excitement, and wealthy members are often given a special voice in decisions. Non-members who attend may be treated as second class.

The situation can create a constant need for resources and take a great deal of time and effort to manage. The setting can be an opportunity for the insecure to find recognition from others as they perform and compete for reputation and social survival, leaning on cultural values instead of their position in Christ. Now, what have we? Of what are these people members? Have we become confused between cultural absolutes and biblical absolutes? Would Jesus fit in?

A great deal of care must be taken to keep the church simple and focused on its biblical teaching and missional task in the world. Humility, harmony, love, and unity are to be its impressions on the world looking on. It will never be perfect as long as the members are people, but we overuse this as an excuse. When the church does not have a reputation for these essentials of the faith, it is not the church God intended and is no longer salt and light in the world. (Pss 51:6, 63:1–8; 84:1–12; Prov 22:4; Mic 6:8; Matt 5:13–16, 7:1–6, 18:1–5; John 4:23–24; Rom 12:3–21, 14:1–8 with 13 and 16–22; 1 Cor 1:10–17; Phil 2:1–4; Col 3:12–17; 1 Pet 1:13–23, 3:8–13)

168. Hanging On

SOME PEOPLE NEED TO talk about some work they have done or accomplishments they feel have succeeded for the rest of their lives. They find ways to mention the kind of car they drive, the neighborhood they live in, or their rank in their profession. In these numbing, monotonous references lies the need for recognition and affirmation, feelings of self-worth and security, and a position of social status that people will respect. There is a deep fear in the hearts of individualists that they might not be recognized for some achievement or not be known for some experience they have had, that their social rank might not be acknowledged. It can drive them to desperation. The thought that others may not know their worth terrifies them.

    God's way is different. When he fulfills a spiritual need or helps us accomplish something for him, he does it for that time in our lives. It is not meant to be latched onto as our achievement for us to talk about for decades or make the center of our feelings of self-worth for the rest of our lives. He himself is to be that center. If he helps us, and we accomplish a task he sets before us, it is done with the doing, and we must be grateful and look to the next thing to be done. We must realize with humility that he makes these things possible, giving us the resources and the grace to serve him. He does not use people to give them a reputation; he uses them to accomplish his purposes in history. Who of us is worthy of proclaiming what we have attained for God? There is no social recognition to be gained, no celebrity status to achieve and cherish in the service of the King. We are his servants and unworthy of his grace. It is a privilege that he should use us at all. Our rewards are yet ahead when we are in his presence day without end. (Ps 37:5–7a; Prov 15:33, 16:18, 18:12, 27:2; Matt 6:1–4; Luke 17:7–10; John 5:44, 7:18; Phil 2:12–13, 3:12–14; 1 Pet 5:6)

169. A Sign from God

SOME CHRISTIANS MAY WANT a sign from God to know his leading, to prove that their inclination is really from him, that he is answering a prayer or giving direction for a decision, to gain his approval or prove they are really his. But it is really very rare that he would provide such a sign. The vast majority of Christians throughout history have never received such special revelation of his will. His way since the beginning has been, instead, that those who follow him should do so with eyes of faith. We are not to put God to the test, trying to make him prove that he is telling us the truth. He prefers to provide us with wisdom from his word and let us make the decisions, trusting him within the promises and boundaries he gives us.

What God does in one person's life is not the pattern he promises to follow for the next person. His part for each one in his purposes is different. The description of Gideon's weak faith in God's promises is not an example to follow. It is an account of God's unending patience with one man, not a prescription for *our* lives. He should not have to endure it again from us who know him through Christ and have his word. So, once again, faithfulness to him is more about being something than doing something. Remembering that his providence is at work. lean into wisdom and faithfulness instead of looking for signs. (Judg 6:16–22 with 36–40; Job 28:20 with 23 and 28; Ps 138:8; Prov 1:7, 2:1–6, 3:3–4, 4:5–9, 9:10; Matt 4:5–7, 6:25–34; Luke 11:29–30; John 21:17–22; Rom 8:31–32; Phil 1:6 with 2:12–13; 1 Thess 5:24; Heb 11:1–3 with 6)

170. Endangered Species

GOD CREATED HUMANS AND animals in different categories as he desired. Humans are far above animals in reasoning, conscience, self-awareness, and knowledge of their creator and his purposes and boundaries. Why would some people want to give up their humanity? They forget their creator and, little by little, give up the gifts he gives and his intentions for them. They strain to harden their conscience. In their efforts to prove that their self-assertive hedonism is the best motive in life, they become inferior to the animals who have the dignity of remaining within the purposes and boundaries God set for them. Each generation is further removed from God than their parents, the family disintegrates, and society crumbles in its pursuit of pleasure, power, and wealth.

Having been denied God's purpose and meaning for life by society, children are confused, alone, and live in emptiness, aimlessly seeking to satisfy their urges and anger or find ways to forget them. Emotionally needy and empty, the society becomes unstable. Deprived of the meaning and value of life, existence becomes cruel to people, and in their rage, they share their agony by killing others without cause. Society blames drugs, gangs, alcohol, and guns, but these have always been with us. They are symptoms and not causes. It is people and their society that have changed. Something inside them is gone. They act without reason or consideration and have none to pass on to their children. They are angry with the life society gives them and want to die, but not to die alone.

After forcibly taking God out of the equation, society expects people to act as if the void was not there. They call it the survival of the fittest, but they have become the least fit for survival. Animals do not have an organized society with social rules or knowledge of God; they cannot reason. However, if humans do not interfere unnaturally with them, they continue to follow the ways God gave them. Humans want to do away with God's ways, but without them, their species is endangered. It has no virtue ruling its institutions. It

170. ENDANGERED SPECIES

cannot flourish; its very survival is threatened. Social "experts" have become enemies of the gospel of God's grace, and society is paying the price.

But all is not lost. In every age, God always has a remnant of followers who are loyal to him. His purposes and promises remain for these faithful ones and will be carried out to their great benefit. They have peace and are neither surprised nor anxious at the world's struggles for survival. Their concern is that more people would turn to God—see the answer to their survival in his grace, receive his salvation, and know the meaning of life and freedom in Christ as he intended. We are among them, and though the world may not know us, we are not unknown or forgotten by God. He is moving in the world to fulfill his purposes, unstoppable, far-reaching, forgetting not a detail, onward to the consummation of all things. And we are part of that movement. In its accomplishment, he will guard those who love him, even the least of us, from the fury of his coming judgment. For come he will. He waits only for more people to turn to him and know his grace. (1 Kgs 19:14 and 18; Pss 1:1–6, 14:1a, 33:11, 115:3; Prov 1:7, 32, 14:8, 12, 15:2, 17:24; John 1:1–18 with 3:16–21, 36; Rom 1:18–25; 2 Cor 4:4, 11:4–15; Eph 4:18, 5:5–10; Phil 3:17–21; Col 3:1–6; 1 Thess 5:1–11, especially 9; 2 Pet 3:1–15a)

171. Conscience Overloaded

THE CONSCIENCE OF MANY Christians is on overload. Many are weighed down by the rules of legalistic movements in Christianity as those under the oral Torah of the Pharisees in Jesus' day. Legalism can build a mound of false guilt so high it becomes a barrier to knowing God's actual purposes, a prison when he intends us to live in the freedom he has given us in Christ. We must not add our human preferences or cultural values to his word nor allow others to tie our conscience down with theirs. God seeks to turn us into a certain kind of people, not give us a list of things to check off—things to do and others that are forbidden to earn his approval. He wants a relationship with us that includes our complete forgiveness, trust in his providence, unwavering loyalty, and life within the boundaries of the wisdom of his word.

Of course, there are things we should not do, behaviors that break the laws of love and selflessness, and attitudes we should not have that disturb our loyalty to our Savior, but it's more about being than doing. Becoming the kind of person God has in mind will result in behavior that honors him, though it will not meet many of legalism's expectations. We have freedom in Christ shaped by humility and bounded by love and gratefulness. It comes from a changing heart and a mind being transformed as we grow in our love of and loyalty to Christ. Don't expect the process to be easy or instant; old habits and coping mechanisms from childhood are particularly stubborn, but expect progress that makes a difference if you are serious. We are products of our culture, experiences, and the fixes we have applied to our childhood insecurities that continue to affect us as adults. Finding out this "why" behind what we think and feel and do today is valuable for handing it over to God.

There is no guilt or shame when his grace has washed us, but he has work to accomplish in us, and our cooperation is essential. His grace and concern for us, his patience and desire for our trust, will give us every opportunity to fill our new wineskin with the new wine of a transformed view of ourselves, others, the world, and all God has put in it for us. His word must become the lens through which we see, his grace the foundation of our freedom in Christ, and his love the motive for the activities of our lives. (Pss 40:6–8, 51:6 with 16–17; Mic 6:8; Matt 12:7; John 8:32, 36; Rom 14:13–23; 1 Cor 10:23—11:1; 2 Cor 3:17–18, 6:12 with 19–20; Gal 5:1 with 13–14; Phil 1:6; Col 2:6–10 with 16–23; 1 Thess 5:23–24; Titus 1:15; Jas 1:22–25; 1 Pet 2:16–17; 1 John 3:16–24, 4:7–21)

172. The Turbulence of Culture

ONE OF THE MOST insightful stories "for children" is *The Emperor's New Clothes*. Written by Hans Christian Andersen in 1837, it is still an accurate estimation of people in our times. Our individualist, self-assertive, competitive approach to survival pushes us to achieve the highest social recognition. This gives us an urgency to belong to the movements of our times. People follow the "progressive" trends at all costs to avoid the way God has given us, even though many have secret fears they may be wrong. They want to impress others as being past the old traditional values and belonging to the new moral order, the "new normal" mindset. It does not matter if it makes no sense; many "important," influential, powerful, wealthy people and celebrities take the new view. The essential need is to distract their minds from doubts about the road they are on and generate good feelings about themselves. People cannot bear that others think they are stupid or even traditional, so they embrace a brain-dead worldview that any amount of commonsense tells them is false and destructive to survival, even without considering God's ways and purposes.

Though those on the outside see Christianity only as legalism, those of genuine faith know true freedom in Christ and peace in the providence of God. They are not of those who have chosen to love this world, though we live in it with them as salt and light. We bring them the message of hope in their context, but we do not adopt their worldview or serve their gods. We are reborn into the true nature of reality in Christ, who is the only way, truth, and life. It will make us countercultural in many ways as we deviate from the social "norms," but we must maintain a relevant message of this gospel for this world. We serve God amid the turbulence of powerful cultural influences. (Ps 37:3–9; Matt 5:13–16; John 3:3 with 16, 19, 8:31–32 with 35–36, 14:6 with 27 and 16:33, 17:13–19; Rom 1:18–23, 12:1–2; 2 Cor 4:4, 5:15–17, 6:14—7:1; Phil 2:12, 3:17—4:1; Col 3:1–4; Jas 1:22–25; 1 Pet 2:12, 15–17; 1 John 2:15–17, 4:1–6)

173. Tragedy and Pain

WHEN SOMETHING TERRIBLE HAPPENS to a Christian, our family, or our friends, we want to know where the God of love is; why would he allow such a thing to happen? Why didn't he stop it? But God is not unaware. He is as grieved as you and I are at such things. Suffering was not his plan for us. It has its roots in what humans have made of our situation. He gave humankind the gift of free will, risking its abuse. He did not want us to know suffering this way. He wanted Adam and Eve to trust him, but not because they were forced to. Jesus wept over the people of Jerusalem who chose suffering over his way for them. He wept at the death of Lazarus. And though the outcome of Jesus' visit would bring joy, Lazarus would eventually die again. Death and suffering are results of the fall of humans from God's desire for them. Set in motion willfully by Adam and Eve, they continue to plague the human situation, even for Christians, until he returns to remove this suffering and make all things right again.

God wants men and women to be free to choose what is good, enjoy love, and know loyalty. He is not punishing us but allowing that freedom to continue in the world so that people can choose to believe and trust him even though others will use that freedom to reject his way. Willful choice brought suffering to the world in the beginning, and continued choices against God multiply it today. But some choose to trust God.

God will not endure the rejection of his grace forever. He comes soon to judge those against him and end the suffering and pain of those who love him. However, we live in that broken world for now, so the choice to know and honor him with our lives is real. In his good providence, he uses even the evil that touches us to bring about his purposes for us. He may use it to shape us for some particular ministry to others or a special relationship. It shows us that his grace is sufficient for us, even in loss or pain. In our weakness, he is still at work to bring about his good purposes. When we endure suffering, it may be to display our unwavering faith in his goodness and grace in this broken world. Each of his children is very special to him, and each is given unique opportunities to be salt and light in a dark world for the short time we are on Earth. What will we do with these opportunities to honor him and help others? (Job 2:9–10, 36:15; Pss 37:23–24 and 28, 119:67–68, 71; Prov 16:9, 24:16; Isa 55:8–9, 65:17; Matt 5:13–16; Luke 19:37–44; John 9:1–5, 11:1–5 with 33–44, 14:27, 16:33, 18:10–11 with 36; 2 Cor 12:7–10; 1 Pet 5:10–11; Rev 21:4)

174. Parents in an Individualist Culture

AN INDIVIDUALIST SOCIETY LIKE ours lays it on each person to achieve their own survival, and many are left to do that alone. As a system of competition, it has no mechanism for selfless survival. It promotes only self-assertion as the way to succeed. This makes it very difficult for parents. Even though they love their children and have the best intentions, even Christians are sometimes so busy competing for and achieving their own mental, emotional, and physical survival and providing for their family's subsistence that they have little time and patience to help their children manage the difficulties, problems, and insecurities in their world. All the while, the world is working to draw the children away from God and their parents to its secular and pagan value system.

Christian parenting must aim to give children reasons to trust their parents and God despite the influences to the contrary around them. It is the central value for anyone to trust God, but often, this crucial issue and trust of parents, in the children's perception, gets eroded. One of the most serious results of poor parenting is the tendency of children to transfer their understanding of their parents, especially their father, to how they understand God. They see him as too busy, someone who doesn't care. Aloof, absent, angry, or demanding, their father is someone from whom it is impossible for them to get approval, assurance, or affirmation. Calling God their father brings up these negative emotions of their experience. This condition may follow them well into adulthood or even last their whole life.

Good parenting takes time, lots of it. God designed it to be a team effort where husband and wife help each other to be good parents while not neglecting one other. They must help each other in our individualist culture to take extra care to avoid its devastating effects on the family, and they seldom have an example to emulate. They often find themselves plowing new ground and figuring out what will produce the best crop. Among many things that can be said, three things stand out as essential for parents.

They must trust the God they talk about—desire his purposes and trust his providence in the everyday events and emotions of life. They must set an example of love by loving each other honestly, openly, and consistently. This will stand behind what they say to their children about God and his love. Finally, parents are only human and must be examples of asking and granting mercy and forgiveness, though discipline may be in order. Children must know their parents love them even when things go wrong, or they fail to show it as they truly desire. They need an example of grace.

This is lifestyle training. Beyond quality time or special talk time, it is all the time. We will not be perfect parents; no one is, but if we set these behaviors as our goals, seek God's help to grow in honesty, humility, and respect, and pray for God's wisdom and his care for our children, we will have done all we can. This training a child "in the way he should go" by example will give them patterns and memories that remain on into adulthood. And though it may take some time for these qualities to blossom in their lives, the deep patterns will remain in the background, never completely forgotten. Children are gifts from God, a responsibility he has granted parents, and very needy of love, trust, and forgiveness between them and their parents. (Prov 9:9–10; 17:6, 22:6; Matt 18:1–6; 1 Cor 7:1–5; Eph 4:20—5:2 and 15–33, 5:22–31, 6:4; Col 3:12–21; 1 Tim 3:12; 2 Tim 1:4–5; Titus 2:1–6; Jas 1:2–8, 17, 3:13–18)

175. The Mind

THINKING SEEMS SO NORMAL. It never stops. But the mind may be the most wasted gift God has given us. Serious reflection can set essential activity in motion, but sketchy thinking tends to be vague and loop endlessly on things that do not matter in the long run. We can become bogged down in small and even trivial worries, often about ourselves. We can become consumed by things we cannot control, our unfinished tasks, or our goals yet to be fulfilled.

When considering God's purposes in the world, we must keep the big picture of his providence in view. We must not become consumed by superficial religious things, petty fits of anger and jealousies, or black-and-white thinking. We must, instead, contemplate the ways of God in his word and the world. He is in control, and he is also mindful of us. We must also reflect on the self as it actually is, not take a popular view of its importance. We must think about God's purposes and put our own in second place. We must consider loving help to others and not using them to our advantage. If we do not think, we will not do, for thinking shapes doing.

Using the mind to its full potential for God is an intentional decision and an ongoing discipline beginning with its renewal. Somewhere between sentimental simplicity and cold rationality is an understanding of God's will and ways, his providence, grace, and mystery, with faith that produces gratefulness, humility, trust, and wisdom. We can learn to set our minds on things above, think on what is true, pure, and worthy, and consider how to love another and love God, but it is an effort of the mind that begins with the heart and must result in action. This is the biblical pattern. We must guard our hearts and minds to this end. (Pss 1:1–3, 7:9, 37:8, 145:3–5a; Prov 4:23–27; Eccl 7:8–12; Matt 22:37–40; Rom 8:5–7, 12:1–3; Eph 4:11–16, 20–24; Phil 2:1–8, 3:17–19, 4:4–9; Col 3:1–4, 12–17; Heb 10:24–25; Jas 1:22–25, 3:13–18)

176. Meditation

FOR PEOPLE IN THE West, it is nearly a forgotten practice, but in many cultures, people still meditate on what they consider essential themes for peace of mind and a sense of well-being. Typically, this is a religious attempt at gaining good karma and adding to self-knowledge and human wisdom. In Theravada Buddhism, meditation is used to relieve suffering and to make progress toward Enlightenment, "the calm of non-existence," in a godless religion. In Hinduism, it is for purity of self among thousands of gods, leading to the attainment of Nirvana. In Taoism, people believe meditation relieves stress and improves health by enabling *chi* to circulate through the body. These are human systems, and they are empty of the true nature of reality. But we who know God and have his truth to reflect on have left meditation out of our lives even though it is a strong biblical theme.

Simple thinking about God is rare enough; meditating on him and his word is almost nonexistent. What do we lose when we ignore the greatness and depth of God by not applying our minds and hearts to his ways? What quiet confidence are we giving up in our busy, noisy world of competition and self-assertion for survival? God waits for us to "enter his presence." That is, to come to his word and remember his kindness to us, to acknowledge our need for him, and think about his purposes, grace, and providence in our lives. We are to renew our minds and set them on things above, trusting the foundation for life he gives. It will take intentionality, time, and effort, but all will be well spent. It provides an anchor in the turbulence of life's ups and downs. It gives the routines of life meaning and leads to emotional energy for relationships along the way. Thinking and dwelling on his truth is the heart of a living, intimate relationship with God that brings the well-being, peace, and rest we need. It leads to wisdom from him for our lives. (Josh 1:8–9; Pss 1:1–3, 19:14, 48:9, 77:11–12, 104:33–34, 119:15–16, 46–48, 97–104, 111:10, 112, 130, 143:5–6, 145:5; Prov 4:5–9, 9:10; Matt 11:28–30; Rom 8:5–9a, 12:2; Phil 4:8–9; Col 3:1–4, 15–16; 2 Tim 2:7)

177. Regrets Changed to Contentment

THERE ARE REALITIES IN life we try to ignore, things that perhaps cannot be changed. Every morning, when we wake up, they are still there. We wish they were not true of us. We may feel physical, mental, material, or relational stresses and strains strangle us from peace and our desired place in life. We may feel guilt, misgivings, uncertainties, or doubts, whether real or perceived. But God is not absent, and he can use even what we regret in his purpose to shape us into the kind of person he wants. With God's help and forgiveness, realities we regret and sometimes their enduring results can be accepted in the light of the abundance of his grace. We may not see how God can use them in his plan. But his providence has been working for a long time with great patience, making way for us to come to him and shaping us to fit his intentions. And his goal is good, so much more important than the opinions of others and so much better than the expectations of our culture. There is nothing to fear in God's purposes for us. The truth about his hand in our lives will set us free. Satan will no longer hold us in his prison of stress and strain, of anxiety, or the fear of rejection. The door is open, and we will finally know contentment. We are his, and he is at work in our lives for his good purposes and, by his unreserved grace, for our benefit now and forever. (Pss 32:5, 33:11, 18, 34:19, 37:23–24, 40:1–5, 91:1–2; Matt 20:13–16; Luke 1:46–48; John 8:31–36; Rom 8:28–39; 1 Cor 1:26–31; 2 Cor 5:15–18, 12:7–10; Phil 1:6, 2:12–13)

178. Emotional Pain

THERE ARE OCCASIONS WHEN our emotional response to a situation goes so deep we fear our very survival if it is repeated. As children or adults, we may be repelled by the possible repetition of the event and avoid new experiences that may bring it to mind, evading the potential person or encounter at all costs, even when everything else about us and our situation has changed. We close ourselves off and distract our hearts and minds to escape another encounter. Anxiety may linger in the background of other aspects of life, and the emotional pain can be etched so deeply in our soul that we cannot grow out of it on our own. Some in Christ's body are trained to help us with these issues. They are gifts to the church, just as pastors, evangelists, and teachers are gifts from God.

We may be called on to trust God in ways that seem beyond our abilities, but with the help of a Christian counselor, we can gain a clearer perspective of our pain and trust God specifically for aspects of it that will help us eventually trust him for the whole. We may not forget the pain or fear, but we will see it in a different light. We will discover that God has our welfare in mind as well as his purposes. It was never his intent that we suffer in these ways. We live in a world broken by human choice where suffering and evil are rampant. Everyone suffers to some extent, but it is more complex for some. God wants us to know freedom from anxiety as we learn to trust him. We will only know contentment and joy when we face our situation with the strength of his grace, embrace his good gifts, and trust him for our well-being. Released from our anxieties, we can help others in the body of Christ to know contentment in trusting God. (Pss 3:1–6, 23:4, 27:1–5, 34:4, 91:1–16; Prov 3:5–6, 14:26–27; Isa 41:10; 2 Cor 5:7, 12:7–10; Eph 4:11–16; Phil 4:6–7; Jas 1:16–18; 1 Pet 5:7; 1 John 4:16–18)

179. To Love Again

WE ARE CHRISTIANS WHO are to be known for our love. But some of us have never had an example of love in our lives. We do not know love or how to express it. It often makes it difficult to accept love from others. For others of us, our love has been betrayed, and we want nothing else but to avoid that pain again. We may have lived our lives protecting ourselves from the need to be loved. Our emotional survival may have depended on it. Letting go of self-protection and the barriers to love is necessary for us to step out of the cold and into the warmth of God's love.

Where human examples fail, God's love is strong, consistent, and unconditional. It is displayed in the greatest of sacrifices: the giving up of his Son to meet our greatest need. We matter to him. He will not now neglect us in our ongoing needs even though his care in our lives may not look like we expect. We belong to him and his plan for the world. He is at work in us for his purposes and our peace. His love is continually expressed by his grace, which he lavishes on us every day.

Our tactics for survival have become natural habits to us over time and are very difficult to change, even when they are no longer needed. But unless we let go of this protection of the self, this survival tactic, we cannot know love for or from God or others. We must put the new wine into a new wineskin. Old things are over, and everything is new in Christ. It may seem like a risk you are unwilling to take, but you have nothing to lose and everything to gain. We each must come to know the unconditional love of God for people such as we are. By his love for us, we can let go of our defenses and learn to love others, leaving all else in God's hands. (Prov 3:27–28; Isa 43:1; Matt 6:31–34, 9:16–17; John 12:24–26, 14:21–24, 15:5–11; Rom 8:31–32 with John 3:16; 2 Cor 5:17; Eph 1:7–8, 2:1–10; Phil 1:6 with 2:12–13; 1 John 3:16–18)

180. Letting God Speak

WHEN WE READ GOD'S word, we may prefer to find what we want or need to find and miss what is really there. Letting God speak for himself takes us to new places in our understanding if we are willing to listen. We will begin to know ourselves better and see life from his perspective. Instead of changing what is there to what we want to be there, we must let him speak, and we must listen. Of course, if reading his word has become an empty habit, we may miss all sorts of things in our effort to accomplish the routine. Reading less and irregularly is better than allowing it to become a ritualistic personal achievement. But, read we must, with hearts and minds open to his purposes in our lives.

Remember that letting God speak for himself means you must be silent. You will need to escape the noise around you and set aside, as much as possible, the mental and emotional interference everyday life brings. We will have to pull the weeds that have taken over the garden of our hearts and minds. The seeds he will plant call for fresh soil. Is there some risk? Yes. You are stepping into the true nature of reality—the way things really are with God at the center and his grace overflowing—and some of your old and favorite values, things you have trusted for your well-being, worth, and identity, will be replaced with his. Your chosen theological system, personal biases, social circle, or need for control may be standing in the way of things God wants you to know and be. You may be reluctant to let go of the old wineskin, but he has new wine for you. Allow him to give you a new wineskin to fill with his purposes for you. His providence—his guiding hand—has brought you to this point in your journey; you can trust him to take you the rest of the way and complete his good work in you. (Pss 1:1–3, 91:14–16, 95:6–7, 103:10–14, 119:11, 105, 138:8; Prov 3:5–7; Matt 9:16–17, 13:1–9; Rom 12:1–3; Phil 1:6, 2:12–13; Col 3:15–17; 1 Thess 5:24; 2 Tim 3:16–17, 4:1–4)

181. Wrong-Way

WE MAY NEVER KNOW how much God hates evil and the resulting pain and suffering in the world. It was never his desire for the world. But the freedom to choose our loyalties and courses of action was his intention for humankind, and we do that every day, as did Adam and Eve. If we know him but choose the wrong way today, God will not abandon us, but he may do or allow things to get our attention again. He does not want anyone to suffer from the evil they choose, nor does he force anyone to do good. He calls us to love and good works with all the encouragement of his word—his providence, power, grace, and will for us—and his Spirit to guide us. We are always choosing to honor God or serve ourselves. But if we are in Christ, no amount of wrong choices can remove his attention to our welfare. We live in a relationship of grace with him, and nothing can change that. He waits for our humble repentance and renewed trust in him, but his love never wavers. (Prov 3:27; Isa 42:1–4; Luke 6:38; John 10:27–30; 1 Cor 10:13; 1 Tim 6:18–19; Titus 3:8; Heb 13:5b, 15–16; 2 Pet 3:9; 1 John 1:9, 3:18; 3 John 11)

182. Good Works in a Bad World

LIVING A "GOOD LIFE" becomes more challenging when the world calls good evil and evil good. As evil takes a militant stance against good, against God's purposes, and especially against Christianity, we must become even more thoughtful about how we live our lives. The world must see our good works and, at least, consider why anyone would want to live out such a life and how they can do so with contentment and peace. They cannot understand the measure of God's grace behind the love and kindness of a selfless Christian, but seeing that love and compassion is the first step in that direction for them.

The purpose of salvation, the inspiration of Scripture, and the church itself is that we might live lives of good works—the fruit of salvation by faith and the outcome of God's word at work in our lives. But we have, many of us, long forgotten these important emphases and intended results. We have become defensive rather than offensive, judgmental instead of loving. We expect non-believers to live like believers before they know the God who changes hearts and motives. We may be making a hard time even more difficult for the gospel. Since the first sin, the world has never been a good place. But God wants us here. We must incarnate the truth we talk about to be light in a dark world. (Prov 3:27–28; Matt 5:13–16; John 17:15–19; 2 Cor 4:6; Gal 6:9–10; Eph 2:8–10, 4:11–13; Phil 2:1–4; 2 Tim 3:16–17; Titus 2:14, 3:1–2, 8, 14; Heb 6:10–12, 13:15–16; Jas 4:17; 1 Pet 2:11–17, 20–25, 3:13–17; 1 John 3:18)

183. Unity around God's Word

Sometimes, Christians will cling to some parts of the Bible and ignore or explain away other parts. Some theological systems are carefully crafted to accentuate the preferences of the theologian and defend against any verses to the contrary. These preferences become exclusive and cause divisions. Jesus' prayer for believers in John 17 is for unity so the world may know God sent him. Love for each other (and those outside the faith) is how they will know we are Christians. But we are divided, and our human preferences cause us to endure church split after church split. What does the world see in this? How are they to understand the gospel? Though there are many false teachers to avoid, heretical twistings of the Bible to teach against, and lies of the evil one in the world that seek to destroy the truth, we must still stand together on the essentials of the true gospel and allow for variations on the nonessentials. For this, what we have made of the church must change. To be arrogant about the theologian we have chosen to follow ignores huge swaths of the Scriptures about divisions in the church, the nature of love, and the attitude of Christ. Our modern tribalism must give way to unity around the truth.

Commentaries are written and complex doctrines formulated by men about God's inspired word. But we must not keep him from speaking for himself. All things in the Bible are given to us for our instruction and training and for correcting those inaccurate views of essential truths and behaviors that deny God. We cannot accept some verses and reject others. Our own thoughts about nonessential issues are not inspired and should be bathed in humility. For there is much we do not know.

To add what we want or expect to God's words is dangerous, sometimes heretical, and perhaps most ruinous when we require others to legalistically accept what we have added. We often give God boundaries he must not cross because of our insecurities. We are afraid for ourselves. But we must not be anxious that God might step outside our logical system, ignore our preferences, or upset our associations. The defense of these boundaries divides believers. Then, we often treat those different from us as enemies. The essentials are before us to stand on together. We must not allow our opinions or insistence on black and white compartments of nonessential right and wrongs to paralyze us and cause division. (Matt 5:38–48; John 13:34–35, 17:20–23; Rom 14:1–23 especially 22, 15:5–7; 1 Cor 1:10—2:5, with 3:1–9 and 13:1–13 and Phil 2:1–8; Gal 5:1–6, 13–15, 25; Eph 4:1–6; 2 Tim 3:16–17; 1 Pet 2:11–12, 3:8–9; Jude 3–4)

184. The Great Deception

THE PARCHED DESERTS OF the world's ways and values cause believers to long for the realities of the spiritual universe. The world would have us believe that they have the truth and that it is empty of any spiritual dimension, that we evolved haphazardly (miraculously) to become human and possess all the wonders of the human body and mind only by chance. They would have us think that no one controls the universe, that science explains everything. Though scientists have discovered a great deal, they know far less about the universe than they lead us to believe. Their guesses about beginnings and teachings that humans are only animals are foolish, though they promote them as wisdom. It is the great deception that began in the garden of Eden.

This humanist system's first doctrine and basic tenet is that there is no God, no supernatural cause (even though their discoveries often point to his necessary existence). The only alternative is their guessing as humans, who are products of the same theory that leaves out any standard of right and wrong, any moral compass at all. Satan uses the world, culture, and selfish human motivations to hypnotize the nations out of the notion that there might be something beyond all this—an ultimate reality that frames the meaning of everything else, that life and happiness might be found outside their theories about our existence.

Many are Satan's followers: deceived and willing workers in his hand to keep a drape over the eyes of men and women that they might not see, that their minds might not think. Nothing is so irritating to them as a believer who knows the truth, who knows God and is confident in his providence and love, his creation and control of the universe. The thriving of the true nature of reality among the stubble of man's created theories gives us life among the dead, light in the darkness. In the world to come, right will no longer be called wrong. (Gen 1:1–31; Pss 10:4, 14:1a, 4–5, 19:1–6, 53:1–3; Isa 5:20–21, 32:5–8, 50:10–11; Jer 17:5–10; Rom 1:21–25, 12:2; 2 Cor 4:4, 11:4–5; Eph 2:4–5, 4:18; Col 2:13–15; 1 John 2:15–17)

185. Traditions Forgotten

CULTURES ARE HUMAN SYSTEMS for the survival of their members. God set them in motion with specific boundaries. This structure included men and women being created for each other with roles for activity, vocation as part of their lives, the ability to reason and make decisions, capacity for reproduction, and the potential for loyalty and love. Though they would find many cultural expressions, these roles were God's will for humankind. He made that clear to his created beings; nevertheless, it was not long before people took God's design into their own hands. Because he did not force them to follow his way, many drifted from his original intentions in Eden. They decided for themselves what worked and did not work for their survival and happiness, even though the results brought pain and suffering.

Once on their own, survival in their situation was often through trial and error. The solutions were hard-won and not ideal. But because some remained more faithful to God's design and followed his ways, however imperfectly, by God's grace, we are here today. These solutions to the problems for survival based on God's revealing of his will in the Bible go back hundreds of generations to that beginning and are still affecting the lives of many today. We refer to these as traditions. But, despite a long dependence on these solutions by many, our individualist cultures in the West today are not favorable toward the conventions that come from them. They think traditional morality and justice are neither personally profitable nor essential to survival. They have manufactured a new situational morality with the self at the center and a new corrupt justice with racial, political, gender, and religious discrimination at the core. They see other people as valuable only if they agree with them and are useful for their purposes. Freedom of speech is seen as a right to propagate their human system of thought and values, but that freedom is denied to others who differ. Their present strategy is to make children their converts. Such is the popular religion of our times—the dark world in which we are to be light.

185. TRADITIONS FORGOTTEN

In general, Western people have a rather hefty appetite for change. New or different is better. Many believe past traditions withhold the pleasures and happiness of doing and being what we want in today's "progressive" environment. "Why should we be bound to the old ways? We know more about human existence today than those who have gone before and want to control our lives without this ancient entrapment." "We're not going back!" So go the foolish words of lost humanity. When we do away with a tradition—a valued practice based on God's word—in this way, we are not thinking about the problems for survival it solved. The effects of some of those problems will return to society like a slow poison in the system. Though some issues that reappear may not be serious, many are terminal. A man's way may seem right to him, but it often ends in death. (Gen 1:1–27 with 2:15–17; Pss 10:1–11, 14:1a, 53:1–4, 77:11–12; Prov 1:7, 2:12–15, 12:15, 13:20, 14:12, 15:24, 16:2, 9, 19:3, 21:2, 22:28, 23:10–11; Rom 1:18–32; Phil 3:17–21; Heb 4:13, 11:38—12:3)

186. God's Ways

GOD'S WAYS AND WORKS cannot be reduced to three points and a poem, a lengthy doctrinal statement, or a multi-volume theology. Despite all we know, there is a great deal that we do not know of his greatness or ways in the world and spiritual universe. He intended it this way because he wants our trust. We know only what he intends us to know. It is misleading when our finite efforts, like those of Job's friends or the Pharisees and their oral Torah, become the final explanation of God's person and works, his weightiness (glory), and wonder. They do not allow for God to be God and miss many of the great mysteries of his infinite person.

Descriptions of God and his purposes in the universe are often symbolic and seem indirect in the Bible. But they may be as clear and direct as our language can express and our human experience understand. Yes, we do know a lot. Wonderfully, we know something of his love and grace toward us to the extent we know ourselves. We know he is the Creator-God and the center of reality in every way. We know that his plan for the universe is centered on the work of Christ. And he has given us so much more. But we can also trust him entirely for things outside our knowledge and experience, the limits of language, and the restrictions of our human weaknesses. Outside these boundaries, mystery remains, but confidence in his love and grace abounds and gives us peace. (Job 5:9, 34:11, 36:11, 38:1—41:34; Ps 103:10-13; Prov 3:5-7, 28:26; Isa 30:15, 40:13-14 with 21-31, 41:10, 42:1-4, 55:8-11; John 21:24-25; Heb 8:12, 11:6; 2 Pet 3:14-18)

187. Human Love Is Inadequate

SOME OF US HAVE amazing spouses and children whose love for us is undeserved, patient, and enduring. But, for the most part, people's experience with love is relatively poor in our individualist society. Some of us may not even have known it from our parents or felt it for them in return. Our lack of an example in childhood often leads to failure at loving others later in life. Even when we know something about love in relationships, we are human, and our devotion can be narrow and conditional compared to God's. We have seldom, if ever, experienced entirely selfless love. We confuse attraction and emotional attachment with unconditional loyalty, trust, patience, and commitment, leading to disappointment and heartbreak. When we say we love God or that he loves us, we are probably using this human experience of love to define what it is like. This puts God's love out of reach for us in its true depth and capacity. We can only understand it partially.

So poor is our human experience of love that some find it hard to accept God's love. But we are no longer talking about human love and its many failures. We now speak of God, whose love is perfect and persistent. This love comes to us in the wilderness and suffering of our lives. It brings us living water, the bread of life, and light in the darkness. This he does at great cost to himself, the sacrifice of his Son for us. It is the love of an infinite God for his finite creatures. He knows us inside out, every weakness and sin, every proud or selfish thought. And yet, in his grace, he loves us with unyielding, enduring, compassionate, though sometimes severe, love. Human ideas and examples of love must be set aside to know and accept God's perfect love. With that realization, we will also finally know humility and gratefulness. We will also finally be able to love others following his example. (Pss 32:10–11, 33:18–22, 86:11–13, 107:1; Matt 23:37–38 with Luke 19:41–44; John 3:16–17, 15:13; Rom 5:8, 8:32–35 with 38–39; 2 Cor 4:6; Eph 1:4–6, 2:1–5; 1 John 3:1, 4:18–19)

188. Seeking Approval

EVERY CHILD GROWING UP has a desire and need for the approval and love of their father and mother. When they know they have it, discipline with mercy furthers correction and helps a child feel assured. There is hardly anything more important than this for growing up with a healthy view of ourselves. We want to feel needed and safe, help others, and be good at something. In our culture, it touches the very meaning of our lives. Approval, love, and careful discipline are God's plans for children in the family, but as important as it all is, it is often lacking, even withheld, between parent and child. Many spend a lifetime trying to gain it, even after their fathers and mothers are gone. Caught in this trap, they hurt themselves, and they hurt others.

The strain of achieving this missing approval can overwhelm a person's approach to life and other people. Such a person may feel the same about God, that his approval seems difficult, if not impossible, to gain. It can be an unbearable burden because its significance is of ultimate consequence. But the situation is entirely different from God's side. He, beyond all human capacity, knows of our deep and desperate need. We cannot be good enough or work hard enough to gain approval from God—to achieve his ideal for us—but all is not lost. Quite the contrary! All is possible. God gives us full assurance of his complete forgiveness and unconditional love in Christ, who has his full approval. We have that approval without deserving it. In this truth, we can rest. His love is deep, his forgiveness is genuine, and his concern for us unending. We will never deserve it. We can only accept it with a humble and grateful heart. (Josh 1:9; Pss 34:4–8 and 17–22; 40:1–5, 139:1–12; Matt 11:28–30; Luke 3:21–22; John 14:21–24; Rom 3:21–26, 4:7–8, 5:8, 8:28–30; 2 Cor 5:17; Eph 2:4–10; 1 John 1:9)

189. Approval Achieved, but Not by Us

WE DO NOT STAND before God in our own achievements. That would be a rather miserable showing anyway. No, we stand before him through the achievement of Christ Jesus, forgiven, loved, and the object of his concern in every way. His providence gives us purpose and all we need to serve him to our fullest capacity, but that is not how we are measured in his presence. We are actually given the position made possible by washing away all sin, every selfish motive, greedy desire, and proud thought. Jesus did that for us in his sacrifice, and as we stand before God, he accepts our faith in that event and our loyalty to his being. We will still fall short, but he is not unaware of our weaknesses. As we repent, he forgives and compensates for every one of them with his grace. Our deepest longing is satisfied in his approval of us in Christ. It is incredible, and nothing can change it. Its accomplishment is finished and stands, carrying satisfaction, contentment, and happiness for us beyond our imagination or hope. (Rom 5:1–2, 8:1–2, 11:6; 2 Cor 12:7–10, Gal 2:20; Eph 1:3, 2:7; Phil 4:19; Col 2:10 with 13–15; 2 Thess 2:16–17; 1 Pet 3:18)

190. Heaven

WHAT ARE OUR IMAGINATIONS of heaven? We have little, and most of it symbolic, information on that realm of existence beyond this one. Much wonder and mystery is on the edges of God's great plan for us. It is of a much greater dimension than our finite minds can envision. But what we know, we treasure. And we trust him for what is yet to be known. Yet our imaginations rest on what it will be like, what we will be like. Some think we will be like angels, having no feelings about anything, indifferent to all but the presence of God and his bidding. But that cannot be the case. We are very different from angels. We will be humans transformed with a history of living in the world God created and having been the crown of that creation as those in his image. We will have had experiences during which we had to trust God without knowing the outcomes that angels know nothing of, relationships with people they could not have, and human emotions and desires foreign to them.

It was God's purpose that we should be different from the angels and animals. We can think and make decisions based on reason and faith. We can know other people intimately and can love as well as hate. Our five senses were created to enjoy that creation, and a great deal of what he called good has been our delight. We have known and loved people around us that we will continue to know in eternity if we think, believe, and choose his way in Christ. Though our record is not perfect, our faith and loyalty have been tested in the world and found true. As such, we enter heaven as beings very different from angels. They are not the crown of his creation, once lost but then redeemed; we are. (Gen 1:26-27; John 14:1-4; 1 Cor 15:40; 2 Cor 5:1; Phil 3:20; Heb 8:5, 9:24, 12:1; 2 Pet 3:12-13; Rev 4:1-11, 21:1—22:6)

191. Ingredients

IF A YOUNG MAN or woman wants to have a biblical ministry to others, the first thought may be that he or she should get a theological degree. But something else is first. There is a misconception that theological knowledge makes a person a pastor or, for that matter, a good Christian. But necessary as it is, theological knowledge is only an ingredient, and not the most important one, in making a person someone God can use in ministry. If the flour has bugs, it won't matter that you have the highest quality chocolate to use in the recipe for a cake. Even if you sift out the bugs, the cake would still taste like them. To be a pastor or missionary who can lead others to know God and walk in his way will take more than education. Among the most essential ingredients are a whole-hearted trust in God's word and providence, genuine humility that comes from knowing oneself, gratefulness for God's grace, a lack of need for social recognition, and consideration for the needs of others. Some social skills and competence in communication are also necessary. As important as theological education is, it must be folded into these other ingredients to be useful. Those of the simplest faith who possess these qualities may have a more significant ministry than the PhD in theology will ever know.

Those with theological training occasionally achieve a ministry position without these other qualities. They become proud of their achievement, enjoy their status, receive earthly rewards, and, in the end, abuse the trust of the people under them and destroy the work of that ministry. Some may tend toward legalism, poisoning the grace of God in the church. Some get lost in their lust for the authority of leadership. Others, whose moral compass was never calibrated by loyalty to God, drift away from him and discredit God's word and work. Others become liberal as they syncretize cultural "absolutes" with biblical absolutes.

Theological education can leave out important subjects such as knowledge of the influence of one's culture on one's life, how to think about and for oneself, or how humility and gratefulness come to be owned. It can be education that replaces spiritual integrity with information. These conditions cause people to distrust the training, which, in turn, damages and weakens the church. To neglect training is to leave out a necessary ingredient. You have to have chocolate to make a chocolate cake, but the other ingredients cannot be left out, or you may end with chocolate crackers flat and brittle. Integrity and wisdom are as essential to ministry as flour and baking powder in a cake recipe if there is to be a ministry honoring God and helping people mature in Christ. (Pss 15:1–5, 19:12–14, 24:3–6; Matt 23:1–7; Luke 18:9–14, 20:46; 1 Tim 3:1–7, 4:7–8; 2 Tim 2:15, 22–26; 1 Pet 5:1–4)

192. Pleasure

THE PLEASURES GOD PLANNED for us on Earth are pretty amazing. We can fill our senses with the stimulation of the beauty of nature, the softness of a breeze, the scent of flowers, the sweetness of honey, and the voice, touch, and music of love. We get up the next day, and it is all there again. We are free as his children to enjoy all our Father has given us within the boundaries of gratefulness to God and love for others. But not all is well; our human appetites are difficult to control. The pleasures God intends can be tainted by wrong choices and self-centered motives, inclinations toward hoarding, misuse, and abuse. Some have taken it away, even violently, from others. It sometimes ends in taking each other's lives. This is the human situation when God is left outside our lives.

We know heaven will not have any of these abuses, and what we will have there will go infinitely beyond the gifts he gives us here. Perhaps our present blessings are a foreshadowing, but if God thinks enjoyment of such things is important on Earth, heaven will be beyond our imagination. Though we have enjoyed his provision of many pleasures here, our lives have often been punctuated with suffering because of human choices. We have not yet known contentment without adversity. We can calm our anxieties with the peace of trusting him while we are here, but we are still living on the porch of his house; the door is ready to be opened to us. We are about to know true delight, happiness without end, and contentment beyond imagination. (Gen 1:31; John 14:1–4; Rom 8:31–32; 1 Cor 2:9, 10:31; Gal 5:13; 1 Tim 4:4–5; Titus 1:15, 2:11; 1 Pet 2:16, 5:10–11; Rev 21:1–6, 22:1–7, 12)

193. The Basics

THE GRANDEST THEOLOGIES IN our libraries have been based on some straightforward basic principles that God has given us. They extrapolate a great deal from these and build complex doctrines, but these basics are the foundation. If the theologian, pastor, or Bible teacher moves away from them, they end at a human destination that leads people astray, away from God instead of toward him. God's word begins with creation and moves on through a series of human failings and judgment, followed by redemption through God's grace until the new creation yet to come. The Old Testament sets the stage and prepares the way. The Gospels reveal his plan for the world through Christ. The book of Acts shows us the beginnings of this plan of Christ for the world. The Epistles explain its meanings and necessary outcomes for us. The Revelation shows us its consummation. The basic theme is that God is moving through history with his plan of redemption and wants us to know and join him, to be part of that movement from creation to re-creation.

Over and over again, in God's unveiling of himself and his plan, we see the nature of man's weakness and limitations when refusing to trust God and his strength and courage when he did trust God. It is the same in all walks of life, in every conceivable situation, and under any and all conditions: man cannot exist or flourish unless he turns from himself and trusts God's goodness and grace. The crowning act of God in expressing his grace is in Christ's birth, ministry, death, and resurrection for humankind. Nothing to fix man's problem of guilt before the living God can substitute for it. It looks backward in fulfilling all he had promised to those of his creation, forgives us and makes us new in the church today, and is the basis for all he will yet do in re-creation.

We live in the grace of God's movement in history if we choose to do so. With simple faith in these acts of God, we can confidently face any situation, knowing that he is in control of our lives for his honor and purpose;

without it, it does not matter how much theology we know. What matters is what we do with what we know. The fact that Jesus is the Son of God and that his sacrifice in our place forgives and justifies us before God the Father is what we need to acknowledge. This is the truth that must change our lives. Paul calls it the truth that leads to godliness. (John 1:1–18, 14:6, 21, 23, 17:3; Rom 1:19–21, 8:21–23; 2 Cor 5:15–21; Eph 2:1–10; Phil 3:16; Col 2:12–14; Titus 1:1–3; Heb 11:1–3 and 6; 1 Pet 1:13–21, 2:9–12, 15, 4:1–2; Rev 21:1–4)

194. Christian "Leaders"

LEADERSHIP AMONG CHRISTIANS IS considered one of the goals of ministry training in our day. But, though highly sought, this goal carries core values the training usually assumes the student already has, which are essential for the responsibilities of leading others. These are attitudes of the heart that every Christian must seek but are required in even greater measure for the man or woman who would lead others.

First, it will mean standing on integrity, humility, unswerving trust in God's person, and loyalty to his purposes. The measuring stick remains the same. Without it, all is chaos, no matter how attractive leadership seems. No ministry built on other values, no twisting of these virtues, will withstand God's final inspection even if it grows in numbers and buildings and in praise of the "celebrity" leading it. The Old Testament prophets did not receive applause for their message. The early church leaders were not social celebrities and suffered a great deal to preach the gospel.

But many in the wealthy West today have sought recognition and built monuments where humility and gratefulness should have been the marks of faithful leadership. They have accumulated treasures on Earth where their hearts are engaged with the passing values of human desires. It is a fearful thing to be a teacher of the word, no matter how we glorify it.

It will seem like high treason to some to say so, but fundamental biblical virtues are far more essential to ministry than any achievements of greatness in men's eyes. The laws of love and compassion, the honest approach to our study of his word, and humble gratefulness for God's grace will never change in their importance for honoring God in Christian ministry. However, it seems they are often more at work in the unnoticed but faithful worker, the humble and overlooked ministry, than in the cathedrals of famous leaders. But again, the first will be last and the last first. (Matt 6:19–24, 18:1–4, 19:29–30 with 20:16, 20–28; Mark 9:33–35, 10:35–45; Luke 18:14b;

1 Cor 1:20–31; 1 Tim 1:3–7, 3:1–7; 2 Tim 2:1–10, 4:3; Titus 1:5–9; Heb 11:1–40; Jas 3:1, 13–18; 1 Pet 5:5–11)

195. Change

NOT ALL CHANGE IS progress. Though we, in our Western culture, have an insatiable appetite for change—thinking different is better—there are essential building blocks for a society that cannot be altered without devastating results. The deceptive thing is that the results of changes to these foundational concepts are not immediate, but by the time they become evident, it is often too late to repair the damage. We may get tired of traditional ways. They may no longer be relevant in society today or become less effective as we lose the virtues and ideals that made them valuable, even indispensable, to a thriving community. But the problem is in the people who want to leave it all behind, not the time-worn principles of God's word. His design for a functional family and a flourishing society resulted in traditional ways of integrating these principles into our lives. These "traditions" are tossed aside as outdated and useless by those who want the change of controlling their own lives without the limitations of God's ways. But all is not well.

As problems mount, a certain desperation sets in, and these people turn to what makes them feel good or important to distract them, as discipline, honesty, humility, and honor slip away from the previous lifestyle. People stop thinking. They make decisions and move on human inclinations. They use animal instinct instead of reasoning and then ask what has gone wrong to cause the problems. In trying to do away with God, these have taken away the meaning of life, the basis for personal worth, the reason to live or respect life, and then they wonder at the degradation of our society. The deprivation is bearing fruit, and it is bitter to the core.

But hope endures in the lives and hearts of those who have held on to the unchanging truths of God, giving them acceptance, identity, freedom, and worth and infusing life with meaning. The experience of these certainties is the irrigation of the dry and dusty desert others have made of life with their "enlightenment," change, and "progress." Those who know God's grace and seek to live by his truths do not thirst or walk in darkness. They are not perfect, but they belong to God, and he has his eye on them. They are central to his purposes in the world and are yet to play an important role in the consummation of his plan for the universe. Yes, the King is coming, and all will be set right again. The pure in heart will indeed see God. (Pss 1:1–6, 10:4, 14:1a, 33:11; Prov 14:12, 22:7–8; Isa 50:10–11; Matt 5:3–10; John 1:4–5, 4:7–14, 6:35–40, 8:12, 31–32, 17:15–17; Rom 1:18–32, 3:22–24; 2 Cor 4:4–6; Gal 6:7–10; Eph 6:14–18; Phil 3:17—4:1; 2 Tim 2:1–7; Titus 1:15)

196. Kingdoms of Darkness and Light

WE LIVE ON A physical planet among things of this life, some soft and beautiful, inspiring, and some coarse and irritating, causing pain. Some people, in our experience, will be kind and helpful, and others unkind and inconsiderate, even bullies. Events for us can be fun and meaningful or difficult and discouraging. This is life as we know it through our social situation. Our cultural lens is supposed to give us human meaning and predictability for survival. We judge or justify behavior as evil or good by its values, as faulty as they may be. A cultural system in itself is both good and bad. It is necessary for human survival and helpful in many ways, but it is human, invisible, powerful, and blind and can either benefit or harm its members. As such, it is a ready tool for Satan to deceive and insulate us from the true nature of reality—God's truth and the spiritual universe beyond this one. It becomes his domain, where he cloaks his operations, shrouds peoples' minds from the light, then blackmails them in the dark.

Cultures give people ways of dealing with the supernatural but always fall short. It may be materialism, religion, or atheism that becomes the answer, blinding people to the actuality of God at the center. Not much different from the pagans of old, people today make their idols and worship them. Members of the culture believe they are right and safe despite the plain evidence that their faith in these cultural substitutes takes them down the wrong road to the destruction of society and the death of its members.

As I have said, cultural systems are human and, as such, experience atrophy at a much faster rate than the elements of the universe. A description of the disintegration of a society, even a civilization, can be summarized in a couple of pages in a history book. As good as some of them were, as their virtues waned, they weakened, and from the void on the inside, they collapsed at the hands of their enemies. Though here today, they are gone tomorrow, along with their great leaders and tyrants. Their religious idols

196. KINGDOMS OF DARKNESS AND LIGHT

broken, cultural values destroyed, material gains flattened, and their hedonism extinguished.

Cultures do not lead us to the gospel; however, they are the vehicles through which it is transmitted and the contexts within which it takes on meaning. Those not under culture's spell who know God through his grace respect its power in people's lives and use what they can of it to their advantage. They will outlive any society, any culture, any civilization. They belong to yet another kingdom, a kingdom of light instead of darkness, that human cultures have tried to smother repeatedly but cannot. It is the spiritual universe, the true nature of reality, not a culture's assumptions about it. Those who believe have a relationship with God that endures without end. To this relationship, they bear witness as salt and light in the world. (Josh 24:14-15; Pss 33:12-22, 34:15-22, 37:20; Prov 21:2; Jer 10:1-16; Ezek 14:6 with 11; Matt 4:12-17, 16:18; Luke 1:76-79; John 1:4-5, 9-14, 3:16-21, 8:12 with 9:5 and 12:34-36, 17:13-19; 2 Cor 4:4, 16-18, 11:14; Eph 5:1 with 8-16; Col 1:13-14)

197. Transported

AT ANY MOMENT, WE can be transported from this ordinary world to that existence beyond the familiar routine and the pain and adversity often accompanying it. One by one now, but a day is coming when God's patience with the world will be exhausted; his time to respond to the world's rejection of his grace will come, and all those who know him will be gathered to him. Times will become difficult for a while, and then all ordinary existence will disappear on "the day of the Lord" as his kingdom comes and a new heaven and earth follow. It will be over. All that people have fought to possess and maintain through personal achievement and oppression of others in this life will be ended. We will stand before God, and the books will be opened. The names will be read. Those who have submitted to his control of the universe and his grace in Christ will go on his right side for eternal life and all others on his left, never to be heard of again. Creation will have completed its cycle to re-creation. The battle with evil—the crucible of our faith—will be over. All will be well again as it was in the beginning. (Dan 12:1–3; Matt 7:13–23, 24:1–51, 25:31–46; John 13:6–10; 2 Cor 5:1–10; 1 Thess 4:13—5:11; 1 Pet 5:10–11; 2 Pet 3:1–15; Rev 21:1–8, 22:1–7. Detailed description: Dan 9:20—12:13; Rev 6:1—22:21)

198. Categories of People

THE BOOK OF PROVERBS talks about several kinds of people as the opposite of those gaining wisdom: the simple, the fool, the stubborn, the lazy, and the arrogant. We would like to think that these are all people outside Christianity today. But that is not the case. These people exist in all walks of life and are sometimes found in churches. They may be weeds among the wheat or weak in their faith, but they will be ongoing irritants to people of genuine faith.

But, while some set their hearts on deceptive or superficial inclinations and lean on human and cultural values, others see life as it really is and set their hearts on the permanent realities of God's ways. We must not judge Christians by just any example we see. Wisdom knows the difference and approaches life and people with patience and discernment. Though we should not attach ourselves to a fool and do well to keep our distance from the arrogant and those who gossip, some who detract from the faith today may become examples of his grace another day. God may interrupt their superficial lives. And we must remember that we were once like them; we who know him are only in his hand by his grace, not by our achievements. (Ps 90:12; Prov 1:29–33, 3:33–35, 6:6–11, 9:4–6, 7–8, 12:16, 18, 14:15, 29, 15:21, 16:2, 18–19, 20:19, 20:27, 23:9; Matt 7:1–5, 15–23, 13:24–30; Luke 6:31 with 37–38, 46–49; Rom 16:17–19; 1 Cor 1:26–31; Eph 2:1–10; Col 2:13–15)

199. Motives for Beliefs

MOST OF US REALIZE that a Bible teacher may take strong doctrinal positions on nonessential issues for reasons other than the unavoidable conviction of their truth. He or she may honestly misunderstand, but individualist values on personal survival can also cause a person in the West to seek status in this way among his or her peers for social survival or feelings of importance. The devices they use to ensure this are directly from the bag of tricks our Western culture offers us: self-assertion, competition, and control of the people and variables around them. The desperate need to belong to a group that affirms one's personal worth is highly emotional and puts reason on the back burner. They are unlikely to look at alternatives to their chosen positions because of the risks to their identity with their group. They are blinded by their rationalizations and will defend these doctrinal positions no matter what other scriptural statements must be ignored. Those who believe otherwise are assumed to have little understanding.

People of this sort become defensive when a question puts their social survival at risk. But, if they are confident in their position because they trust God and his word as he gave it to us, they are not threatened by questions. They can discuss convictions on nonessentials and alternatives without emotional risk. We must all be sensitive to this inclination toward social survival and monitor our motives and emotions when discussing doctrines we see as biblical. Churches should not be exclusive social institutions defending their group's preferences and partialities. Each should be a body of people who hold to the essential doctrines with confidence and the nonessential with humility. (Matt 7:15–23; John 13:34–35; Rom 12:3, 10, 16, 13:8, 14:13, 15:7; Gal 5:15, 26; Eph 4:2, 32; Phil 2:1–11; 1 Thess 5:11; Titus 1:10–16; Heb 10:24; Jas 4:4, 5:9)

200. The Works of Legalism

LEGALISM IS A SYSTEM of rules and regulations added to the Bible to achieve God's approval, salvation, or a reputation for righteousness. It is based on extrabiblical preferences attached to biblical truths through unbiblical interpretations that ignore contrary verses. Under the guise of being literal, Bible verses are twisted and used as leverage to shape the regulations. Strict adherence is then required of everyone to be insiders in the group. A passion for legalism may come from fear of punishment, insecurity, the need for approval or control, or a desire for black and white, quantitative objectivity out of fear of ambiguity. It is one of the main criticisms of Christianity by unbelievers, and with good reason. They wonder where the goodness and love of God could be in such a system.

Jesus did not talk to Nicodemus the same way he talked to the woman at the well, or the rich young ruler, or Bartimaeus, or Zacchaeus. He spoke to each one in terms of their own needs in considering his message. His point was that he was the way, the truth, and the life (John 14:6), the Messiah, and he wanted them to follow him. But each needed to hear that message differently. The Pharisees had their theological box closed and locked to this peasant preacher born in a barn. (We have numerous theological boxes among us as well.) The messianic thinking of every Jew was inside that box, but each had their personal needs, and Jesus took the door in each case that opened to their hearts. We have a tendency to formulate concise doctrines. But the Bible is not full of ironclad propositional statements. Some foundational truths are stated directly. John 3:16 or 14:6, Eph 2:8–10, and 2 Tim 3:16–17 are examples. But a great deal about God and his ways is revealed through historical accounts, stories, parables, and conversations—not black and white information—giving us boundaries for the truth in different directions.

Legalism is lethal to the well-being of a church and contradicts God's grace and the work of Christ. One cannot add works to grace for salvation, which are instead to be its result. Legalism also denies the freedom we have been given in Christ. The law came through Moses, but grace and truth came to us through Jesus Christ, and they set us free. Jesus spoke much about legalism when he criticized the Pharisees in Matt 23. We must find ourselves far from it, bound by our love for God and those around us and his overarching purpose of bringing the world into a grace relationship with himself. (Prov 21:2-3; Hos 6:6; Matt 12:1-8, 23:23-26; John 1:14-17, 3:16-17, 8:31-32, 36; Acts 20:24; Rom 4:1-9, 14:5-8, 16-18, 22; 1 Cor 6:12, 10:23-24; Gal 3:23-25, 5:1, 6, 6:14; Eph 2:8-10; 2 Thess 2:16-17; 2 Tim 1:8-9, 4:3-5; Titus 2:11; Jas 1:22-25; 2 Pet 3:9)

201. The Sacred Gift

CERTAIN VIEWS OF GOD and his word cause confusion and twist our understanding of God's purposes to meet our needs. When our Western need for logic and order is joined with our uneasiness with ambiguity, dread of uncertainty, and fear of mystery, it can bring out attitudes and doctrinal positions that satisfy these Western needs and requirements. The mystery and danger of the sacred gift of human freedom do not seem to fit with God's control of the universe. But we think as humans and give our understandings more credibility than they deserve.

We have many absolute truths, giving us clear boundaries for the rest of our theological thinking. But we can also limit God to our finite world of human reason and logic. It is evident in Scripture that God is ultimate and absolute in the spiritual and physical universe. He has also given us the freedom to pray, decide on his way or reject it, choose good or evil, love or hate. He has sovereignly decided to grant humankind the freedom to be part of his plan and bring their petitions to him who answers. We must not let our preferences for a black and white understanding of God cause us to limit his wisdom and ways. We can and must choose to let God be God. Of course, when we do, the answers to our prayers may not look like we expect them to from our vantage point; his providence may not seem to be from him. For his ways are not our ways, and there is a time for his purposes that may not be our time. But we can and must trust him in all these things. (Prov 3:5–7 with 26:12 and 28:26; Eccl 3:1; Isa 46:10, 55:8–11; Matt 7:7–11, 19:21–24; John 4:28, 6:66–68, 14:13, 15:7; Rom 11:33–36; Eph 3:12; Heb 4:14–16)

202. Accepting Freedom

MANY NATURAL AND SOMETIMES severe results of our choices are allowed by God because he has given humans the blessing and danger of choosing courses of action. In many cases, he does not interfere. Still, he can and does intervene at other times. It is a grand but mystery-laden blessing—his providence on our behalf and his response to our prayers, even though neither may meet our personal and cultural expectations.

Not only do God's mystery and providence boggle our minds, it also bothers many Christians that Christ brought both grace and truth. The two do not seem to mix very well. Most of us lean toward one or the other. Many emphasize truth more than grace and prefer to see our relationship with God as obedience or sin. Others stress grace by bringing in lofty-softy sentimentalism, divesting God of his severity toward willful rebellion.

Truth and grace must be kept together. When we do so, we can see and accept that this combination brings a freedom believers did not have before the death and resurrection of Christ. We can do all things seasoned with gratefulness to God and love for our neighbor. Again, this makes the Western soul uncomfortable. Some combat this uneasy state with God's sovereignty, total depravity, or legalism, anything to do away with mystery or freedom, anything but letting God be God. But relationships do not work that way. God's grace should fill us with humility, gratefulness, and wonder at his greatness, mercy, and the freedom he has given us framed by love for him and those around us. Wisdom is the way forward and cannot always be defined by black and white reasoning. This grace, freedom, mystery, and love do not submit to formal logic. They demand a heart of trust in God. (John 1:14 and 17, 8:31–32, 36; Rom 11:33–36; 1 Cor 6:12, 10:23–33; Gal 2:4, 5:1 with 13 and 14; Eph 3:12, 14–21; 1 Tim 4:3–5; Titus 1:15–16; Jas 1:22–25; 1 Pet 2:16–17; 1 John 5:13–15)

203. God's Intentions in God's Way

OUR WESTERN CULTURAL PREFERENCES are an automatic frame of reference for the meaning of information and experience. Even though the Bible is written with a Middle Eastern frame of reference, most of us are limited to our Western values and inclinations when reading the text. Without knowing it, we twist and squeeze it into something that makes sense to us; we wring information out of phrases in a way that may miss the particular intent in that Middle Eastern culture, giving it meaning that goes outside its purposes in that social context. In short, we find what we expect if it were said, if the event took place, in our own Western context today. Though the essential truths about the gospel stand out to us without understanding the social values of that time, this Western approach to the Bible can come up with some strange applications leading to legalism, mysticism, or syncretism. Bible teaching in schools and churches must consider this and help us put our own culture aside long enough to look into the Bible through the windows of the cultural and social context of the times—that of the original audience or participants in the events.

The Bible is different. It is not a reference book of answers to our every question, nor is it intended to speak to every possible behavior of the human being, labeling it good or bad. It was not designed to fit an ideal system of categories and logic that Western man usually brings to it. We can expect it to defy our packaging, frustrate our reasoning, and sometimes offend our sensibilities. It is a revelation of God himself, his works in the universe, and his will for the human race. It is intended to shape us into people who live our lives under his grace, honor his ways, love those around us, and face life's decisions with sensitivity and wisdom. This is countercultural in a context valuing self-assertion and personal achievement to establish one's identity and worth.

God repeatedly tells us that he looks at people's hearts—their motives, intentions, and desires—rather than their outward appearance, vocabulary, achievements, or display of "spirituality." The Old Testament talks about the "fear of the Lord"—an inward recognition and respect for his lordship over the universe and our lives. It is found deep in the heart and bears fruit in our attitudes and actions. It will result in behaviors that will vary among true Christians, but their heart's intentions are always the same—to honor their God, remain loyal to his way, and care about others the way we would want them to care about us. (1 Sam 16:6–7; Pss 40:6–8, 51:6 with 16–17, 147:11; Prov 1:7, 3:5–7, 9:10, 16:2, 17:3, 20:27, 21:2–3; Eccl 3:1–8; Hos 6:6; Matt 7:12, 15–23, 9:13, 12:7)

204. Knowing and Doing

HUMANKIND CHOSE TO KNOW good and evil with the act of Adam and Eve in the garden. The result was a shattering of the perfection of God's creation that we have lived with ever since. We continue to know good and evil every day. Our prayers are often for God's help navigating the difficulties of living in this broken world. Though we sometimes do not recognize his answers, other times, we pray already knowing what he wants of us.

Only a fool prays for a good harvest without planting and cultivating the crop. When we do what God has already laid before us for his honor and glory, there are fewer things to pray about, and they tend to be of more eternal consequence. To put our hand to the vocation God has provided, to love the family he has given us, to see our neighbor's helplessness as needing our hand, these need little prayer. As important as prayer is, the length of our prayers is no indication of deeper spiritual commitment. Doing God's will, as we already know it, is the duty before us. (Josh 7:10–13; Prov 20:4, 27:23–27; Mic 6:8; Gal 6:9–10; Eph 2:8–10; Phil 3:16; 1 Thess 4:11; 2 Thess 3:10; 2 Tim 3:16–17; Titus 2:11–14, 3:14; Jas 1:22–25 with 4:17; 1 John 3:16–20)

205. What, No Options?

THE PERSON WHO REJECTS Jesus as the only way to God for a religion (including the extensive faith of atheism and the replacement of God in evolution) does so on other grounds than an honest reading of the documents of the New Testament. Religions usually boast of some ultimate, supreme remedy for the problems of humankind. But when you read their original documents and talk to those people, you will find it depressingly futile. You may find some truth about man's nature and suffering and some temporary emotional relief, but there will be no actual solutions and, in most cases, no honest answers. You will find the opposite of a remedy—endless ritual behavior that brings further suffering. This is the deception of Satan.

The exclusiveness of Jesus' words may be offensive to many, but the way to any necessary solution is usually exclusive at the core. Try some other alternative to sleeping, eating, or paying your taxes. There are no alternatives for water or air or maintaining a minimum body temperature to stay alive. Seats in the airplane are given exclusively to those who have tickets, and you have to drive on the right side of the road unless you are in England. Why are these elements and rules demanded so exclusively? Is it really fair that we have no other options?

Requirements for the survival of the human being are mirrored by those for the survival of a society. There are minimum requirements that cannot be short-circuited without drastic results. We may try to make the human situation the way we want it, but our human ideas fall short of meaningful survival, let alone flourishing. It is the same concerning God. No two people come to Christ in precisely the same manner—but come to him, they must. If you want to put your car in the garage, there aren't many alternatives to opening the door. If you want to get to God, you will have to take the way of Jesus. It is not a popular choice because the doorway is small, and you have to bow down to enter—a humbling of our independent self. The blessing is that, by his grace, there is a way, and it is open to all. There, you will find not subjugation to a harsh master but forgiveness and freedom in a relationship with God—forgiveness of our sin against God and freedom from that old self and its history. We will have freedom from cultural demands to care about others, to own an identity with Christ, and to live with new meaning and purpose. It is highly worth taking the exclusive way of Christ. No other options lead to God and the destiny of eternal life. (Isa 55:8-9; Matt 7:13-14, 24-27; John 1:12, 3:16-21, 8:12, 31-32, 12:24-26, 14:6; Acts 4:12; Rom 3:22-24, 6:19-23; Gal 5:1; Eph 2:1-10; 1 Tim 2:5; 1 Pet 3:18; Jude 3-4)

206. The Source of Thinking

IF HUMAN RATIONALITY COMES from a totally irrational, non-intentional, utterly blind process of chance, then human thinking cannot be trusted to give us an explanation or theory of how it came about. Humans ultimately cannot talk about truth, good and evil, right and wrong, morality, or say anything of meaning. Life from a mud ball excludes all significance of that life and any meaningful thinking about it.

Like the emperor's new clothes, the masses have been duped by the schemes of those trying their best to exclude God from the universe. They have removed significance from life, and the results are obvious in our disintegrating society. Those in charge of maintaining the theories—those "in the know"—are desperately casting blame here and there for the ruin they have caused. They are looking for remedies for their guilt everywhere except where they can be found. But there are some, even among the simple, who know there is a great deal of significance to life—those who know where it comes from, who can think, and who see the emperor is naked. It all begins with the God of creation and finds its fulfillment in the life, death, and resurrection of Christ, the way, the truth, and the life. It will take both courage and humility to find his way. But the mind and heart created by God can fully engage both to choose life over death. Those with eyes of faith know the difference. (Gen 1:1—2:25; Ps 1:1–6; Prov 5:21 with 6:16–19, 9:10, 14:12, 34, 16:19, 26:12, 23–28; Luke 16:19–30; John 14:6; Rom 1:21–22; 1 Cor 1:23–29; 2 Cor 4:4–6, 11:13–15; Eph 2:1–5; 1 Pet 5:8–9)

207. Wisdom over Culture

CULTURES ARE HUMAN SURVIVAL systems with good, harmful, and neutral elements. Good parts or values are just that, sometimes praiseworthy, sometimes just practical ways to accomplish a wholesome life. Bad aspects may be evil, or they may be just unhelpful. They may not look wrong, but they may be harmful to survival in the long run. Most of the time, they are the perversion of good things God has given us. The largest category of culture is the area of neutral elements with no moral dimensions in themselves. They may be used for good or evil behavior. It depends on our personal values concerning them.

Good parts of culture might emphasize humility; hospitality; generosity; relationships; a daily fish, seaweed, and kimchee diet; and how people honor the aged. Harmful elements might be witchcraft, materialism, competitive self-assertion, legalism, the evil eye, or the constant fear of capricious nature spirits. Neutral elements might be means of transportation or how people build houses or care for newborns. Marriage celebrations, what is used for currency, or how people express sadness, embarrassment, or joy may also be neutral. Institutions for economics, education, and government are neutral but can be highly corrupted by the greedy, the immoral, or the unjust.

Wisdom is having a discerning eye and discriminating ear concerning cultural values and assumptions. God must be at the core of our worldview if we are to have this wisdom. Then, we can decide how to use our culture's good and neutral values to honor him. This fear of God, this recognition of and respect for the infinite God of the universe, opens our eyes and ears to the way, the truth, and the life. Mixing the abuses of good values or the harmful elements of culture with the truth we have in God's word becomes a destructive syncretism in our lives and churches. Wisdom from God's word rather than cultural expediency must be our consideration. (Pss 8:1–9, 9:7–10; Prov 3:5–6 with 26:12 and 28:26, 4:23, 9:10, 21:20–21; Luke 12:15–21;

John 1:4–5 with 8:12 and 14:6; Rom 12:1–2; 1 Cor 10:31; Eph 5:15–17; Phil 1:9–11; Col 3:17; 1 Tim 4:4, 6:6–11; Titus 1:15)

208. Freedom and Its Limits

THE MOST CHALLENGING AREA to navigate in culture is the use of its neutral elements. While it may not matter if you use one neutral solution or another to accomplish things in life, they can generate a great deal of suffering and evil when abused. People misuse money, authority, the internet, or recreation. These elements are neutral in themselves but have a great potential for either good or evil.

It is possible, however, to feel some neutral elements are always sinful if they are often abused, are associated with non-Christian use, or are simply unfamiliar. Some Christians even find ways of making the Bible say these elements are sinful. In their negativity, they prefer other forms of expression that seem to be without the potential for sin. But since sin begins in the heart, even virtuous activities may be carried out with the wrong motives, exposing the gravest of sins—pride or selfish ambition.

Someone's use of neutral elements as a Christian may seem unpleasant to you, but that does not make them evil. We are free in Christ to choose and use any neutral or good elements of culture if we are grateful and our intention is to honor God and respect others in the activity. Except for the guidance of children, we are not free to make that decision for another person, and we must sometimes curb our freedom for the sake of other Christians. Our freedom is not without limits, and the intentions of others are not known to us. This means sensitivity and humility become critical factors in expressing or curbing our freedom. They should characterize our lives. (Matt 7:1–5 with 12; Luke 6:37–38; John 7:24, 17:20–23; Rom 12:9–16, 14:1–8, 13–23, 15:5–7; Gal 2:4, 5:1 with 13–15; Phil 2:3–4; Col 2:6–23; 1 Pet 2:16)

209. Thinking about What We Know

SOME PEOPLE ACCUMULATE INFORMATION about God but miss its meaning. They may think their accumulation of a great deal of information sets them apart as more spiritually mature from those of a simpler faith. But this is a dangerous frame of mind. It is possible all that information, as important as much of it may be, will remain superficial in their minds. We must, instead, think about what we know. Those who think about a small amount of biblical information and see its meaning for them will be a great deal further in their spiritual lives than those who know a lot but only as information. Knowledge must become wisdom that directs the life of the person. Those who think deeply about God's purposes, his providence, and his grace, who trust him only, are the great ones among us, though, in other ways, they may appear simple. I have been privileged, as have many others, of knowing a few of these people in life and in their writings. Let them be our examples. (Ps 90:12; Prov 3:5–7, 27–28, 26:12, 28:26; Eccl 9:17–18; Isa 66:2b; Mic 6:8; Matt 5:3–10, 11:25–26, 20:25–28; 1 Cor 1:20–31; Eph 2:8–10; 2 Tim 3:16–17; Titus 1:16; Heb 11:6; Jas 1:22–25, 3:13; 1 John 3:16–20)

210. The Great Decline

WE TALK ABOUT THE decline of Christianity in our day, but we may not be accurate in this judgment. That is, it is not the decline of true Christianity. We have been used to large numbers, but that has been the number of people attached to Christianity, people attending churches. We cannot be sure how many people of true faith are in such numbers. Church attendance is not the only and not the best indicator of loyalty to God. Many of those who have attended church fall away quickly when it is no longer popular or profitable for them. Others who have true faith will leave a church when it no longer helps them grow spiritually, for not all churches are equal. So, church attendance does not tell us the whole story. And, we must remember that, though large numbers of the faithful are encouraging, they are not the expected course of things here on Earth. Jesus told us that few find the small gate, the narrow way.

The most serious aspect of our situation is that of false faith among those who claim to be Christians. When love is not real, proud judgments common, and selfish ambitions obvious, outsiders are kept away from the realities of the truth and grace of God. Not every church is an authentic expression of biblical faith. Syncretism, legalism, sentimentalism, and mysticism often thrive in visible Christianity. Institutional professionalism may take over its purpose and mission. Not everyone who calls him "Lord" will enter the kingdom of heaven. Jesus would suggest the use of a millstone for those who lead others away from God. So grievous is their counterfeit faith.

So, the popularity of visible Christianity is shrinking among the Western population. The pendulum is swinging to lower numbers in response to these unbiblical examples of superficial faith, love for the world, and the deception of Satan. People may leave because many churches do not offer the teaching and biblical worldview they need. They have not found the institutional church they have known helpful in their journey, or it has become irrelevant to a living faith. Many who leave remain loyal to God but seek the teaching they need elsewhere.

We live in a generation throwing off the shackles of tradition for a life of "freedom" without God. And we must not be deceived; it will take more than a romantic notion about Jesus to convince those of the world around us to step into ours. Loyalty and allegiance must be bathed in grace and truth, love must result in action, faith must show empathy, and freedom in Christ must reveal an authentic relationship with God. If Christianity declines in new people coming to Christ, the cause is not always outside the church. God's grace is quite resistible, and never more so than when its example is made into a system of works for his approval, extroversion becomes a sign of salvation, spiritual leadership a mask for selfish ambition, or the size of the building the symbol of its success. We must be done with faithless, sentimental, proud, legalistic, selfish, or mystical and insecure leadership in our churches. It is time for a resilient but humble faith that leads people into a trusting relationship with God through his grace to us in Christ. (Matt 7:13–14, 15–23, 13:24–30, 18:1–6; Mark 10:21–27; Luke 18:9–14; John 1:14 and 17; Acts 20:28–31; 1 Tim 2:5–6; 2 Tim 3:1–5; Titus 1:16; Rev 2:1—3:22)

211. In Love with Christianity

IN CHRISTIANITY, WE MUST grow toward trust in God, gratefulness for his grace, humility in our words and actions, love of those around us, unity with believers, and compassion for a lost world. Following his word, we must be people of truth and grace. But this identification is threatening to some and has brought about unbiblical reactions. The message about freedom in Christ and the grace of God has been ignored by some and replaced by a perfectionist insistence on propositional truth and obedience to rules that earn God's approval. Others have turned to a superficial, romanticized faith—love without substance—or mysticism that needs constant miracles for assurance of God's love and direction. But salvation is neither earned by works nor realized through emotional displays or confirming wonders. And it is not gained by association with "spiritual celebrities." These groups are in love with a sort of "Christianity," but not with the God of grace and truth revealed in the Bible.

The world reacts against these displays of "faith." Grace and compassion with truth and obedience are often seen as mutually exclusive. But the church was never meant to be held together with the chains of legalism, the sticky syrup of romantic feelings, or the bandages of constant signs and wonders. The message that has been missing for some time now in many churches is a humble faith in Christ as the only way evidenced by good works lived out in the freedom Christ gives us. It is not works without faith or faith without works, but an unbending loyalty to God demonstrated by a costly and treasured freedom in Christ to be lived out in love for others and gratefulness for his grace. It is faith revealed by works. By this, we will be the salt of the earth, a light in a dark world. (Isa 66:2b; Matt 5:13–16; John 1:14, 17, 8:31–36, 13:34–35; Rom 12:9–21, 14:19–23; 1 Cor 8:9; 2 Cor 3:17; Gal 5:1; Eph 5:8–9; 1 Tim 4:4, 6:18–19; Heb 13:15–16; Jas 1:22–26, 2:14–26; 1 Pet 2:16; 1 John 3:16–20)

212. Popular Christianity

I HAVE OFTEN SPOKEN of the categories of Christianity as being biblical, popular, or folk Christianity. The main distinction concerns syncretism—how much cultural values, personal experience, and self-assertion are mixed with a person's "faith." Popular Christianity is among us all in our churches. It is a matter of devotion to Christianity or the church as a solution to emotional and social needs rather than knowing and trusting God. These people appear to be Christians and are often very good people. But, while none of us is perfect in our walk with God, there is a fundamental difference in loyalty and allegiance to God between biblical Christians and popular Christians. Without this settled trust in God, popular Christianity will not get a person through the storms of life, and it may not get them to heaven. That being said, we cannot often tell who is a biblical Christian and who is a popular Christian since faith is a matter of the heart. Our disagreement with another Christian's expression of their faith is not a reason to brand them a popular Christian. God reserves the right to make decisions about our faith. He asks us to look for the log in our own eye before looking for the speck in another's.

The strength for forward motion comes from engaging with God. It amounts to an unwavering trust in God's grace, a dogged loyalty and allegiance to his providence and purpose in our lives, and a continual restraining of the influences of self-assertion, perfectionism, and cultural expectations in our lives. This is not something we do as well as we might think, as it makes humility a central part of the equation. Without his grace, none of us is worthy of this relationship with him. (Prov 3:5–7, 4:23, 28:26; Matt 7:15–29, 15:7–9, 18:1–4; John 12:41–46; Eph 4:1, 5:1, 15–17; Phil 3:12–16; Col 1:10–12; 2 Tim 3:5, 7; Titus 1:16; Heb 11:6; 1 John 2:15–17)

213. Spiritual Adultery

PEOPLE ARE TIRED OF it. They are put off by the exhibitions of superficial Christianity. They are repelled by legalism and tired of the giddiness of popular Christianity. Their search for meaning in life in that direction is over. The door is closing to an era of opportunity for Western Christians. Those tired of the hypocritical display click the locks on that door, hoping to keep it closed. The question is, How much are we Christians helping to close that door? Has the salt become tasteless, the light gone out? As in the days of Malachi and the worthless sacrifices the priests offered to God, perhaps Christians too, in the institutionalization of the church, and then the maneuvers to keep it going, have left their first love, allowed the life to go out of their faith. Have Christians taken a mistress? Have they fallen in love with their church building on the side? Have they committed the spiritual adultery of syncretism with their culture? Have they divided their faith, loyalty, and affection and given God the leftovers? God is looking for those who worship him in spirit and truth. Faith in his goodness and trust in his grace have always been matters of the heart. (Pss 5:21, 14:8, 51:6, 16–17, 145:18–19; Prov 17:3, 21:2–3; Hos 4:12; Hab 2:18–20; Mal 1:10; Matt 7:15–29, 12:7, 15:7–9; Luke 18:8; John 4:23–24, Rom 1:22; Eph 5:8; Titus 1:16; Jas 4:4; 1 John 2:15–17; Rev 2:1—3:22)

214. The Choice of Loyalty to God

THERE IS SOMETHING ABOUT the curse that man brought upon himself in the garden that we must never forget: it is here to stay in this life. We get glimpses from God of what will one day be the normal state of affairs without it, but for now, it goes on, and we live a life of faith in that broken world. Even when enjoying the beautiful gifts freely given to us in his creation, the pain and suffering from sin are never far off. Mankind was deceived by Satan, and planting doubt is still his tool to discourage our trust in God. Suffering is not God's choice for us, and he will one day end it all, but it makes up the conditions under which we can exercise genuine trust in his grace, confidence in his providence, and assurance of his power today. God made possible the choice to be loyal to him in a rebellious world. In this way, we can know his grace and providence under the contrary conditions of this life in which we desperately need him. The freedom of that choice is only possible by his grace, which he has put before every man and woman.

Every day of our lives, this choice is before us. We are either desiring loyalty to God and living in the truth, showing grace to others as its sign, or living for ourselves. On our own, we may be thinking we are the only ones who are right, wondering why everyone else is so wrong, or worrying about how imperfect we are and that someone may find out. But those loyal to God know very well they are not perfect and that his grace and truth are. (John 1:1–5 with 10–12, 3:16–19, 14:25–31, 15:18–21 with 16:33 and 18:36, 17:13–19; Rom 12:1–22; 1 Cor 1:20–31; Eph 4:17–24, 6:10–18; Col 3:1–10; Titus 2:11–14)

215. Eyes of Faith

WHAT WOULD HAPPEN IF God granted people every prayer as asked? Who would not ask for the wrong things? And if God met all our human, cultural, and selfish demands as we expected, who would not be a "Christian" for the wrong reason? Do we know so little about ourselves, our human finitude, and selfish preferences? Are we that unaware of our culture's strong influence on us and how weak we are toward its expectations? Before we cry out "unfair!" to the God of the universe, who promised to answer our prayers, we might consider that his ways are not our ways, his thoughts are not our thoughts, and his purposes may be outside our logical understanding. Even our theological framework can get in the way. Many things God does defy human reason, and his answers to our prayers are often better than what we asked for in our limited perception and with our human expectations. But many of those answers go unrecognized, much of his providence unnoticed, until later in life.

As we look over God's activity in the Bible, if we had done those things, we would have done them differently. Our logic cannot compare to his wisdom; we do not fully understand his intentions; we must have eyes of faith concerning the mystery of what we do not know. Humanly speaking, God is not very conventional, and we can find it frustrating to see that, in reality, he does not always fit our human preferences for him. But for all the things we do not know and are incapable of understanding—the paradoxes of his ways and the mystery he reserves for himself—this God is intensely interested in us and our welfare, and he wants our trust. He may seek to get it for our ultimate good by giving us opportunities to express it in ways we do not appreciate or may not understand at the time.

Though God loves us and knows our needs, he often waits for us to ask him for help. In his power to save and bless, he is waiting for our permission, our faith, to move ahead. A relationship with God begins with trusting him, who is totally trustworthy. We must look to him with eyes of faith and ears of hope. He always hears us, though the timing and nature of his help may be outside our expectations. Relax. This God is on your side if you want his purposes fulfilled in and through you. You do not have to know the how and why of everything. You just need to trust him. In the brightest or darkest times of life, he is there to accomplish his purposes with your welfare in mind. (Isa 40:28, 55:8–9; Jer 17:9–10; Matt 6:5–8; John 14:13–14; Rom 1:17, 11:33–36; 1 Cor 1:20, 25; Eph 3:12; Phil 1:6 with 2:12–13; 1 Thess 5:23–24; Heb 11:6; 1 John 5:13–15)

216. God Does Not Run Out of Time

THE WESTERN PERSPECTIVE ON time is a powerful controlling factor in our lives. Many other cultures have a long-term view of time and expect delayed gratification, but we have short-term expectations for fulfillment. We are often impatient and frustrated. Many prayers are for things we want and need now and are a desperate cry for immediate help. But God may still take months or even ten or twenty years to bring about his ideal response to us. David was anointed king by Samuel at God's insistence, but he did not become king until twenty painful years later. God is neither rushed nor limited by time.

We must look back, often over a lifetime, and reflect on how God has been at work in our lives. His hand has probably moved many mountains into the sea in response to our prayers, even when our faith was weakest. Even the worst events of our lives, though we evaluate them with our personal preferences and desires and judge them with our cultural frame of reference, from our finite perspective, have a part in our lives that he turns into his purposes for us. And that may take time we are unwilling to allow. Patience is not one of our cultural virtues. But the psalmist tells us to wait on the Lord, as does Jeremiah in his lamentations. His time is the best time. We must trust him, for our times are in his hands. (1 Sam 16:6–13 with 2 Sam 5:4; Pss 13:1–6, 27:13–14, 31:14–16, 37:7, 40:1–3, 43:5, 46:10, 90:4 with 12 and 17, 119:71, 121:1–4 with 4:3, 127:1–2, 130:1–6, 138:8; Lam 3:22–26; Rom 8:22–25, 28; Phil 1:6, 2:13, 4:6–7; Jas 5:7)

217. Knowing and Not Knowing God

WHEN PEOPLE DISTRUST THE Bible and do not experience God's love and grace, they live with a different worldview than those who have trusted Christ's work on their behalf and know God through his word. We cannot and should not expect them to live as if they have what we have—an assurance of God's hand in the world, his grace and forgiveness, his providence in our lives, and his personal care. Our expectation that people who are not Christians can and should act like Christians is illogical. It burns up emotional energy we should use to serve God and reach out to them. And God has told us that to fret about their behavior makes things worse, for our anger does not accomplish his will. Our expectations of them may push the unsaved further from knowing God.

Are some unbelievers more kind or moral than others? Yes, but they still lack the essential element of knowing God through Jesus. Their world is built on something else. We cannot make the transformation of knowing God happen in their lives. But we can prepare the soil for it by incarnating God's truth, grace, and love, using the plow of good works, the harrow of kindness, praying that God will soften the soil of their hearts. When it is ready, we can plant the seeds of the truth and water them from time to time. However, we cannot count on their immediate transformation. They may never accept God's grace or may take time, even a lifetime, coming to know him. It is a process more than an event; we must entrust them to God while seeking to be light in the darkness, showing them the way. (Pss 37:8–11, 23–24, 28, 91:14; Jer 9:23–24; Matt 5:13–16; Mark 2:13–17; Luke 8:4–15; Eph 4:26–27; Titus 2:9–10; Jas 1:19–20; 1 Pet 2:12 and 15)

218. The Interference of Culture

CULTURE IS A FORMIDABLE influence in our lives. That influence begins at a level we cannot easily examine, the level of our worldview—understandings of reality that are never questioned. Unfortunately, we are given these understandings assumed by our culture as the truth and do not automatically escape their influence when we become Christians. Though not all bad, our culture is an interpretive framework, and we experience our faith in God within the realm and under the influence of that lens. A Western person does not spontaneously stop being the individualist, egalitarian, achievement-oriented, time-conscious, monochronic, low-context product of their culture when accepting God's grace in Christ. But some of these values or their intensity are harmful to our trust in God. If we do not pay attention or examine the controlling influence of our culture, we will not live out our faith in a biblical way. We will instead live a life of syncretism, that is, a life of mixed values, some cultural and selfish and some biblical, and some terribly twisted by that mixture. Our Christian conscience will be culturally conditioned, and the lens through which we read God's word will be smudged and unclear.

If our faith becomes encrusted by our cultural worldview and values and we do not know how to scrape off the barnacles, it will be weighed down by these parasitic assumptions, beliefs, and values. If we build a life, a marriage, or a ministry on this foundation, it will not be what God intends. Putting your culture on the operating table takes considerable trust and courage. But we must take the scalpel to the malignant tissue that, if left intact, may infect the entire body. Knowing God involves a transformation of the mind. We must turn from trusting in our culture and its survival methods to trusting God and his providence. (Pss 18:2, 20:7, 37:3–7a, 118:6–9; Prov 3:5–7, 26:12, 28:26; Matt 7:24–27, 9:16–17, 18:1–5; John 12:24–26; Rom 12:1–2; 2 Cor 4:4–7; 1 John 2:15–17, 4:1–6)

219. Cultural Wineskins

AMERICAN CULTURE IS NO better or worse than many others. Though it has its unique values and freedoms of independent, democratic capitalism, because it is human, it is not perfect. It is easily abused by selfish and evil intentions, pushed around by politicians and celebrities, marred by intentional immorality, influenced by self-destructive fads and trends, and a prisoner of its neurotic efforts to insert meaning and contentment in the void left by a rejection of God. It is intended to serve, like all cultures, each with its many subcultures, as an integrated system for human survival at its core, but that core is eroded, and it is losing its integration. Many believe life will be better if they just cancel it all. But they do not know where they are going.

No one can live without a functioning cultural system to organize behavior, give life purpose and relationships meaning, and make communication possible. But that is the problem. On the one hand, Western culture is losing that necessary integration and, with that loss, a good deal of its functionality. On the other hand, culture is so necessary to our survival that we are reluctant to step outside the boundaries of its disintegrating values, even when they pull us away from biblical values.

We are naturally disinclined to question the assumptions and values from which feelings of security and self-worth have come in the past. But as Christians, we must be aware of the danger of allowing cultural absolutes to outweigh biblical absolutes in our new life. For personal, emotional, social, and mental survival, we have employed self-assertion, achievement, social affirmation, and logical systems of understanding in our lives, our relationships, our careers, and, unfortunately, in our faith. It is time we took inventory of the influences on our lives and examined the worldview behind them.

Our pride and desperation for approval, identity, and self-worth have built a barricade around the kind of person our culture has allowed and helped us to become. But all those needs are now fully met in Christ. We were at ease with the old, familiar values. But now have new wine, and putting it in the old wineskin will not work. We must pour the new wine into the new wineskin—step into a new worldview with God at its center. Though we still walk in this physical world, we are now alive and alert to the spiritual universe, the kingdom of God. We live with a purpose beyond mere survival. Our identity and self-worth come from the sturdy and constant source of God's love, grace, and forgiveness. It is countercultural to the individualist, survival of the fittest, god of our own life kind of thinking we were given in our socialization. We now trust the righteousness God has given us in Christ. It meets his standard of justice and gives us his complete acceptance. Think of it. We have a relationship with the God of the universe. Purpose and meaning in life are restored. We now live to honor him and rest in his care. (Prov 16:2, 25, 26:12, 28:26; Luke 5:33–39; Rom 6:4–7, 12:1–2; 2 Cor 5:15–17; Eph 2:1–5, 10, 4:22–24; Phil 1:27, 2:3–4; Col 1:9–13, 3:17; 1 Pet 1:13–21, 4:1–2; 1 John 1:9)

220. God Speaks?

IT HAS ALWAYS BEEN the case that some theologians think they know more than God gives us about various subjects. Liberal theologians come to the Bible with assumptions and expectations about what is there, ought to be there, or must be there. They toss what they think should not be there and come up with what they are looking for. Popular Christians also see what they want or need in the Bible. They do not let God speak for himself. But, if we think he needs our help or always agrees with our opinions, we have yet to know God. Those who find what is not there are influenced by cultural expectations, their need to control, insecurity, and personal and emotional requirements. Desperate to lessen God's demands and enhance their social survival, they fall into syncretism, a mixture of both that resembles neither. Then, the mixture hardens. The longer it goes unattended, the harder it gets. You no longer have Christianity but a religion that reflects the culture's demands and social expectations. If you do not control your culture's influence, it will control you in subtle and deceptive ways.

No. We must let God speak for himself and see the relevance of his words to our lives and culture today. He intends to accomplish his purposes regardless of our preferences. Of course, there is mystery in God's ways, much that is beyond our finite understanding. But we must open our hearts and minds to all God gives us and trust him for what he does not. It will open the door to the freedom we can know in Christ. (Pss 1:1–3, 53:1; Isa 29:16; Matt 7:24–27; John 8:31–36; Acts 20:28–31; Rom 1:16; 2 Cor 4:4; Col 2:13–23; 1 Tim 1:3–7; 2 Tim 3:16, 4:1–4; Titus 1:10–16; Jas 1:22–25; 2 Pet 2:1–3; 1 John 2:15–17, 3:18)

221. All Sin Matters

WE HAVE A WAY of condoning some sins and highly criticizing others. We rank them on a list according to what we consider their level of seriousness, and when we get lower on the list, our concern tapers off. We also have a way of inventing sins by filling in information that God does not give us, reading between the lines what we think must be the intent in his word. All this ranking of sins mentioned in the Bible and devising others that are not his words come from human sources.

Most of us have a culturally influenced Christian conscience. That is, we let trends in our culture define what God means when he reveals his will in the Bible, often watering down the truth or producing false guilt. Some of us fear an angry God who, for us, is an image of a demanding father or mother in our lives, one whose approval is impossible to achieve. Yet others of us have personal needs to control others so we can feel better about ourselves. If we can make it seem that God demands more than meets the eye in the Bible, and we alone have the answers, people come under our control.

These thoughts about sin are motivated by insecurities. We find it hard to trust a God of grace and freedom. This way of judging God's word regarding what we find acceptable or not in his priorities for us and his definition of sin has hurt Christianity and caused a gulf between Christians and the world around them. Legalism, gossip, envy, pride, and greed are grave sins in the Bible, as are murder, injustice, theft, and adultery. But when we say that all sin matters, we must also remember that God can and does forgive all sin if we come to him through the sacrifice of Christ. Failure does not have the final word. Grace does.

When we ask if God only notices the "big" ones and overlooks the "small" ones, we neglect important principles in God's word. The first is that God is more concerned about what we are than what we do. Secondly, the New Testament talks about freedom in Christ for those who trust him— freedom bounded by our desire to honor him and love for those around us.

Thoughts and actions are not sins for us because our culture or legalistic Bible teaching says they are. Finally, grace and truth came together with Jesus. The truth is that we all sin, and his grace is such that he forgives all sin, beginning with the thoughts and intents of the heart, when we come to him honestly and humbly accept that grace. This is a significant point of Jesus washing the disciples' feet in John 13. He showed them that we do not need a total bath, but we need our feet washed to maintain our fellowship with him.

Sins are not smaller or greater; they are matters of the heart and show our trust in God is still weak. But he already knows that and reminds us constantly that he is there for us and is all we need. And he does that because we all need to be reminded. When we realize our weakness and turn to him, we do his will, and his grace covers us with forgiveness. It should produce a great deal of humility in us, for all our sins are on the same list, and their rank is equal to all others, yet God's grace washes our feet each day as we come to him. (1 Sam 16:7; Prov 5:21, 16:2, 21:2–3 with 27, 26:23–26; Jer 17:9–10; Matt 7:1–6, 15:7–9; Luke 6:37–38 with 43–45; John 4:23–24, 5:24, 8:31–32, 13:6–10, 21:17–22; Rom 12:1–3, 14:5–8 with 16–18 and 22; 2 Cor 9:8, 12:7–10; Col 1:22, 2:13–15; 1 Pet 5:6–7 with Phil 4:6; 1 John 1:8–10, 21)

222. Time with a Fool

THE PROVERBS GIVE US the realities of living a life of wisdom and its alternatives. It mentions several categories of people. We find there the naïve, the senseless, the stubborn, the proud, and the lazy, and all of them reap the unhappy results of their choices. All are called fools and begged to correct their ways, but they do not listen; they die for want of wisdom. Fools do not know the purpose of life, how to live it in relationships, or why they do what they do. They cannot see down the road to the outcomes of their irrational and reckless ways.

The result of spending time with a fool, however clever he or she may seem, is losing days, weeks, or months of forward motion in the important things of life. Fools are people and deserve the respect we should have for all human beings created in the image of God. We may seek to influence them for Christ, but we cannot afford to let them suck the life out of us, smother our spirit, or eat up our emotional energy until we are worn down and incapable of putting our hand to the good and essential things God has set before us. Other people also need our attention and love. (Pss 1:1–3, 53:1; Prov 1:7, 32, 12:15, 13:16, 20, 15:2, 16:19, 22, 25, 17:12, 18:2, 6–7, 23:9, 26:4–5, 11, 12, 27:22, 29:11, 26; Eccl 2:14, 4:5, 10:1–3; Isa 5:20–21; Matt 7:6 with 12; Luke 9:1–6; Rom 1:21–22)

223. The Conscience of a Nation

EVERY CULTURE HAS THE component of conscience: ideas of things considered good or bad to do or think, social sins, right or wrong, moral or immoral, virtue or vice. Each culture gives its members expectations of each other to follow the rules of their group conscience. Among these are essential rules everyone needs to pay attention to for the group's survival. Such ideas as do not murder, do not steal, do not assault another, or respect other's rights, protect the needy, and serve your country become parts of the law for the people. The society criticizes and maybe imprisons those who break these laws. They also praise those who carry them out at a high cost to themselves. It becomes a matter of honor or shame, innocence or guilt, virtue or mayhem in the culture to follow or disregard the code. Many of these rules have their roots in God's plan for humankind, though some cultures are further removed from that than others. Nevertheless, it feels natural to the people—the way things ought to be.

But, eventually, the members of a culture try to generate new issues for the group's conscience or remove those traditional morals they do not like. They want these adjustments to become part of a new moral and ethical code, the law of the land, and they get governing authorities to enforce them since they are not naturally part of the traditional ways of going about life. This mixed "moral" code—natural and manufactured—often divides the people. Though some of the changes are good, what was once pagan and hedonistic may take on the shiny new façade of not just acceptable but virtuous behavior enforced by law. It may be given the height of attention while the "old" moral code will be depicted as socially sinful. What once protected the society and enhanced its survival will be removed for destructive values outside God's will.

The health of society depends on the consistency of justice, virtue, and integrity in relationships regarding the standards we see in God's word. But social conscience is never perfect, and it always wanes. It is sort of a social

223. THE CONSCIENCE OF A NATION

law of thermodynamics at work. It always tends toward disintegration. Many members of society think they are enjoying freedom from the earlier collective conscience as it breaks down. But they have no idea in their naiveté that disintegration and destruction are around the corner. When biblical standards of virtue and integrity, mercy and punishment, or moral and immoral behavior evaporate in the conscience of the governing power, the resulting corruption seeps into every crook and cranny, eventually destroying the basic unit of the family. It will ultimately punish the good people and give freedom and rewards to the bad. That culture is in critical condition, stage four self-destruction.

Human nature inevitably turns against God and toward tribal or self-survival without him at any cost. It never ends well. Though this is natural in human societies, God gives us the ultimate moral standard—motives, values, and priorities that would preserve a people and cause their community to flourish. He offers forgiveness and freedom, life with renewed purpose and meaning, providential care, and a perfect destination without end. Some may think they are okay without God. But culture's rewards are thin and temporary, and we cannot trust in ourselves, our money, or our social standing for long-term survival. Everyone stands at a fork in the road and must choose life or death. (Prov 11:28, 16:2, 28:26; Matt 24:4–14; Luke 6:43–45; John 3:16–21 with 36, 5:24, 8:12, 31–32, 11:25–26; Rom 1:18–22; Eph 2:1–2; Phil 3:17–21; Col 2:13; 1 Tim 1:18–20, 4:1–2; 2 Tim 3:1–5; 1 Pet 3:13–17)

224. The Golden Rule

IN CHRISTIANITY, OUR MORAL and ethical basis for relating to those around us rests on God's word. It can be reduced to Jesus' words that we should treat others as we want them to treat us. The understanding of this is sometimes spelled out in detail in his word, such as in the parable of the Good Samaritan. More often, however, we are given a boundary within which good over bad, profitable over unprofitable, and helpful over unhelpful must be our choice, given the situation or people involved. *Agape* love, seeking another's highest good, is the baseline from which we are to measure the decision for any activity. It creates the biblical norm for us, giving us expectations of each other. It is the high road and often means personal sacrifice to take it. And yet, knowing all this, we all fall short of God's desire for us in our day-to-day lives.

We are not good at this. We need to realize our weaknesses and confess our sins, embracing the humility this gives us before we seek to criticize or find fault in the shortcomings of others. Jesus said, "First, take the plank out of your own eye, then you will see clearly to remove the speck of sawdust from your brother's eye." It is very possible that once you see clearly, there may not be a speck in your brother's eye after all. Love should be the result, a proof of our faith and hope. For a good tree does not bear bad fruit. (Matt 7:1–5, 12, 15–20; Luke 9:23–25, 10:25–37; John 13:34–35; Rom 12:3 with 9–19; 1 Cor 8:9, 10:23–31, 13:13; Gal 3:12–14, 5:13–14; Eph 2:3–4, 4:32; Col 3:12–14; Jas 3:13–18; 1 Pet 2:16–17)

225. Survival

HUMAN BEINGS HAVE A survival instinct for self-preservation. We usually think about this in terms of physical survival and the "fight or flight" instincts that serve us in dangerous situations. But our human nature and culture also give us ways to survive mentally, emotionally, and socially. For example, Western culture gives us rational logic for our minds, ways to demonstrate achievement, granting self-worth and identity for our emotional health, and ways of competing and asserting ourselves for social survival and material success. Self-preservation is still the essence, and the ways culture gives us to manage survival in these domains become instinctive, however unbiblical they may be.

In an individualist society, protecting the self in these ways can take on desperate dimensions. But these ways of survival are human and seldom mirror biblical truth. Because of their importance to our survival, we do not find it easy to shed these cultural strategies to adopt biblical understandings when we become Christians. As a result, institutional Christianity includes or condones many values and behaviors that are human and cultural. Churches in individualist cultures overlook a great deal of selfishness and competition. Those in collective cultures call for a great deal of acquiescence to the group and submission to its hierarchy to maintain a virtuous status and feelings of belonging. Neither is the biblical norm for true believers. It takes a great deal of trust and courage to risk human survival, as our society sees it, and choose God's way even though it leads to our every fulfillment in him. His grace, promises, providence, and protection give us forgiveness, freedom, hope, and meaning. (Pss 33:16–22 with 20:7 and 147:10–11 and Prov 21:31; Pss 40:4, 127:1–2, 146:3–6; Prov 11:28, 26:12, 28:26; Jer 9:23–24; Matt 5:1–10, 7:13–14; Luke 9:23–25, 12:13–21; John 12:24–26; Rom 8:31–39, 12:1–3; 2 Cor 5:15; Gal 5:13–15, 22–26; Col 3:1–4; 2 Pet 1:3–11; 1 John 2:15–17)

226. Fear and Anxiety

Most everyone has experienced some trauma in their lifetime. Christians are no exception. Whether it comes in early years in the home or later in life, unfortunate things happen in this broken world, and we are affected more than we realize. The memories of these events, whether they took place over a long term or were a single incident, can gain control of our lives. Some people manage to push the memories of these negative experiences away from their waking thoughts, but the anxiety and fear they have left with us more often lingers, sometimes for years and, for many, a lifetime. When these memories return, the fears of those events burned deep into our emotions return. They drive us to anxious thoughts and the behaviors they seem to demand of us that seek to compensate for them or help us escape them. Our memories of these damaging events and the fear and anxiety they trigger cause us to forget things in the present. They distort us and bring emotions and thoughts that distract us from the important things we might be doing, the people in our lives we might be loving, and the rest and peace God promises to those of faith.

But God is not surprised nor angry at our anxiety. He knows we were born into a broken world, and his compassion is unending. He desires to draw us closer to himself and reminds us over and over to give these anxieties to him and let his grace and love replace them in our lives. He reminds us because we all need reminding, not once but over and over, when the complexities and difficulties of life bring confusion and forgetfulness, and the bad memories return. We must let these anxious and fearful memories be gradually replaced by realizing his love and grace for us just as we are, by awareness and gratitude for his blessings surrounding us today, and by attention to his words of encouragement to trust him in all things. It takes time; we may never forget or understand why, but those memories that linger can bring our minds back to his work, blessings, and present grace in our lives.

226. FEAR AND ANXIETY

Though some may think that anxiety and fear are sins and that God is upset by them in our lives since he tells us not to be anxious, it is not so. He forgave our sins when we turned to Christ and continues to do so as we walk with him. Like Christians everywhere, we now need to come to maturity in him. He now wants us to know his peace in our relationship with him by growing in our faith and trusting him with our inner world of thoughts and feelings. It is not a sin to need to grow in Christ. He gave us his word to nurture us as his children. His goal is for us to grow in him; it is how he cares for us. He brings freedom from the chains of these thoughts and fears. We may not forget the experiences, but we no longer have to let them control us. It may be that without such memories, we would not learn to trust him. (Ps 103:6–18; Prov 3:5–7; Matt 11:28–30, 12:20; John 8:31–32, 14:21–27, 16:33; Rom 8:31–32; 2 Cor 12:7–10; Gal 5:1; Phil 4:4–9; Col 2:13–15; 2 Tim 3:16–17; 1 Pet 1:3–9, 5:6–11; 1 John 3:19–24)

227. The Christian Life Is Not Natural

I RECENTLY READ IN two different books that a lifestyle of living for Christ, a walking "worthy of the gospel," is a natural result of believing in Christ as God and our Savior. But that is not true. It is anything but natural. It is an intentional choice of the believer each day, a constant awareness of where we fall short, where we are weak and need his forgiveness, need to trust him, and need to change a way of thinking, an attitude, or a behavior. Walking worthy of the gospel is walking in the Spirit and is an ongoing process of change and reinforcement of that change in us. We are reminded of it on every page of the New Testament. It is based on our love and loyalty to God and a humble heart that knows it is not perfect—gratefully depending on him and his grace each day.

Will some aspects of it become natural? Yes. We will eventually remember lessons learned, turn to him more readily in troubles, and further realize the importance of trusting him. But there is no end to our growing more in Christ and learning to trust his work in us—his good providence. But we are not alone in this endeavor to walk worthy of him. He is always with us through the Spirit he has given us. His grace and forgiveness, his love and providence, the freedom of our relationship with him, his trustworthiness, and our eternal salvation are our strong encouragements. His word reminds us of all of this and shows us how he has worked in the lives of his faithful ones.

We can depend on his providence to be at work in our lives for our good and for his good purposes at every step of the way. We are free from the guilt of our sin and free from legalism, but we are not free from our need to walk in his way of love and grace, trusting him for our worries and seeking to honor him with our lives. We must be faithful to what we know of his ways as he has shown them to us in his word and trust him for what we do not know. (Pss 23:4, 139:5–12; John 8:31, 32–36; 2 Cor 12:7–10; Gal 5:1 with 13–15, 16–26; Eph 4:1–6, 21–24, 5:8–10, 15–18; Phil 1:27 with 1:6 and 2:12–13, 3:12–16; Col 2:13–15; Heb 11:1–40; 1 John 1:5–10)

228. God Loves the World

I WAS READING SOMEONE today who was saying they did not believe in a God who sends men and women to eternal and conscious torment for not believing the right things. He said God is a God of love and beauty and would not do such a thing. Well, he is right that God would not do such a thing. I don't believe God is like that either. Human suffering here and hereafter is not God's choice for people. Humankind chose not to trust God in the garden of Eden. He created Adam and Eve with free wills to choose a path of knowing good with his blessings or evil with the consequences of suffering in this life and the next. He called it death. God loves the world and longs for all to come to salvation through his grace. He constantly gets blamed for our choice of this suffering, but he gave the ultimate sacrifice—his Son—so that all who believe in this act of his grace might avoid the eternal suffering they are headed for on their own. He made a way back to himself, and he wants everyone to know about it.

This same author brought up the fact that millions have died without knowing about the gospel of Jesus. He did not believe that God would send them to hell. And he is right; God is not sending them to hell. They are already headed to that destiny. He does not want anyone to perish in such a way. The reason they have not heard the gospel is mankind's choice not to listen to God, not to trust his way, and therefore not to teach others to listen but to substitute a religion or philosophy for God's word and his desire for them. Jesus is highly critical of those who would lead people away from God or cause them to sin. He talked about the better option of millstones tied around their necks and being thrown into the sea. The eternal destiny of those they lead astray was and is at stake.

We do not know God's heart concerning the eternal fate of those who have never heard of Christ themselves to make their own choice nor concerning those who may have concluded there is a God from their observation of the creation who never heard of Jesus. He has not told us all things.

But we do know he is a God of justice and will be just with these. We also know that their situation is one more result of the rejection of God by others, not God's design. Those who reject him and his way have chosen their own destiny, and leading others away from God only increases their torment. Our main task is getting the good news to those who have not heard it. We must trust God for what he has not told us.

The "eternal fire" was created by God for Satan and his demons, not for humankind. It gives God the utmost sorrow when people choose Satan's side and his destination for themselves and even more when they lead others to follow them in their decision. He greatly regrets their choice but does not tread on the sacred gift of free will he gave them to make that decision. The way to God through Christ is described by Jesus as being narrow with a small gate. It is that way because of the humility and submission to God and his grace that are its conditions. People have to bow low to enter that gate, but they are proud and want to control their own lives. They feel it is too much to ask, or others have made them think so. They have been deceived and deceive others to seek instead to destroy the way of Jesus or to replace it with traditional human religion or atheism—the crown of human religions. God's way in Christ is open to all; the choice is before each person. But there is only one way. That is what God has told us: nothing more and nothing less. (Gen 1:26–28 with 15–17 and 3:1–13; Deut 32:4; Pss 89:8, 14, 97:1–2; Matt 7:13–23, 18:1–6, 19:16–24, 25:41; Luke 12:47–48, 16:19–31, 17:1–2, 18:18–25, 19:37–44; John 1:10–13, 3:16–17, 35–36, 8:42–45 with 1:12, 14:6; Rom 3:21–24; 2 Cor 4:4; Gal 6:7–10; 1 Tim 2:1–6; Titus 1:1–3, 2:11–15; 2 Pet 2:9–19, 3:3–11 with 14–18)

229. The Knowledge That Leads to Godliness

PAUL TELLS TITUS IN the first few verses of his letter to him that he was chosen by God to instruct and encourage the people of God in their faith and in their knowledge of the truth that leads to godliness—"a faith and knowledge resting on the hope of eternal life." Two lines of activity in the spiritual universe accompany growing in Christ. One is that we will be humbled as God shows us there is a great deal he has not given us to know. We will come to appreciate and even enjoy the mystery God has chosen to maintain in our relationship of trust with him. In this way, God nurtures trust in himself. Adam and Eve did not know why, in God's creation of all the trees in the garden for them, there should be one from which they were never to eat. We will realize many questions are not answered for us in his word. In these areas, we move ahead with sheer trust, or we do not move ahead at all.

Secondly, as we progress in our Christian lives, we will become more aware of our sins. It will become a wonder to believe that God could love us, save us, be at work in us, and want us to serve him and be a part of his work in the world. But he has and does and will always do so. It creates a deep gratefulness for his grace. Sometimes, in our progress, God shows us what we don't know or don't want to know about ourselves—our sin of trusting the old survival strategies for our insecurities and their resulting patterns in our lives. He is showing us what we need to change in our thinking, attitudes, and actions that do not reveal him in our lives. Sometimes, it is Satan trying to discourage us using even what God is revealing to us, accusing us to make us feel defeated and guilty. Sometimes, it is God using what Satan is reminding us of to show us his "grace is sufficient" and his "power is made perfect in weakness."

Seeing ourselves more clearly as our weaknesses become more evident comes as either a purifier of our faith in God's lavish grace or a discouragement of our forward movement in the godliness Paul speaks of in his initial words to Titus. Satan would like the latter; God is intending the former. God is using a messenger of Satan to give us a deeper understanding of his grace and work in our lives. Paul tells the Corinthians that he asked God three times to remove the torment this "thorn" was to him, but he came to delight in it as God's hand on him. He said God used it to produce humility and gratefulness in his heart. It gave him an enduring trust in the power that was working in him, spiritual and emotional resilience in serving God in what he had given him to do, strength for the suffering it would bring his way, and rest in God's providential way in his life and work. This is an example of what Paul tells the Philippians about God at work in us. God's loving grace is everything to us. It brings humility, gratefulness, and security in the worst of times. God will continue his work in us for his good purposes until the day we see Christ. (Pss 20:7; 33:16–22; Prov 3:5–7, 11:28, 28:6; Zech 3:1–2; Matt 5:3–10; Acts 9:13–16; Rom 7:14–25, 11:33–36; 2 Cor 12:7–10; Gal 2:17–21 with 3:23–25; Eph 2:1–10; Phil 1:6 with 2:12–13; Titus 1:1–3; 1 Pet 5:6; Rev 12:10–11)

230. Dealing with Doubt

CHRISTIANS MAY OCCASIONALLY HAVE doubts about God. Perhaps they have not seen his hand or felt his presence in their lives for some time. They wonder if, after all, God is not very interested in them. And, of course, those who are not Christians are so because they have doubts, or maybe even what they call certainties, that there is no God. I have some advice for those who are not Christians: Hadn't you better make sure? It is a pretty big deal if there really is a God, and you are refusing to believe it based on your feelings. Or maybe you do not think God is there based on secondary evidence given to you by people about whom you know nothing of the integrity of their own search. Many who don't believe in God have that view because they do not want there to be a God. They want to be gods themselves—a familiar theme from the very beginning. But everyone should want to find out the truth. It is too important of a search to be satisfied with anything less.

You won't find God with a microscope or a telescope. If you want to know the truth, you will have to use the ways he has given us to know him. That is by an honest reading of the Gospels with an open heart and mind—not the conditions of most secular research concerning God—all the while praying that he would make the truth about himself and his grace known to you. You should know the truth, not someone else's idea about it. It may take you some time, but don't be satisfied with less than your own discovery. He will not leave you alone in your search for him and will not fail the honest heart seeking him. But a humble honesty will be needed. After all, you do need to know. And when you find the truth, it is up to you to choose your allegiance. Will you bow before the God of the universe or raise your fist?

Christians who have doubts from time to time need only to trust what they already know. Satan is our accuser before God and in our own hearts, and we are tested and tempted in this world to look away from God when we do not feel his presence. But we cannot rest on feelings; we must rest our faith on facts and God's unrelenting providence in our lives. When he allows spiritually dry days and weeks, it is to give us the opportunity to practice our trust in him.

Paul was tormented by a messenger of Satan that God would not remove because he had a purpose for it in Paul's life. It was there to produce true humility, resolute trust, and resilient endurance. In the end, God told him it was his hand on him and that his grace was sufficient. Paul then came to delight in his weaknesses and difficulties that revealed God's strength, grace, and help. Though feelings are only a small part of it, it is still a matter of the heart where God is looking for trust when we do not understand or when we do not see or feel his presence. (Ps 42:1–5; Prov 3:5–7; Isa 14:12–15, 42:3; Jer 29:12–14; Ezek 28:11–17; Zech 3:1–2; Rom 8:28–39; 2 Cor 9:8, 12:7–10; Rev 12:10–11)

231. Help for the Weary

THERE ARE MANY WEARY and tired people. They have experienced the hard things of this life. They may be people in poverty or in lands stricken with the ravages of war. They may bear the brunt of unjust or brutal rulers over them. Or it may be more personal suffering from an unfaithful spouse in marriage, sickness, disability, being mistreated as children, forgotten in old age, or feelings of guilt from wrongs they have committed. If you are among them, you may feel like a plant with a broken stem beginning to wilt, a short candle with only a spark left on the wick; all may seem useless, but there is One who cares more than you know. You may be young or in the autumn of your life, but God is mindful of that broken stem and lonely spark and offers forgiveness, grace, and hope. He forgives our sins through faith in Jesus, satisfying his justice through the sacrifice of Christ for us. He gives us grace and hope in our suffering where there was none in the world around us. He gives peace and rest to the weak and downtrodden. He will one day vindicate those wrongfully accused, abused, or oppressed and bring ultimate justice to the world. We are not forgotten. He knows our names and writes them in his book. They can never be erased; no one can take us from his hand. We rest in him who trust and delight in the Lord, who commit our way to his good providence. (Ps 37:3–9; Isa 42:1–3; Matt 5:3–10, 11:28–30; John 1:12, 3:16, 14:27, 16:33; Rom 8:35–39, 12:12, 15:13; 2 Cor 5:17; Eph 2:1–10; Col 1:3–6, 2:13–15; Heb 4:9–11, 11:1; 1 Pet 3:18; 1 John 1:9; Rev 2:17, 20:11–15)

232. Mystical Experiences from God

THERE SEEM TO BE three types of Christian people in the family: There are those who have mystical experiences they say are from God that make them feel special to him. For them, special signs are evidence of his presence and affirmation. Then there are those who desperately wish they would receive a special sign or experience of God's presence to strengthen their faith and affirm their worth in his eyes. Finally, there are those who don't feel the need for special revelation from God to keep their faith vibrant but who know that God is active in their lives and can bring about any miracles he wants to fulfill his purposes. These trust God's truth and providence with soul and spirit and experience contentment in his love and gratitude for his grace. In humility, they let God be God and don't confine him to the courses of action their definitions and boundaries might set for him. The framework for their faith is his word, their trust in its eternal truths, and their loyalty to its purposes as given to them by God himself.

We decide which kind of person we will be. But we have help to do so. The first group of people should realize that it is not given to us in God's word to seek signs and wonders for ourselves. Instead, in the Bible, we see God acting in special events with miracles and signs of his own accord and for his purposes in the lives of selected people. It was never normative for the lives of Christians—never required or recommended for the believers in the churches. Our trust is in the same God, but his work in our lives is not of such a nature. The central theme in God's word for us is to trust his ways, power, and grace in everyday events and see his caring providence in the normal course of life and ministry.

The second group is told in the Bible to let go of their fears and anxieties by trusting God's ways and abiding in his grace and love. We already know we are his and do not need special signs to affirm it, though we may get them. Our feelings about him and his work in our lives are not the point. He wants our trust. Feelings of assurance and security, contentment and peace often accompany this trust, but we can trust him without them as Daniel's friends did before the blazing furnace of Nebuchadnezzar. This life is our opportunity to do so.

It is the third type of person who finds his or her way laid out for them in God's word. It is his will for us. When we take his course, gratefulness for his grace and confidence in his providence will overcome fear and anxiety. But we must let him be God and trust him entirely in the world and in our lives. We will not be perfect at this kind of trust, but he is not demanding perfection. That has been accomplished for us in Christ. He is looking at our hearts and intentions and is gracious to us in times of weakness. In him, we have absolute certainty of his love, can look forward to his continual work in and through our lives, and can share this confidence with others he brings into our lives.

Paul's advice for today is laid out in his letters to various churches in the New Testament. Though all of them are important, his last advice to the new churches is given in 1 and 2 Timothy and Titus, giving us a picture of God's heart for his people. There, the emphasis you will find is walking worthy of the gospel and doing good works. The letters to the Ephesians, Philippians, and Colossians are also helpful in considering how we should now live as Christians regarding the three types of people we talk about here. The kind who are at peace in their walk with God are mentioned by Jesus in Matt 5–7. It is all in his word; we have all we need there. (Pss 37:1–8, 119:105; Prov 3:5–7; Dan 3:15–18; Matt 5:1–10; Eph 6:10–20; Phil 1:6, 2:12–13, 4:4–9; Col 3:1–25; 1 Tim 4:1–26; Titus 1:1—3:15; Heb 12:1–3; 2 Pet 1:3)

233. Knowing Yourself Is Important for Knowing God

THOSE WITHOUT CHRIST ARE indeed blinded by Satan to the grace and freedom of the gospel. But it is also true that many Christians who have responded to the gospel are still numb to its blessings and benefits, awake but too groggy to see the way before them. They are unaware of what keeps them from fully enjoying the peace Jesus promises, the rest of being in the yoke with him. Of course, there may be other reasons for this, but the main one is living on a false narrative in the mind, a story with origins that may be painful or even unknown to the person. They live on an auto-pilot programmed by their experiences, culture, personal preferences, and appetites in our broken world. Their compass and altimeter are faulty; their pitch, roll, and yaw out of calibration; and they feel uneasy about it, not really knowing themselves and what drives and motivates their behavior and shapes their outlook. Their GPS is not locating their destination, and they sense they are lost. They wound themselves and injure others as they stumble along, crippled by difficult experiences from as far back as childhood. They read the Bible seemingly without effect and pray but do not see God's answers. "But I am a Christian! What is the matter with my faith?" It is a kind of Christian sleepwalking—self-defeating and hurting our relationship with God and those around us.

The believer needs to truly wake up to God's interest in them and what he has for them through an awareness of their history, the influences that have shaped them, and the residual effects on them today. This is not always a fun process, but as they grow in that awareness, they can move on to know how God has made them unique for himself and how he can use that history to shape them to live for him today and represent him in the world. We are not the cookie-cutter Christians we have been taught to be. Each is different from the others and forms a part of the body with functions and talents that others do not have. By the same token, you cannot do all that other Christians can, but you and I matter in that body of Christ. We matter to God.

We must ask God to help us discover what our past has taught us to value and believe, what our culture has demanded of us, and what hidden desperations shape the faulty lens through which we see him and his relationship with us. Some of our memories and experiences were and may still be painful. But God wants to remove that pain. As we identify these blinding influences and replace them with what God gives us in his word, we will begin living under a new authority and understand more and more of the forgiveness, freedom, and peace God is offering us. We will value being "in Christ" more and more and start to see the special place he has given us in his plan. This road to giving the self to God is fraught with the disillusions and lies Satan has planted in our minds. The way is strewn with his traps, but we now have eyes that see. It is longer for some than others, but God is with us every step of the way. This is the beginning of the wisdom God has always wanted for us. (Pss 23:4, 91:1–4, 139:1–12; Rom 12:1–2; 2 Cor 4:4–6; Eph 5:8–9, 13–16, 6:10–18; Phil 3:12–16; Col 2:13–15, 3:1–4; Jas 1:2–8; 1 Pet 5:6–9; 1 John 5:19)

234. Anger, the Enemy

ANGER CANNOT BRING ABOUT God's will in our lives or those around us. We know little of patience in our Western way of immediate gratification. It makes frustration and anger part of our everyday lives. This is especially so for the perfectionist who wants everyone else to do his will. But anger is our enemy and defeats God's purposes for us. Though love is often the opposite of anger and impatience, controlling anger is a matter of wisdom as much as a matter of love. Knowing the futility of anger, realizing the pain it can cause others, recognizing the selfish motive of our hearts, and understanding the nature of love and God's desire that should characterize our lives are matters of the heart that should guide our decisions and actions. There is a righteous anger that hates the injustice and violence in the world. But it is not anger for selfish reasons—for loss of personal possessions, profit, or recognition. It is anger expressed because of love for others.

"The end of a matter is better than its beginning, and patience is better than pride. Do not be quickly provoked in your spirit, for anger resides in the lap of fools." Pride often leads to anger, and Proverbs tells us that is the reaction of a fool, the opposite of wisdom. Conflict often pushes us to that foolish anger. Patience waits for a better ending of the matter. A patient man or woman, longsuffering in their love, is greater than a warrior "who takes a city" or a competitor who wins the argument. Winning is not the goal. The need to win, to always be right, will eventually produce anger. Love is the goal in relationships, and it demands patience and understanding—wanting the best for the other person. God showed patient grace to you and me. Anger is the opposite of this grace and spoils the opportunity to show we care. Wisdom gives us perspective and patience, making way for grace. It "makes one wise man more powerful than ten rulers in a city." It is a rare jewel in our times. (Ps 37:7–8; Prov 15:1, 16:32; Eccl 7:8–9, 12, 19; Isa 66:2; Mic 6:8; 1 Cor 13:4–7; Eph 4:22—5:2; Phil 2:1–4; Jas 1:19–20, 3:13–18)

Scripture Index

GENESIS

1:1—2:25	290
1:1–31	132, 259
1:1–27	216, 260
1:15–17	319
1:26–31	73
1:26–28	48, 319
1:26–27	168, 266
1:26	201
1:27–28	85, 95
1:31	40, 51, 85, 95, 131, 168, 201, 236, 269
2:15–25	48
2:15–17	47, 203, 260
2:15–16	201
2:20b–24	95
2:24	211
3:1–24	73, 233
3:1–19	18, 97
3:1–13	319
3:1–7	33, 48, 201
3:1–5	215
3:6–7	226
3:6	58, 155
3:8–13	29
3:14–15	180
3:16–19	40
15:4–6	118
22:1–18	118
22:1–2	52
37:28	52
45:4–8	52
50:18–21	29, 50
50:19–21	38, 174, 192

EXODUS

1:15—2:10	50
3:9–10	50
13:3	105
20:1–6	164

LEVITICUS

11:45	105
22:33	105
25:38	105
26:13	105

NUMBERS

11:4–6	176
15:41	105
23:19	21

DEUTERONOMY

4:20	105
6:12	105
10:12	104
20:1	105
31:6–8	63
31:6	26, 58, 96
31:8	26, 58, 96, 107
32:4	47, 58, 63, 67, 319
32:35	67

JOSHUA

1:8–9	250
1:8	110

JOSHUA (continued)

1:9	264
7:10–13	287
23:14	107
24:5–7	105
24:14–15	157, 160, 164, 201, 233, 276

JUDGES

6:16–22, 36–40	239

1 SAMUEL

2:3–9	196
2:3b	104
2:4–9	91
2:7	166
2:8c	48, 51
13:14	22, 102
16:6–13	303
16:6–7	126, 200, 285
16:7	102, 166, 309
16:13	102

2 SAMUEL

5:4	303
24:10	185

1 KINGS

8:56–61	107
19:14, 18	240

2 KINGS

6:8–23	174
6:15–17	80, 136, 170

1 CHRONICLES

29:17a	13, 78, 186
29:18b	13, 78, 186

2 CHRONICLES

7:14	40, 109, 186, 203, 224
32:7–8	118

ESTHER

1—10	50
2:8–9	52

JOB

2:9–10	29, 135, 158, 245
5:9	46, 262
13:15	96
28:20, 23, 28	239
34:11	262
36:11	262
36:15	245
38:1—41:34	262
38:36	227
42:1–2	203

PSALMS

1:1–6	181, 240, 274, 290
1:1–3	19, 110, 209, 217, 221, 223, 249, 250, 254, 308, 311
3:1–6	252
4:3	303
4:5–8	214
4:8	33
5:3	217
5:21	299
7:9	249
8:1–9	95, 291
8:3–9	45, 48, 168
9:7–10	15, 16, 291
9:9–10	129
10:1–11	260
10:4	259, 274
11:4	174
13:1–6	303
14:1	290
14:1a	205, 235, 240, 259, 260, 274
14:2	92, 174
14:4–5	259
14:8	299
15:1–5	78, 181, 183, 267
16:1–11	15, 110, 153
16:5–11	13, 57, 84
16:8	43
17:2	74
18:2	305

18:27	128
18:30	58
19:1–14	95, 216
19:1–6	40, 259
19:12–14	267
19:14	250
20:7–8	90
20:7	21, 33, 43, 96, 118, 155, 165, 214, 231, 305, 315, 321
21:7	33, 90, 214
21:8–9	172
22:3–5	231
23:1–6	90, 217
23:4	29, 37, 40, 43, 80, 96, 158, 252, 318, 328
24:1–6	76, 181
24:3–6	183, 267
25:1–21	59, 192
25:1–3	90
25:4–5	77, 194
25:8–10	231
25:8–9	24, 194
25:9	100
26:12	129
27:1–5	252
27:1	63, 110, 129
27:13–14	58, 67, 74, 138, 151, 155, 194, 303
28:6–9	21, 105
28:7	33, 129, 152
29:1–11	58
31:14–16	303
32:1–5	27, 63
32:4–5	76
32:5	251
32:8–10	143
32:10–11	263
32:10	203
33:6–22	174
33:11	78, 126, 145, 165, 194, 203, 211, 217, 231, 240, 251, 274
33:12–22	276
33:16–22	16, 21, 90, 118, 155, 165, 315, 321
33:16–19	96, 231
33:18–22	263
33:18–19	126
33:18	200, 251
33:20–22	74, 231
34:1–22	61, 129, 165, 201
34:4–10	80, 152, 194
34:4–8	118, 219, 264
34:4–7	192
34:4	217, 252
34:8	214, 226
34:15–22	276
34:15	200
34:17–22	194, 264
34:17–19	74, 192, 217
34:19	207, 251
34:22	186
36:7–10	107
37:1–11	16, 26, 67, 118, 135, 138, 224
37:1–9	74, 150, 174
37:1–8	134, 143, 326
37:1–7	151, 201
37:1–6	15
37:3–11	194, 196
37:3–9	244, 325
37:3–7	97
37:3–7a	105, 231, 305
37:3–6	33, 38, 42, 61, 110, 157, 181, 214, 219
37:3–5	21
37:4	203, 204
37:5–9	152
37:5–7a	155, 238
37:5–6	27, 91
37:6–9	60
37:7–11	35, 122
37:7–8	330
37:7	303
37:8–11	304
37:8	249
37:16–17	219
37:16	203
37:20	276
37:23–24	16, 45, 52, 55, 66, 74, 76, 89, 105, 107, 110, 118, 133, 143, 165, 186, 207, 217, 245, 251, 304
37:23	204
37:27–28	74
37:28	16, 89, 105, 107, 118, 143, 217, 245, 304
37:34	135

PSALMS (continued)

Reference	Pages
37:34a	74, 143, 194
40:1–5	251, 264
40:1–4	80, 96, 212
40:1–3	129, 303
40:3	217, 224
40:4	21, 92, 157, 236, 315
40:6–8	22, 183, 242, 285
42:1–5	80, 323
42:5–8	158
42:5	15, 26, 32, 151, 217
42:11	194
43:3–5	50
43:5	303
44:23–26	151
46:1–11	122, 152
46:1–3	37, 129, 151
46:7a	129
46:10	47, 151, 303
46:10a	129
48:9	250
51:5–6	102
51:6	61, 69, 127, 237, 242, 285, 299
51:16–17	13, 61, 63, 69, 102, 127, 128, 183, 186, 242, 285, 299
51:17	22
52:7–9	200
52:7	235
52:8–9	157
53:1–4	260
53:1–3	259
53:1	64, 235, 308, 311
55:22	96, 133
56:3–4, 11	157
57:7–11	95
61:2–4	107
62:1–2	37, 151
62:5–8	37, 165
62:5–7	151
62:11–12	37
63:1–8	26, 43, 219, 237
66:16–20	110
69:32	100
71:14–18	151
73:21–28	110, 151, 192
77:11–12	250, 260
78:7–8	22
78:8	133, 164
78:35–39	139
78:35–37	22, 133, 164
80:8	105
84:1–12	32, 155, 237
84:10–12	118
85:10–12	35
86:5	226
86:11–13	263
89:5–18	48
89:8	45, 68, 319
89:14	42, 68, 319
90:4	95, 168, 303
90:10–17	32
90:10–12	59, 134, 168
90:10	95
90:12	90, 95, 110, 120, 169, 219, 279, 294, 303
90:14	110, 168, 219
90:17	110, 168, 219, 303
91:1–16	26, 37, 214, 252
91:1–4	32, 43, 80, 118, 328
91:1–2	16, 63, 107, 129, 219, 251
91:1	45, 77, 139, 190, 217
91:5	69
91:9	45, 107, 139
91:14–16	16, 45, 57, 69, 76, 80, 107, 139, 152, 190, 208, 217, 228, 254
91:14	304
92:9–15	172
94:12–13a	117
95:1–7	230
95:6–7	45, 75, 208, 254
96:6–9	58
97:1–2	94, 319
99:1–5	42
100:1–5	32, 104, 230
100:3	45, 75
100:5	128
102:11–12	168
103:1–5	236
103:6–18	27, 168, 209, 316
103:9–14	128
103:10–18	167, 190
103:10–14	36, 60, 66, 69, 126, 179, 184, 186, 212, 254
103:10–13	262
103:12	63

104:33–34	250	139:1–4	174
105:4	194	139:5–12	318
107:1	263	139:6	46, 58
107:13–16	37	139:7–12	26, 29, 40, 43, 107
107:14	64	139:7–10	212
111:4–7	33	139:13–17	82
111:10	57, 61, 90, 169, 205, 250	139:13–16	45
112:4–7	109	139:13–16a	168
112:6–8a	214	139:14–16	235
115:1–8	217	139:23–24	21, 88, 95
115:3	33, 50, 174, 203, 240	143:5–6	105, 250
115:11	96, 118	145:3–5a	249
116:1–2	90	145:5	250
118:6–9	90, 305	145:13–14	24
118:19–27a	216	145:13b–14	152
119:11	254	145:17–19	102
119:15–16	250	145:18–19	76, 128, 152, 183, 299
119:46–48	105, 250	145:18	40
119:67–71	29	146:3–6	21, 96, 118, 155, 315
119:67–68	245	146:5–10	151, 152
119:70–72	111	146:5–6	165
119:71	97, 105, 126, 135, 245, 303	147:2–6	100
119:75–77	117	147:3	29
119:92–93	29	147:10–11	21, 100, 315
119:97–104	250	147:11	133, 152, 285
119:103	124, 126	148:1–14	216
119:105	80, 124, 126, 254, 326		
119:112	250		
119:130	80, 250		

PROVERBS

121: 1–8	122, 129, 152	1:5	160
121:1–4	303	1:7	57, 61, 90, 120, 127, 152, 235, 239, 240, 260, 285, 311
124:1–8	152	1:28–33	160
125:1–2	33	1:29–33	279
127:1–2	33, 92, 194, 303, 315	1:32	240, 311
130:1–8	66, 69	2:1–11	77, 204
130:1–6	74, 303	2:1–6	239
130:3–8	63	2:5–6	160
130:3–6	30, 76	2:12–15	260
130:3–4	11, 18, 24, 27	3:3–4	27, 230, 239
130:5–6	40, 67, 134, 138, 151, 194	3:5–10	231
135:6	50, 203	3:5–8	26, 90, 217
138:6–8	29, 52, 126, 192	3:5–7	15, 16, 21, 32, 33, 57, 96, 105, 107, 114, 118, 129, 134, 135, 138, 139, 143, 150, 166, 169, 190, 200, 205, 214, 219, 254, 262, 283, 285, 294, 298, 305, 316, 321, 323, 326
138:8	55, 77, 105, 194, 239, 254, 303		
139:1–18	21, 47, 88, 95, 111		
139:1–12	69, 164, 192, 205, 209, 214, 264, 328		
139:1–6	14, 24, 45		

PROVERBS *(continued)*

3:5–6	59, 192, 204, 252, 291,
3:6–7	37, 38
3:9	23
3:11–12	117
3:13–18	169, 205, 217
3:27–28	150, 159, 185, 200, 208, 222, 253, 256, 294
3:27	255
3:33–35	279
4:1–13	124
4:5–13	90
4:5–9	120, 205, 239, 250
4:5–7	169
4:6–9	134
4:20–27	85, 124, 227
4:23–27	249
4:23	85, 291, 298
5:15–23	211
5:21–23	94
5:21	16, 143, 290, 309
6:6–11	279
6:12–19	209
6:16–19	290
7:20	14
8:6–21	124
8:10–21	59, 134
8:17–21	207
9:4–6, 7–8	279
9:9–10	247
9:9	127
9:10	57, 61, 90, 152, 205, 239, 250, 285, 290, 291
10:4	110
10:9	22
10:13	160
11:2	100
11:7	151
11:15	23, 209
11:25	109
11:28	21, 23, 117, 157, 207, 214, 236, 312, 315, 321
12:4	211
12:15	260, 311
12:16	235, 279
12:18	230, 279
12:25	153, 230
13:7	219
13:16	209, 311
13:20	260, 311
14:2	94
14:8–12	235
14:8	240
14:12	11, 104, 124, 219, 240, 260, 274, 290
14:15	235, 279
14:26–27	152, 252
14:27	57
14:29	279
14:34	290
15:1	330
15:2	240, 311
15:3, 8–9, 11	201
15:13	230
15:14	160
15:15	230
15:16–17	219
15:21	279
15:24	260
15:25	92
15:33	59, 90, 100, 128, 152, 238
16:1–6	94
16:2	11, 13, 16, 78, 80, 104, 126, 127, 143, 186, 200, 235, 260, 279, 285, 306, 309, 312
16:9	32, 35, 38, 45, 50, 52, 55, 59, 64, 76, 77, 89, 90, 96, 105, 107, 118, 135, 150, 151, 190, 208, 214, 235, 245, 260
16:18–19	224, 279
16:18	238
16:19	76, 196, 219, 290, 311
16:22	311
16:24	153, 230
16:25	59, 127, 223, 228, 233, 306, 311
16:32	48, 74, 94, 330
17:1	74, 221
17:3–4	94
17:3	102, 200, 285, 299
17:6	247
17:12	311
17:22	230
17:24	160, 217, 235, 240
18:2, 6–7	311
18:12–13	100

18:12	128, 238
18:22	211
19:3	42, 226, 235, 260
19:9	167
19:15	110, 235
19:22	230
20:4	287
20:19	279
20:22	67, 74, 134, 138
20:24	15, 38, 77
20:27	80, 126, 200, 235, 279, 285
21:1–3	94
21:1	68
21:2–3	120, 183, 186, 191, 281, 285, 299, 309
21:2	61, 67, 80, 104, 126, 127, 138, 260, 276
21:3	13, 22, 24, 42, 102, 140, 228
21:13	208
21:20–21	291
21:27	309
21:30	16
21:31	21, 315
22:4	104, 128, 181, 183, 237
22:6	85, 95, 247
22:7–8	274
22:9	23, 109
22:24–27	209
22:24	223
22:28	260
23:4–5	23
23:6–8	109
23:9	279, 311
23:10–11	260
24:3	204
24:15–16	45
24:16	55, 66, 89, 118, 133, 186, 245
24:21–22	68
24:29	74
25:4–5	94
26:4–5, 11	311
26:12	114, 129, 134, 138, 157, 235, 283, 290, 291, 294, 305, 306, 311, 315
26:14–16	110
26:23–28	209, 290
26:23–26	309
27:2	114, 238
27:19	200
27:22	311
27:23–27	53, 287
28:6	219, 298, 321
28:26	13, 15, 16, 21, 23, 24, 33, 57, 59, 90, 98, 100, 105, 109, 117, 129, 134, 157, 186, 200, 214, 235, 262, 283, 291, 294, 305, 306, 315
29:4	94
29:11	311
29:23	100
29:25	214
29:26	311, 312
30:5–6	85, 102
30:7–9	98, 131
30:21–31	216
31:10	211

ECCLESIASTES

2:14	311
3:1–8	285
3:1	283
4:5	311
5:1–3	100
5:8–10	68
5:8–9	94
5:10–15	219
5:11–12	131
7:8–12	249
7:8–9	67, 74, 174, 330
7:12, 19	330
7:20	78, 132, 176, 179
9:17–18	59, 293
10:1–3	311
10:18	235

ISAIAH

1:18	63, 69
5:20–23	201
5:20–21	259, 311
6:1–8	104
6:1–7	57
6:5	198
9:2, 6–7	64
10:1–4	67
14:12–15	48, 323

ISAIAH (continued)

14:26–27	50
26:3–4	32, 33, 165, 166, 227
26:8–9	152
29:13	183, 184
29:16	87, 308
30:15	110, 118, 152, 214, 262
30:19–22	143
32:5–8	259
32:17	90, 111, 118, 143, 152
33:6	90
40:8	124
40:13–14, 21–31	262
40:28–31	45, 52, 58, 74, 165, 217
40:28	46, 301
40:31	134, 151
41:10	15, 45, 52, 165, 217, 252, 262
41:13	15
42:1–4	255, 262
42:1–3	13, 14, 32, 37, 63, 64, 67, 76, 84, 186, 325
42:3	323
43:1–3a	15, 21, 174
43:1	19, 50, 84, 111, 118, 172, 184, 214, 253
43:1b	37
43:10–14	203
43:10–13	91, 174
43:11–13	52
43:25	63
44:6–8	52, 58
44:8	45
44:9	122, 174
44:18	80
45:5–6, 9–12	50
45:12	48
46:9–10	46, 47
46:10	15, 50, 52, 91, 174, 283
48:17	45, 50, 91
50:10–11	15, 64, 87, 91, 164, 259, 274
50:10	21
52:13—53:12	224
53:1–6	71
55:6–7	205
55:8–11	38, 52, 91, 124, 262, 283
55:8–9	33, 58, 138, 166, 245, 288, 301
56:11–12	94
59:12–15	94
65:17	18, 29, 245
66:1–6	139, 200
66:2	181, 183, 330
66:2b	13, 100, 104, 110, 128, 196, 205, 294, 297

JEREMIAH

1:4–5	82
2:5–13	48
2:13	87
9:23–24	57, 157, 196, 228, 236, 304, 315
9:24–25	139, 200
10:1–16	276
15:16	124
17:5–10	109, 259
17:5–8	96
17:7–8	152
17:9–10	201, 301, 309
17:9	114, 116, 124
17:11	203
29:10–14	38, 105
29:12–14	323
29:13	36, 57, 78, 88

LAMENTATIONS

3:22–26	64, 67, 303
3:22–24	194
3:25–26	151
3:26	74
3:31–33	94
3:40	11, 36, 50, 66

EZEKIEL

14:6, 11	276
28:11–17	323
33:29–33	183
33:30–33	139, 184

DANIEL

1:1–7	50
2:48–49	50
3:8–18	68

3:15–18	174, 326
3:16–18	52, 96, 158
4:34c–35	50
4:35	203
9:20—12:13	278
12:1–3	278

HOSEA

4:1	131
4:12	131, 299
4:12b	78
6:6	13, 61, 102, 127, 131, 140, 143, 228, 281, 285
14:9	59, 160

AMOS

5:14–15	201

MICAH

4:5	21, 174
6:6–8	190
6:8	13, 22, 24, 42, 61, 91, 94, 100, 102, 104, 110, 127, 128, 140, 143, 148, 181, 183, 191, 203, 205, 212, 228, 231, 237, 242, 287, 294, 330

HABAKKUK

1:1–6	68
1:4	94
1:5–6, 12	52
2:4	21
2:9–11	94
2:18–20	299
3:16–19	43, 52
3:17–19	55

ZEPHANIAH

3:7–8	67

HAGGAI

1:13	107

ZECHARIAH

3:1–2	321, 323

MALACHI

1:10–14	183
1:10	299
2:1–2	139
2:14–15	85
3:10	231

MATTHEW

1:21	71
3:8	191
4:5–7	239
4:12–17	80, 276
5:1–10	80, 194, 224, 315, 326
5:3–12	135
5:3–10	76, 88, 100, 102, 179, 196, 219, 274, 294, 321, 325
5:3	24, 128
5:8	51, 78, 128, 228
5:10–12	172
5:13–16	122, 132, 150, 153, 162, 175, 208, 237, 244, 245, 255, 297, 304
5:14–16	145, 191
5:16	140, 194
5:38–48	122, 172, 257
6:1–8	61, 127, 228
6:1–4	238
6:5–8	301
6:9–13	38, 40
6:10	136
6:14	27
6:19–24	272
6:19–21	23, 43, 122, 157, 207, 219, 231
6:24	164, 188
6:25–34	16, 23, 31, 43, 165, 205, 207, 219, 221, 236, 239
6:25–33	216
6:31–34	26, 111, 134, 136, 253
6:33–34	51
6:33	50, 88, 110, 112, 126, 138, 157, 194, 231
7:1–6	209, 237, 309
7:1–5	182, 279, 293, 314

MATTHEW (continued)

Reference	Pages
7:1–2	75
7:6	27, 311
7:7–12	35, 36, 88
7:7–11	23, 283
7:12	47, 209, 285, 293, 311, 314
7:13–29	60
7:13–23	89, 278, 319
7:13–14	19, 71, 87, 92, 139, 176, 205, 225, 233, 288, 295, 315
7:15–29	162, 164
7:15–27	225
7:15–23	61, 127, 129, 138, 175, 178, 186, 200, 223, 279, 280, 285, 295
7:15–20	191, 314
7:21–23	69, 87, 112, 139, 172
7:21	71
7:24–29	176
7:24–27	126, 157, 221, 288, 305, 308
8:5–13	82, 228
8:23–27	15, 26, 43
9:9–13	13
9:13	285
9:16–17	24, 29, 166, 170, 188, 198, 253, 254, 305
10:16	209
11:25–30	15, 91, 179
11:25–26	224, 294
11:28–30	16, 32, 37, 84, 97, 118, 165, 166, 170, 214, 221, 250, 264, 316, 325
11:28	66
11:29	217
12:1–8	281
12:7	242, 285, 299
12:15–21	151
12:20	316
12:50	112
13:1–9	254
13:8–9	120
13:11–17	94
13:18–23	109
13:24–30	129, 178, 186, 200, 279, 295
13:36–43	60, 172, 178, 186, 200
13:44–46	100, 162, 205, 207
14:22–32	84
14:28–32	33, 129
15:7–20	126
15:7–11	183
15:7–9	186, 298, 299, 309
15:8–9	139, 228
16:1–4	231
16:5–12	26
16:18	276
16:24–28	87
16:24–26	205
16:26	214
18:1–9	175
18:1–6	60, 228, 247, 295, 319
18:1–5	237, 305
18:1–4	24, 100, 104, 116, 128, 164, 176, 188, 198, 224, 272, 298
18:6	186
18:12–35	63, 74
18:12–14	11
18:21–35	75, 121, 209
19:16–30	87
19:16–26	43, 82, 102
19:16–24	36, 225, 226, 233, 319
19:16–22	201
19:21–24	283
19:23–30	196
19:29–30	166, 231, 272
20:9–15	179
20:13–16	251
20:16	166, 196, 272
20:20–28	196, 272
20:25–28	166, 294
22:15–22	68, 122
22:34–40	75, 95, 98, 102, 133, 201
22:37–40	249
23:1–15	172
23:1–7	223, 267
23:11–12	100
23:12–13	223
23:23–26	281
23:25–28	98
23:37–39	233
23:37–38	263
23:37	92
24:1–51	278
24:4–14	312
24:4–5, 10–12, 23–24	178
24:10–12	178
24:23–24	178
25:31–46	60, 69, 98, 209, 278
25:31–33	198

25:34–40	208	9:1–6	311
25:41	319	9:23–25	29, 31, 59, 90, 155, 157, 162, 166, 188, 205, 314, 315
26:22, 50–54	122		
27:45-54	42	9:23–24	174
28:18–20	95, 120, 132, 140, 145	10:25–37	55, 98, 153, 179, 314
28:18	16, 26, 80	10:38–42	165, 221
28:18a	107	11:9–10	35
28:20b	26, 29, 80, 107	11:23	188
		11:29–30	239
		11:52	136, 186

MARK

		12:6–7	14
2:13–17	304	12:13–21	43, 109, 165, 188, 235, 315
7:6–7	102	12:15–21	92, 221, 291
9:33–37	11, 166	12:15	23, 207
9:33–35	19, 272	12:16–21	87
10:6–9	211	12:22–34	43
10:17–31	116	12:47–48	319
10:21–27	295	14:11	100
10:29–31	166, 196	14:15–24	169
10:31	112	15:1–24	82
10:35–45	272	15:3–7, 8–10	36
12:28–34	55, 58	15:11–31	128
		15:11–24	36, 66, 92, 152, 179

LUKE

		16:13–15	11, 188
		16:19–31	92, 136, 235, 319
1:37	50	16:19–30	290
1:46–55	196	17:1–2	172, 186, 319
1:46–48	251	17:3–4	74
1:51–52	224	17:7–10	238
1:76–79	276	18:8	299
3:21–22	264	18:9–14	13, 75, 98, 128, 148, 178, 190, 198, 222, 224, 267, 295
5:8–11	140		
5:8–9	198	18:14b	272
5:22–26	186	18:18–25	319
5:33–39	306	19:1–10	11, 133
5:37–38	176	19:37–44	245, 319
6:31	182, 279	19:41–44	203, 263
6:35–38	172	20:46	267
6:37–38	75, 182, 209, 279, 293, 309	22:14–27	212
6:38	255	22:23–34	19
6:43–45	22, 309, 312	22:24–26	11
6:46–49	31, 87, 126, 174, 279	24:36–49	33
7:11–17	126		
7:36–50	121		

JOHN

8:4–15	225, 304		
8:9	87	1:1–18	40, 71, 240, 270
8:22–25	118	1:1–14	80
8:23–25	87	1:1–5	64, 184, 203, 300

JOHN (continued)

1:3	164
1:4–5	57, 274, 276, 291
1:4	19, 82
1:9–14	276
1:10–18	11
1:10–14	111
1:10–13	57, 82, 170, 319
1:10–12	87, 179, 203, 300
1:10–11	164
1:12–13	89
1:12	88, 181, 226, 288, 319, 325
1:14–18	18, 88, 102
1:14–17	281
1:14	207, 284, 295, 297
1:15–18	121
1:16–18	184, 207
1:17	135, 223, 284, 295, 297
1:29	82
2:1–11	51, 52
2:12–16	148
2:13–17	172
3:1–21	36, 170, 228
3:3	244
3:5–7	215
3:7	176, 226
3:14–21	11, 87
3:16–21	18, 60, 64, 66, 116, 203, 240, 276, 288, 312
3:16–19	300
3:16–18	69, 82
3:16–17	162, 166, 215, 225, 263, 281, 319
3:16	145, 151, 181, 226, 244, 253, 281, 325
3:17–18	186
3:17	84, 185
3:19–21	94, 164, 233
3:19	170, 244
3:22–30	101
3:23–24	58
3:35–36	319
3:35	16
3:36	11, 60, 64, 82, 186, 203, 216, 228, 233, 240, 312
4:4–26	36
4:7–26	179
4:7–14	274
4:14	82
4:19–26	102
4:23–24	46, 104, 183, 228, 237, 299, 309
4:28	283
5:13–16	76
5:24	11, 166, 179, 181, 186, 212, 309, 312
5:44	238
6:35–40	118, 274
6:66–68	283
7:18	238
7:24	293
8:1—10:42	46
8:1–11	102
8:3–11	36
8:12	19, 57, 64, 71, 80, 82, 84, 136, 164, 170, 179, 181, 184, 215, 225, 274, 276, 288, 291, 312
8:31–36	179, 184, 223, 251, 297, 308, 318
8:31–32	89, 112, 120, 135, 158, 188, 226, 244, 274, 281, 284, 288, 309, 312, 316
8:32	129, 160, 228, 242
8:35–36	244
8:36	89, 112, 120, 129, 160, 228, 242, 281, 284
8:42–45	319
9:1–41	29, 50, 181
9:1–38	36
9:1–5	245
9:4–5	162
9:5	276
9:26	225
10:9–10	71
10:10	82, 179
10:10b	51
10:27–30	36, 43, 255
10:28–30	18, 57, 118, 203, 228
11:1–5	245
11:17–43	64
11:25–26	212, 312
11:33–44	249
12:20–26	31
12:23–26	155, 174
12:24–26	29, 127, 166, 188, 205, 253, 288, 305, 315

12:34–36	61, 276	15:11	230
12:35–36	170	15:12	75, 98, 159
12:41–46	298	15:13	263
12:43	203	15:18–21	96, 97, 135, 300
13:1–17	11, 78	15:19	162
13:3	16	16:33	15, 16, 18, 21, 31, 32, 33, 64, 76, 80, 96, 97, 118, 122, 127, 129, 132, 135, 151, 162, 165, 166, 201, 207, 233, 244, 245, 300, 316, 325
13:5–9	133		
13:6–10	19, 77, 155, 212, 278, 309		
13:8–10	84, 186, 228		
13:34–35	75, 98, 101, 133, 145, 146, 208, 222, 257, 280, 297, 314	17:3	57, 58, 152, 169, 179, 183, 270
13:34	159	17:13–19	42, 132, 152, 162, 233, 244, 276, 300
14:1–4	14, 42, 122, 165, 192, 266, 269		
14:1	21, 33, 201	17:15–19	16, 29, 40, 76, 111, 135, 145, 155, 256
14:6	15, 19, 48, 57, 82, 87, 122, 157, 164, 215, 217, 224, 225, 244, 270, 281, 288, 290, 291, 319	17:15–17	274
		17:15	33, 97, 151, 192
		17:20–23	55, 145, 146, 169, 179, 214, 257, 293
14:13–14	38		
14:13	283	17:21, 23	101
14:15–24	183	18:10–11	122, 245
14:15–18	107	18:36	122, 245, 300
14:15	22, 133, 158	19:11	68
14:18	96	20:19–20	15, 32, 37, 97, 111
14:20–23	14	20:24–28	33
14:21–27	316	21:17–22	182, 239, 309
14:21–24	22, 57, 225, 228, 253, 264	21:17, 20–22	196
14:21–23	169	21:24–25	262
14:21	158, 179, 270		
14:23–24	59		
14:23	42, 80, 179, 270		
14:25–31	300		

ACTS

1:8	140
2:46–47	53
4:12	157, 164, 201, 288
5:1–11	22
5:29	27
9:13–16	321
10:15	131
11:9	85
13:22–23	22
13:22	102
18:9–11	107
20:24	281
20:28–31	69, 89, 178, 186, 223, 295, 308
26:15–18	64, 105, 136

14:27	15, 31, 32, 37, 66, 80, 84, 96, 97, 111, 114, 118, 127, 135, 162, 165, 179, 201, 207, 244, 245, 325
15:1–11	188, 214, 228
15:1–10	167
15:1–8	169, 198, 231
15:4–8	109
15:4–5	48
15:5–11	253
15:5–8	32, 35, 40, 138, 179
15:5	157
15:7–8	38
15:7	283
15:9–14	22, 158
15:9–13	133
15:9	111

ROMANS

Reference	Pages
1:16	308
1:17	118, 142, 301
1:18–32	260, 274
1:18–25	87, 240
1:18–23	203, 244
1:18–22	60, 64, 312
1:18–22a	201
1:19–21	270
1:21–25	259
1:21–22	235, 290, 311
1:22	299
2:1–11	182
3:20–24	11
3:21–28	184
3:21–26	57, 63, 69, 76, 264
3:21–25	73
3:21–24	42, 186, 212, 226, 228, 319
3:22–24	66, 274, 288
3:23–24	116
4:1–9	281
4:6–8	60, 212
4:7–8	186, 264
5:1–8	76
5:1–2	24, 42, 57, 265
5:3–5	29, 32
5:6–19	73
5:6–11	11, 60, 63, 69, 207, 212
5:6–8	88
5:8	105
6:4–7	306
6:5–14	78
6:6–7	31
6:8–14	66, 114, 167
6:11–14	168
6:19–23	288
7:14–25	19, 50, 77, 228, 321
7:18–25	36
8:1–2	265
8:5–17	114
8:5–9a	250
8:5–8	227
8:5–7	249
8:18–25	48
8:21–23	270
8:22–25	97, 303
8:24	151
8:28–39	26, 29, 45, 107, 151, 251, 323
8:28–32	214
8:28–30	140, 264
8:28	50, 55, 105, 194, 303
8:31–39	43, 315
8:31–35	33, 186
8:31–32	23, 38, 48, 59, 207, 215, 219, 239, 253, 269, 316
8:32–35	263
8:32	35, 150
8:35–39	36, 325
8:38–39	263
9:33	214
10:1–4	198
11:6	265
11:33–36	24, 27, 36, 38, 40, 46, 58, 91, 138, 152, 166, 222, 283, 284, 301, 321
11:33	57
12:1–22	300
12:1–21	160
12:1–8	143
12:1–3	227, 249, 254, 309, 315
12:1–2	29, 31, 32, 55, 112, 118, 166, 170, 176, 198, 204, 223, 231, 244, 291, 305, 306, 328
12:1	168
12:2	120, 250, 259
12:3–21	237
12:3	24, 208, 235, 280, 314
12:9–21	208, 222, 297
12:9–19	48, 159, 314
12:9–16	55, 146, 293
12:9–13	133, 182, 194
12:9–10	101
12:10	280
12:12	325
12:16	280
12:17–21	74
12:21	96
13:1–7	68, 122
13:3–5	27
13:8–10	75
13:8	280
14:1–23	184, 257
14:1–22	48, 182
14:1–8	13, 237, 293
14:1	185

14:5–8	85, 142, 281, 309	8:8–9	13
14:5	185	8:9	297, 314
14:13–23	160, 242, 293	9:19	142
14:13	13, 237, 280	10:13	255
14:16–22	237	10:22–31	24
14:16–18	13, 85, 236, 281, 309	10:23—11:1	85, 131, 185, 242
14:19–23	297	10:23–33	284
14:22	13, 142, 185, 281, 309	10:23–31	48, 182, 314
15:5–7	257, 293	10:23–24	19, 23, 101, 142, 159, 233, 236, 281
15:5–6	55	10:26–31	231
15:5	142, 146	10:31–33	101, 233
15:7	280	10:31	19, 23, 51, 53, 216, 269, 291
15:13	71, 97, 151, 325	12:4–11	148
16:17–19	172, 279	12:10	196
16:17	223	12:24b–27	146
16:20	215	12:27–31	148
		13:1–13	23, 148, 208, 257

1 CORINTHIANS

1:10—2:5	257
1:10–17	237
1:18–31	59
1:20–31	162, 169, 196, 224, 272, 294, 300
1:20	301
1:23–29	235, 290
1:25	301
1:26—2:5	194
1:26–31	91, 102, 160, 179, 251, 279
2:6–10	224
2:8–10	111
2:9–10	77
2:9	18, 29, 35, 269
2:14–16	91, 132, 136
2:16	224
3:1–9	257
3:10–15	186
3:11–15	201
3:16–17	176
3:18	114
6:7	75
6:12—7:5	85
6:12	19, 131, 166, 281, 284
6:19–20	31, 74, 166, 168
7:1–5	211, 247
7:17, 20–24	140
8:1–13	184
8:5–6	164

13:4–7	31, 194, 330
13:6–7	158
13:7	133
13:13	314
15:3	73
15:10a	175
15:12–19	151
15:20–28	73
15:40	266
15:50–58	97
15:51–54	48
16:17–20	209

2 CORINTHIANS

1:21–22	88
3:7	142, 297
3:15—4:7	18
3:17–18	242
3:17	89, 128, 155, 160, 184, 215
4:4–7	85, 136, 175, 198, 305
4:4–6	121, 215, 225, 274, 290, 328
4:4	87, 94, 116, 132, 226, 227, 240, 244, 259, 276, 308, 319
4:6–7	95, 100, 181, 194
4:6	64, 80, 256, 263
4:7	142
4:16–18	276
5:1–10	278
5:1	266

2 CORINTHIANS
(continued)

5:6–9	29
5:7	252
5:15–21	270
5:15–18	112, 251
5:15–18a	186
5:15–17	24, 82, 89, 117, 128, 166, 176, 244, 306
5:15	31, 101, 315
5:17	48, 84, 215, 217, 228, 253, 264, 325
6:12	242
6:14—7:1	244
6:19–20	242
9:6–11	23
9:8–9	215
9:8	150, 153, 309, 323
10:5	227
11:1–4	118
11:4–15	240
11:4–5	259
11:13–15	155, 178, 198, 215, 290
11:14–15	116
11:14	276
11:24–29	118
12:7–10	29, 32, 132, 151, 167, 194, 228, 231, 245, 251, 252, 265, 309, 316, 318, 321, 323
12:20–21	146
13:5	88
15:9–10	88

GALATIANS

2:4	284, 293
2:14	223
2:17–21	321
2:20–21	205
2:20	101, 114, 265
2:21	223
3:12–14	314
3:23–25	281, 321
5:1–9	184
5:1–6	55, 181, 182, 223, 257
5:1	13, 47, 142, 230, 242, 281, 284, 288, 293, 297, 316, 318
5:6	281
5:6b	142
5:13–16	13
5:13–15	47, 101, 146, 257, 293, 315, 318
5:13–14	133, 160, 184, 242, 314
5:13	51, 112, 223, 269, 284
5:14	284
5:15	280
5:16–26	148, 318
5:16	53
5:22–26	315
5:22–25	164
5:25–26	101
5:25	53, 257
5:26	280
6:3–5	24, 235
6:7–10	274, 319
6:9–10	120, 143, 153, 191, 256, 287
6:14	98, 170, 281

EPHESIANS

1:3–10	222
1:3–8	11, 88, 121, 207
1:3	265
1:4–6	263
1:6–8	27
1:7–14	174
1:7–10	24
1:7–8	212, 253
1:9–10	48, 50
1:15–21	120
1:17–23	21
1:17–19a	160
1:22–23	16
2:1–10	11, 13, 18, 24, 63, 64, 73, 121, 128, 133, 179, 198, 207, 215, 253, 270, 279, 288, 321, 325
2:1–5	27, 58, 78, 105, 209, 263, 290, 306
2:1–2	136, 312
2:3–4	314
2:4–10	184, 264
2:4–7	88
2:4–5	76, 259
2:6–7	212
2:7	265

2:8–10	134, 145, 181, 191, 223, 226, 233, 256, 181, 287, 294
2:10	77, 143, 153, 208, 221, 235, 306
3:12	35, 52, 134, 158, 160, 162, 179, 184, 283, 284, 301
3:14–21	284
4:1–7	140, 164
4:1–6	257, 318
4:1–3	22, 133, 143, 194
4:1	223, 298
4:2	100, 280
4:11–16	140, 190, 249, 252
4:11–13	114, 146, 175, 256
4:17—5:2	22
4:17–24	300
4:17–18	116
4:18	240, 259
4:20—5:2	247
4:20–24	227, 249
4:21–24	318
4:22—5:2	330
4:22–24	31, 116, 217, 306
4:26–27	304
4:32—5:1	209
4:32	74, 121, 153, 280, 314
5:1–2	159
5:1	276, 298
5:5–10	240
5:8–33	216
5:8–17	59
5:8–16	276
5:8–10	145, 208, 318
5:8–9	297, 328
5:8	299
5:13–16	328
5:14	37, 87, 225
5:15–33	247
5:15–21	13
5:15–20	53, 169
5:15–18	114, 116, 204, 318
5:15–17	143, 291, 298
5:17–18	164
5:18	212
5:20	110
5:22–33	211
5:22–31	85, 247
5:22–27	24
5:25–27	179
5:31–33	95
6:4	247
6:10–20	326
6:10–18	136, 198, 300, 328
6:14–18	274

PHILIPPIANS

1:3–11	146
1:6	29, 33, 45, 47, 52, 55, 64, 74, 75, 76, 77, 96, 105, 120, 176, 179, 182, 186, 192, 194, 207, 209, 214, 239, 242, 251, 253, 254, 301, 303, 318, 321, 326
1:9–11	21, 88, 112, 120, 143, 160, 170, 198, 204, 222, 231, 291
1:12–14	174, 192
1:15–17	175, 223
1:20–30	122
1:20–21	114
1:21	101
1:27	114, 133, 143, 146, 222, 223, 306, 318
2:1–11	280
2:1–8	148, 249, 257
2:1–4	101, 109, 133, 143, 146, 182, 188, 208, 209, 222, 236, 237, 256, 330
2:3–8	175
2:3–4	31, 78, 110, 153, 159, 217, 293, 306
2:3	100, 211
2:5–11	164
2:8–9	281
2:12–16	150
2:12–16a	22, 146
2:12–13	29, 32, 33, 45, 47, 50, 52, 74, 75, 76, 77, 88, 105, 152, 176, 182, 185, 186, 194, 198, 207, 209, 235, 238, 239, 251, 253, 254, 301, 318, 321, 326
2:12	244
2:13	64, 107, 120, 192, 303
3:7–19	205
3:7–11	152, 162
3:7–9	90, 122, 198, 205
3:12—4:1	45, 143, 231
3:12–16	77, 84, 89, 227, 298, 318, 328
3:12–14	112, 212, 238

PHILIPPIANS (continued)

3:13–14	61, 140, 142, 166, 190
3:15	146
3:16	270, 287
3:17—4:1	138, 244, 274
3:17–21	60, 87, 201, 203, 240, 260, 312
3:17–19	249
3:20	266
4:3	14
4:4–13	142
4:4–9	26, 37, 96, 110, 111, 118, 165, 208, 249, 316, 326
4:4–7	16, 40, 192, 219
4:5–7	129
4:6–8	227
4:6–7	15, 31, 38, 66, 114, 214, 252, 303
4:6	309
4:7	71
4:8–9	31, 250
4:10–13	194
4:12–13	157
4:13	43
4:19	265

COLOSSIANS

1:3–6	97, 132, 151, 325
1:6	82
1:9–14	21, 55, 143, 150
1:9–13	306
1:9–12	22, 145, 204
1:10–12	223, 298
1:13–14	105, 136, 186, 276
1:13	209
1:15–20	40, 73
1:15–17	50
1:16	216
1:21–23	208
1:21–22	186
1:22	309
1:27	24
2:1–3	77, 207
2:2–3	46
2:3	169
2:6–23	293
2:6–10	181, 242
2:6–7	36
2:10	265
2:12–15	82
2:12–14	270
2:13—3:4	209
2:13–23	188, 308
2:13–15	58, 63, 179, 215, 259, 265, 279, 309, 316, 318, 325, 328
2:13	105, 312
2:16–23	13, 89, 120, 181, 184, 242
2:20—3:4	139
2:21–23	133
3:1–25	326
3:1–17	166, 167
3:1–10	300
3:1–6	240
3:1–4	13, 31, 43, 88, 110, 112, 170, 190, 198, 215, 227, 244, 249, 250, 315, 328
3:1–3	14, 32, 84
3:10	190
3:12–21	247
3:12–17	55, 111, 142, 230, 237, 249
3:12–14	74, 159, 314
3:12	100, 153
3:13–15	27
3:13–14	121
3:15–17	254
3:15–16	250
3:15	15
3:16a	170
3:17	19, 23, 53, 190, 291, 306
4:5–6	53, 145
4:12	143, 204

1 THESSALONIANS

1:2–7	146
1:2–3	55
2:11–12	55
2:12	22
3:11–12	132, 135, 236
4:11–12	110, 140, 145, 148, 150
4:11	53, 68, 78, 121, 287
4:13—5:11	278
5:1–11	64, 240
5:4–8	148
5:8–11	60

5:9–11	186, 233
5:11	280
5:12–15	194
5:15–18	230
5:21–22	233
5:21	19
5:23–24	33, 45, 77, 107, 176, 192, 242, 301
5:24	47, 55, 64, 105, 194, 239, 254

2 THESSALONIANS

1:5–10	60, 116
1:11–12	21, 45
1:11	55
2:16–17	26, 37, 215, 265, 281
3:6–15	167
3:6–13	53, 221
3:6–10	236
3:10–13	110
3:10	287
3:16	37

1 TIMOTHY

1:3–7	61, 89, 127, 133, 146, 178, 184, 272, 308
1:5–7	22, 148
1:5	185
1:12–17	11, 84, 121, 179, 209
1:15–17	226
1:18–20	312
1:18–19	140
1:19	185
2:1–6	145, 164, 225, 319
2:1–4	53, 68, 150, 221
2:5–6	82, 295
2:5	201, 288
3:1–7	267, 272
3:2	148
3:12	247
3:16	24, 91
4:1–26	326
4:1–16	148
4:1–4	48, 92
4:1–2	312
4:2	185
4:3–10	192
4:3–5	284
4:4–8	142
4:4–5	51, 131, 269
4:4	19, 40, 47, 85, 216, 233, 236, 291, 297
4:7–8	267
6:3–6	139
6:6–11	291
6:6–10	23
6:17–19	109
6:18–19	143, 153, 191, 255, 297
6:18	120

2 TIMOTHY

1:4–5	247
1:8–10	225
1:8–9	140, 281
2:1–10	272
2:1–7	274
2:1–6	236
2:7	250
2:15, 22–26	267
3:1–5	89, 139, 196, 295, 312
3:5	298
3:7	139, 298
3:16–17	153, 191, 221, 223, 233, 254, 256, 257, 281, 287, 294, 316
3:16	308
4:1–5	60
4:1–4	138, 178, 225, 254, 308
4:3–5	281
4:3	272
4:5	148
4:9–10	160
4:14–15	172

TITUS

1:1—3:15	148, 326
1:1–3	270, 319, 321
1:5–9	272
1:10–16	60, 280, 308
1:13–16	153
1:15–16	19, 139, 178, 186, 188, 223, 184

TITUS (continued)

1:15	23, 51, 78, 85, 131, 142, 185, 228, 236, 242, 269, 274, 291
1:16	69, 200, 294, 295, 298, 299
2:1—3:14	153
2:1–8	53
2:1–6	247
2:7	120, 191
2:9–10	304
2:11–15	120, 319
2:11–14	287, 300
2:11–12	145, 150
2:11	11, 225, 269, 281
2:14	191, 256
3:1–2	132, 150, 256
3:1	68, 120, 122, 191
3:2	100
3:3–8	121, 184
3:8	120, 132, 150, 191, 255, 256
3:14	53, 120, 132, 145, 150, 191, 221, 236, 256, 287

HEBREWS

3:12–15	88, 233
3:12–13	176
4:1–2, 8–11	37
4:9–11	32, 84, 97, 118, 170, 214, 325
4:12–13	47, 124, 127
4:13	260
4:14–16	11, 66, 84, 121, 158, 209, 283
4:15–16	78
6:10–12	256
6:10	132, 191
6:12	53, 145
6:18–19	153
8:5	266
8:12	262
9:8–15	116
9:11–15	66
9:11–14	184
9:23–28	116, 186
9:24	266
9:26b	66
10:6, 11	233
10:24–25	249
10:24	153, 280
10:26–27	11
10:32–38	29, 207
11:1–40	272, 318
11:1–39	21, 165
11:1–13	190
11:1–3	136, 239, 270
11:1	97, 118, 150, 151, 181, 325
11:6	38, 52, 97, 118, 128, 134, 136, 150, 181, 239, 262, 270, 294, 298, 301
11:11–16	151
11:13	97, 150
11:38—12:3	260
12:1–12	29
12:1–6	117
12:1–3	162, 192, 326
12:1	266
12:28–29	46, 92, 142, 145
13:4	85, 211
13:5–6	14, 23
13:5b–6	107
13:5b	255
13:7–8	165
13:15–16	120, 143, 153, 165, 191, 255, 256, 297
13:15	150
13:20–21	71, 88

JAMES

1:1–8	134
1:2–12	117, 135, 192
1:2–8	29, 32, 33, 67, 97, 111, 134, 247, 328
1:2–4	26
1:5–8	84, 118, 136, 143, 194
1:5–6	204
1:6–8	52
1:9–11	196
1:12	122, 134, 194
1:13–25	167
1:13–18	18, 42, 233
1:14–15	94
1:16–18	35, 85, 88, 131, 226, 236, 252
1:16–17	23, 207
1:17–18	203

1:17	58, 61, 100, 223, 231, 247	1:3–9	16, 40, 97, 111, 207, 230, 316
1:19–27	98	1:3–7	26, 67, 208
1:19–20	74, 209, 217, 304, 330	1:6–12	29, 32, 33
1:22–26	297	1:6–7	118
1:22–25	13, 48, 61, 82, 89, 97, 120, 121, 124, 126, 127, 129, 158, 160, 182, 184, 200, 208, 225, 242, 244, 249, 281, 284, 287, 294, 308	1:12	48
		1:13—2:3	167, 190
		1:13–23	237
		1:13–21	114, 227, 270, 306
		1:22–25	168
1:26–27	228	1:24–25	124
2:1–9	196	2:1–3	61, 236
2:7	191	2:4–12	64
2:12	160	2:9–12	270
2:14–26	297	2:11–17	132, 150, 256
2:14–17	116	2:11–12	153, 208, 257
2:14–16	200	2:12	53, 140, 244, 304
2:18–19	121	2:13–17	68
3:1–2	175	2:13–14	122
3:1	272	2:15–17	244
3:9–12	168	2:15–16	13
3:13–18	31, 59, 78, 109, 131, 142, 143, 146, 160, 169, 175, 200, 204, 217, 223, 247, 249, 272, 314, 330	2:15	53, 153, 191, 270, 304
		2:16–17	142, 160, 242, 284, 287
		2:16	47, 51, 112, 269, 293, 297
3:13–14	222	2:20–25	256
3:13	100, 153, 159, 294	2:21–25	215
3:17–18	90	2:23–25	226
3:17	159	2:24–25	24, 33
4:1–7	155	3:1–7	85, 211, 216
4:1–5	157	3:8–17	185
4:3	104	3:8–13	237
4:4–10	92, 299	3:8–12	201
4:4	280	3:8–9	257
4:6	36	3:10–17	122
4:7–10	188	3:13–18	29
4:7	96, 104, 109	3:13–17	120, 143, 153, 191, 256, 312
4:10–12	182	3:14–18	175
4:10	11, 16, 21, 36, 46, 59, 61, 76, 100, 104, 109, 116, 128, 135, 142, 196	3:14–17	67
		3:14b	27
		3:18	24, 27, 42, 66, 71, 73, 76, 101, 114, 121, 128, 186, 215, 265, 288, 325
4:13–17	95, 168, 219		
4:17	256, 287		
5:1–6	23	3:18a	179
5:7–11	67, 151	4:1–2	114, 270, 306
5:7–8	92, 194	4:2	101
5:7	303	4:6–11	31
5:9	280	4:7–11	148

1 PETER

1:3–12	42, 192
4:12–19	117, 226

1 PETER (continued)

4:12–17	122
4:12–16	135
4:19	151
5:1–11	188
5:1–4	267
5:5–11	272
5:5–8	98
5:5–6	100, 109
5:5	101
5:5b–6	212
5:6–11	29, 33, 64, 80, 128, 192, 316
5:6–9	222, 328
5:6–7	15, 16, 26, 37, 66, 96, 114, 129, 142, 165, 214, 219, 309
5:6	76, 111, 116, 145, 148, 196, 238, 321
5:7–11	40
5:7	208, 252
5:8–11	109, 155
5:8–9	198, 215, 290
5:10–11	16, 18, 42, 48, 67, 73, 97, 151, 207, 226, 245, 269, 278

2 PETER

1:1–2	71
1:3–11	29, 98, 143, 145, 150, 167, 170, 207, 215, 223, 315
1:3–9	194, 198, 227
1:3–8	43
1:3–4	23, 24, 59
1:3	88, 179, 326
2:1–3	178, 308
2:2	223
2:9–19	319
2:19–22	188
2:19	178
2:20–22	176
3:1–15	116, 278
3:1–15a	162, 240
3:1–12	60
3:1–9	92, 224
3:3–11	183
3:3	139
3:8–14	145
3:8–10	67

3:9	64, 94, 111, 203, 209, 225, 255, 281
3:10–14	186
3:11–13	48
3:12–13	266
3:14–18	262, 319
3:15	225
3:18	121
4:2–19	97

1 JOHN

1:1–5	132
1:3–6	158
1:5–10	42, 63, 64, 212, 318
1:5–7	124
1:8–10	24, 66, 184, 186, 228, 309
1:8–9	36, 84
1:9	27, 57, 69, 76, 77, 78, 109, 116, 226, 255, 264, 306, 325
1:21	309
2:3–6	179
2:9–11	64, 75
2:15–17	11, 19, 82, 88, 92, 112, 131, 136, 145, 155, 157, 162, 166, 170, 176, 222, 244, 259, 298, 299, 305, 308, 315
2:17	42
3:1–3	27, 190, 192, 208, 209, 212
3:1	263
3:11–13	97, 172
3:16–24	185, 222, 242
3:16–20	75, 101, 109, 150, 159, 287, 294, 297
3:16–18	191, 253
3:16	201
3:17–19	23
3:18	116, 121, 126, 158, 182, 200, 208, 255, 256, 308
3:19–24	316
4:1–6	42, 97, 162, 170, 178, 244, 305
4:1–3	223
4:4–6	112, 155, 224
4:4	96
4:7–21	242
4:7–12	75
4:7–8	226
4:9–11	159

4:13–21	217
4:16–18	252
4:18–19	179, 263
4:19–21	75
5:1–5	96, 224
5:11	58
5:12	57
5:13–15	35, 38, 284, 301
5:19	328

2 JOHN

3	71
4–6	22

3 JOHN

11	255

JUDE

3–4	257, 288
17–23	45

REVELATION

2:1—3:22	146, 295, 299
2:17	14, 91, 325
3:4–6	96
3:17	198
4:1–11	266
6:1—22:21	278
7:16–17	111
12:7–10	215
12:10–11	321, 323
19:11–16	224
20:11–15	325
20:15	14
21:1—22:6	266
21:1–8	278
21:1–6	233, 269
21:1–5	48, 111, 145
21:1–4	18, 29, 69, 80, 151, 165, 270
21:4	33
22:1–7	269, 278
22:1–6	233
22:12	269

www.ingramcontent.com/pod-product-compliance
Lightning Source LLC
Chambersburg PA
CBHW071226230426

43668CB00011B/1327